Collins

AF662431

Canvas Book 4 Semester 1

Published by Collins Learning
A division of HarperCollins*Publishers* India Limited

HarperCollins *Publishers*
A-75, Sector 57, Noida, Uttar Pradesh 201301, India
1 London Bridge Street, London SE1 9GF, United Kingdom
2 Bloor Street East, Toronto, Ontario M4W 1A8, Canada
Lvl 13, 201 Elizabeth Street (PO Box A565, NSW, 1235), Syndney NSW 2000, Australia
195 Broadway, New York, NY 10007, USA

Browse the complete Collins catalogue at
www.collins.in

First edition 2016 , Reprint edition 2019

ISBN: 978-935-177604-8

Printed and bound by Saurabh Printers Pvt. Ltd.

MRP ₹ 460.00

Preface

Learners in the primary levels exhibit a natural tendency to learn by weaving all the areas of learning into one string. *Canvas—an integrated semester course* for classes 1 to 5 provides a comprehensive learning experience for the young learners. This series of ten semester books present learning materials through the integrated, interlinked and interwoven approach combining all the disciplines together. The core subjects—English, Mathematics, Science, EVS/Social Studies and General Knowledge are presented in an interactive way for the learner's holistic development. *Canvas* provides learning experiences with sufficient opportunity for exploration to young minds in their formative stage.

The interactive approach of this series integrates multiple intelligences and brain-based methodology applied in every classroom across all levels. Cross-curricular links have been created across the areas of learning for experiential and comprehensive development. The enquiry and skill based approach of the books contributes to the trans-disciplinary structure and comprehension. The books maintain a good balance between teacher-led and learner-initiated activities. *Canvas* enables learners to understand the interdisciplinary nature of knowledge and apply this approach to problem solving.

The well-graded course materials develop a link between natural, cultural and social environment. The course content across the subjects develop basic language skills through analysis, application and appreciation; develop critical and analytical thinking; develop scientific temperament and create a strong sense of human values.

Some of the pedagogical elements integrated across all subjects are Learning Objectives, Warm up, New Words, Do it Yourself, Think and Answer, Eco Zone, Life Skills, Value Zone, Activity and Connect for cross-curricular links.

Canvas series aims to develop 21st century skills including critical and creative thinking skills, effective communication skills, interpersonal and collaborative skills, and information and media skills in the young learners.

This series is supported by comprehensive Teacher's resources in the form of an interactive e-book with animations and interactivities, answer keys, lesson plans and a Test Generator for creation of quick test.

We value any feedback on this series. Please e-mail us at kanav.agnihotri@harpercollins_india.com

Key Features

Mathematics

Concepts explained in simple and easy-to-understand language
- **Exercises and Revision Exercise** within each chapter to recall and revise the concepts learnt
- **Mental Maths** to help practise calculation skills and deductive reasoning
- **Worksheets** to reinforce practice with fun exercises
- **Cross-curricular Links** to integrate knowledge across subjects
- **HOTS (Higher Order Thinking Skills)** and **Challenge** to sharpen the thinking skills beyond textual knowledge
- **Maths Lab Activity** to test skills for investigation, observation and analysis

Social Studies

- **I Know** assesses the prior knowledge of the learners.
- **Observe and Reflect** has pre-reading tasks that allow the learners to infer and relate to the topic.
- **Fact Zone** provides interesting titbits of information and **Find Out** tasks encourage referencing skills
- **Do It Yourself** contains application-based activities for experiential learning
- **Eco Zone** sensitizes learners towards conservation of environment
- **Word Zone**, **Remember** and **Review Zone** at the end of the units facilitate understanding, recall and reinforcement, and assessment.
- **Think Zone** focuses on Higher Order Thinking Skills.
- **Life Skills Zone** equips learners with the basic skills they need to excel in life and **Value Zone** helps to build the right attitudes and values in learners.
- **Activity Zone** has varied creative tasks and **My Zone** helps in self-assessment and provides interesting **Pin It Up** activities.

ELT

- Syllabus designed to meet the latest CBSE curriculum framework, with carefully graded units to ensure clear progression through the grammar syllabus
- Each unit based around reading passages that cover a wide range of genres and text types
- Includes a variety of writing tasks to challenge learners
- Language skills and vocabulary sections to encourage the use of dictionaries and enrich the learner's language
- Particular emphasis on listening and speaking skills
- Project and life skill pages to encourage group work and aid in formative assessment
- Clear and accessible layout and design

Science

- **Revise and Recall, Think and Answer** test application of the concepts learned.
- **Science in Context** gives interesting extra information on the topic being discussed.
- **Summary** provides snapshot of the chapter content which helps students in quick revision.
- **Cross-curricular learning link** integrates knowledge across subjects.
- **Life Skills** test awareness, empathy and attitude towards self and others.
- Relevant **activities** hone experimental and deduction skills.
- **Project** questions link the concept learned to real-life applications.

Acknowledgements

ELT

The authors and publishers wish to acknowledge the authors listed below, and thank the following for permission to use copyright material:

Unit 1: *Twelve Silver Cups* from *The Twelve Silver Cups* by Enid Blyton, permission granted by Hodder & Stoughton, 338 Euston Road, London NW1 3BH; Unit 3: Vivian French for *Collins Big Cat: Mountain Mona* (HarperCollins Publishers); Unit 4: Angie and Andy Belcher for *Caring for Our Planet* from *Collins Big Cat: Oceans Alive* (HarperCollins Publishers); Unit 5: Mark Carthew and Michael Rosen for *Kaleidoscope* from *Collins Big Cat: Kaleidoscope* (HarperCollins Publishers); Unit 5: *Fabulous Beast* © Sampurna Chattarji is reprinted with the permission of the author, and was originally published in *The Fried Frog and other Funny Freaky Foodie Feisty Poems* by Sampurna Chattarji (Scholastic, first edition June 2009, reprinted September 2009, May 2010, ISBN-13: 978-81-8477-285-2)

Every effort has been made to trace copyright holders and to obtain their permission for the use of copyright material. The authors and publishers will gladly receive any information enabling them to rectify any error or omission in subsequent editions.

Illustrations

Unit 1: *Twelve Silver Cups*, Richa Kinra; Unit 3: *Mountain Mona*, Chris Fisher; Unit 4: *Caring for Our Planet*, Angie Belcher; Unit 5: *Kaleidoscope*, Amit John

All other illustrations: Q2A Media Services Private Limited

Photograph

Shutterstock.com: Danny E Hooks

Social Sciences

All illustrations Quadrum Solutions

Images

strmko; fotoVoyager; schita, Aelita17; Mykhailo Muzyka; Gannet77, Rafal Cichawa, Rattham, Shweitank; Bartosz Hadyniak, Danielrao, Danielrao; PeteDraper; Lya_Cattel; Marcus Lindstrom; UdayanSankarPal, Rattham, Danielrao; Luciano Mortula; pixelfusion3d, shylendrahoode, werusq, mrinalnag; davidevison; mwphotos; f9photos; DavorLovincic, djgunner; OSTILL, Roberto A Sanchez; EcoPic, photka; RichardHayman13, naveen0301; pjmalsbury, mahroch; AravindTeki, iannomadav, girishacf; spyder24; Sujay Govindaraj; yaseenin, turtix, siraanamwong, cinoby; powerofforever, FaraAk, Aleynikov; RNMitra; SoumenNath, menonsstocks; LSP1982, gehringj, yanikap; thinair28; intst; ertyo5, DamianPEvans; botulinum21, Anna Bryukhanova, pjrimages; VasukiRao; yogesh_more; fabio lamanna, vesnyanka; TarpMagnus, MosayMay, sandsun, Yurchello108; voraorn, kokouu; sandsun; julianwphoto; mshch, Tatiana Belova; mshch, skhoward, apomares; julianwphoto, Jeremy Richards; Musat; L.L. Prasanna Ranatunga, Anna Yu, CornelisNienaber_, eROMAZe, yoglimogli, Zwilling330, Andyworks, girishacf, girishacf; Maps © Collins Bartholomew Ltd 2016

Science

All illustrations AptaraCorp Ltd.

Images

MR. SUWIT GAEWSEE-NGAM, apiguide, Jakkrit Orrasri, Sealstep; CoolKengzz, O lympus, Super Prin, Kokhanchikov; Grigorev Mikhail, Ruud Morijn Photographer, roundstripe; Nelson Sirlin, Nithid Memanee; asif waseem, themorningglory, wichitpong katwit, Pakhnyushcha; a9photo, Decha Thapanya, dabjola, Julia Pivovarova; Nithid Memanee, a9photo, Nelson Sirlin, Kokhanchikov, wichitpong katwit; Nithid

Memanee, Grigorev Mikhail, Decha Thapanya; outdoorsman, Daniel Prudek, Gillian Holliday; Xavier MARCHANT, worldswildlifewonders, MNSKumar, rickyd; Wanchai Orsuk; FourOaks, Ratchapol Yindeesuk, Stephane Bidouze, Cathy Keifer; neelsky; Gillian Holliday, Daniel Prudek, Xavier MARCHANT, outdoorsman, Cathy Keifer, MNSKumar, Stephane Bidouze, Ratchapol Yindeesuk; Multiart, glasscuter, v.s.anandhakrishna, highviews, Anna Breitenberger, windu, mygoodpix, Elena Larina; EvgeniaSh., Hurst Photo; Robyn Mackenzie, zkruger, Kondor83, Hong Vo, Dancestrokes, Tischenko Irina, Evgeny Karandaev, Elena Schweitzer, Christine Langer-Pueschel; 64: Ljupco Smokovski, Laborant, grynold, Madlen, monticello; Kondor83, Robyn Mackenzie, Elena Schweitzer, Tischenko Irina, Evgeny Karandaev, Dancestrokes, Christine Langer-Pueschel, Hurst Photo; tacar, Freer, VladislavGudovskiy, Dancestrokes, Elena Schweitzer, Tischenko Irina

Contents

English

Mathematics

Science

Social Studies

GK

ENGLISH

CONTENTS MAP

Unit	Title of text	Reading	Vocabulary	Grammar	Language skills	Listening	Speaking	Writing
1	Twelve Silver Cups	Factual, inferential, extrapolative	Sports	Articles: *a*, *an*, *the*; types of noun	Ordinal numbers	Fill the gaps in the conversation	Role-play reporting a stolen cycle to a police officer	Write a different ending to the story
	My Shadow	Poem appreciation						
2	The Selfish Sparrow	Factual, inferential, extrapolative	Character adjectives; bird protection	Pronouns: subject, object, reflexive	Dictionary work: guide words	Tick what people should or shouldn't do	Ask and answer questions about doing things yourself and give advice	Write a story using the given phrases
3	Mountain Mona	Factual, inferential	Verbs of movement	Subjects and predicates	Pronunciation: /əʊ/ and /aʊ/	Match the people with what they are good at	Ask and answer questions about what you are good at	Write a paragraph about your school's Annual Day
	Town Mouse, Country Mouse	Poem appreciation						
	Revision 1							
	Activity							
4	Caring for our Planet	Factual, extrapolative	Environment; conservation	*should*, *shouldn't*; present continuous	Spelling: apostrophes to show belonging	Match the people with the advice	Give advice using *should* and *shouldn't*	Write paragraphs about caring for the environment using the given words and phrases
5	Kaleidoscope	Factual, extrapolative	Jobs and equipment	Comparative forms of adjectives	Spelling: adjectives ending in *-ful*	Tick the correct adjective	Make comparative sentences using the adjectives given	Plan an invention and write about it
	Fabulous Beast	Poem appreciation						
	Revision 2							
	Activity							
	Grammar Practice							
	Project							
	Life Skills							
	Listening Texts							

1 Twelve Silver Cups

In this unit, I will...

- learn some sports-related words
- learn about types of nouns
- practise using articles *a*, *an* and *the*
- write and say ordinal numbers (1st, 2nd, 3rd, etc.)
- practise asking for and giving information

Warm-up FA

Look at the maze. Help Rajat win the gold cup.

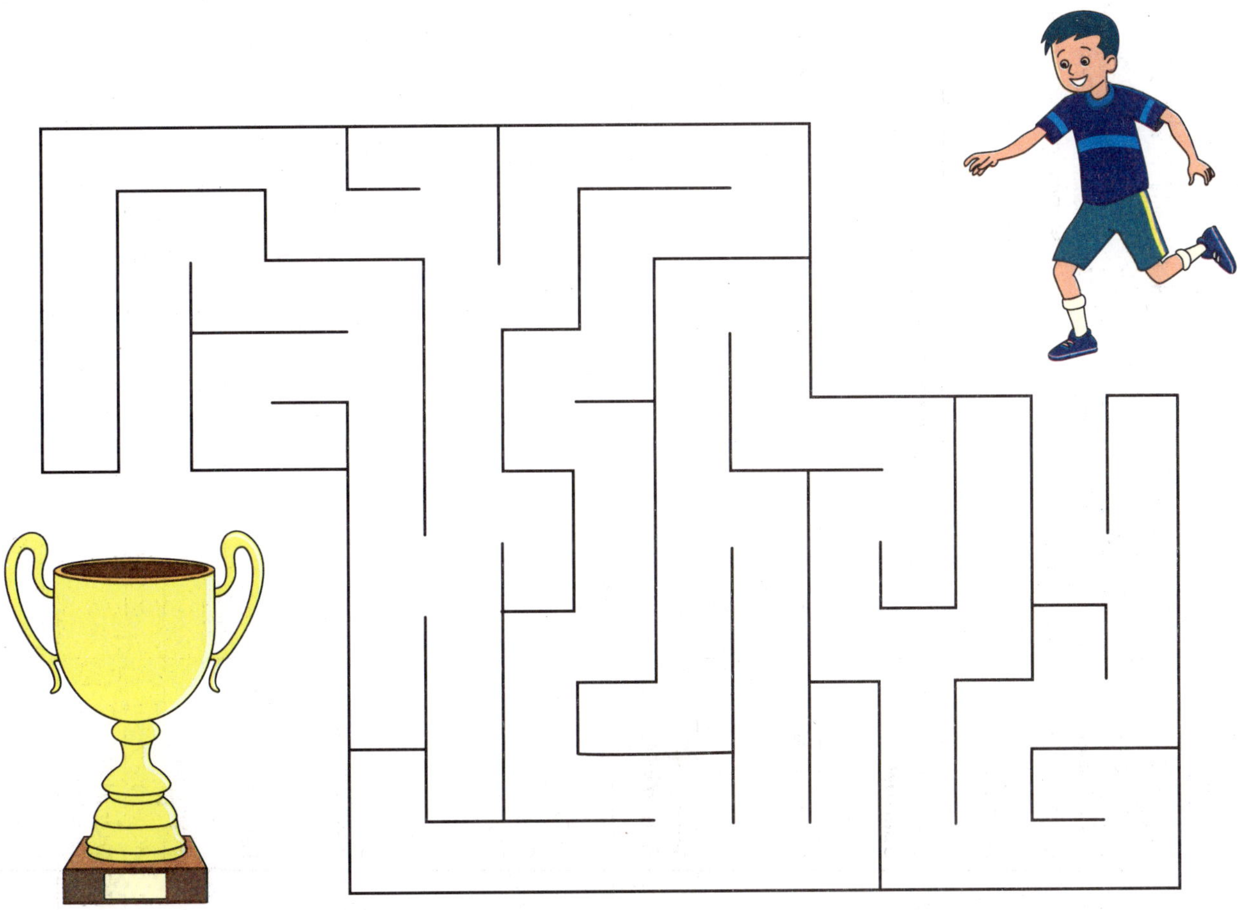

Reading

Read this story about a boy who won twelve silver cups... and then lost them!

Jeffery was a splendid[1] runner, and at his school sports, he always won all the running prizes.

He already had eleven cups. So that year, when he again won the prize for running, he had his twelfth silver cup. How pleased he was!

And then, what do you think happened to those twelve silver cups? One night, a burglar[2] got into the house and stole them all! He hadn't time to take anything else because Spot, the dog, began to bark. Daddy woke up and heard a noise and tore[3] downstairs – just in time to see a dark figure running down the garden.

Daddy switched on the light, and saw that Jeffery's cups were gone. He ran into the garden – but the man had disappeared. So Daddy rang up the police.

But nobody seemed to be able to get back those cups. Jeffery was very unhappy because they were his, and he had been proud of them.

The policeman took a lot of notes and asked a great many questions. But he didn't catch the thief, though he said he felt sure he knew who it was.

Two weeks went by and nothing was heard of the twelve silver cups. Then another bit of bad luck came to Jeffery. He lost his tortoise!

Wordfile

1. **Splendid** means wonderful or excellent.
2. A **burglar** is a person who steals things from someone's house.
3. If you **tear** downstairs, you run downstairs quickly. The past tense of **tear** is **tore**.

He had had Slowcoach, his tortoise, for six years, and was fond of the quaint[4] old creature. Slowcoach would let Jeffery tickle him under the chin, and would always poke his head out when Jeffery whistled a special whistle. Now he was gone!

'Oh, Mother, where do you think he can be?' said Jeffery. 'I've hunted over every bit of the garden.'

'He must have escaped into someone else's garden,' said Mother. 'You know how tortoises wander, Jeff.'

Jeffery went to look at the fence, and he looked very carefully indeed. Mother was right! The wire was not so strong, and Spot had scraped at it, and bent it back in one place so that he might get into the big ploughed[5] field at the back.

'His brown shell is so like the earth that I don't believe I'd see him if he was right under my nose[6]!' said the boy. 'Hey, Spot! Come and help me! Find Slowcoach! Maybe your nose will find what my eyes can't!'

Spot squeezed through the hole in the wire and danced over the field, yelping. He sniffed here and there and then he and Jeffery both saw the same thing! In the middle of the field, a piece of earth flew up into the air – and then another!

Jeffery ran over the furrows[7] – and when he got to the place, he laughed.

'It's old Slowcoach burying himself for the winter!' he said. 'What a long way you've walked over the field, Slowcoach!'

'Wuff!' said Spot, and danced around the tortoise. There was nothing much to be seen of him except one hind leg, for he was now half buried.

Jeffery pulled Slowcoach gently out of the soil.

Wordfile

4. If something is **quaint**, it is different and pleasing.
5. In a **ploughed** field, the soil has been turned over, ready for planting seeds.
6. If something is **under your nose**, you can see it in front of you.
7. A **furrow** is a line that a farmer digs in a field.

Wordfile

8. **Moss** and **bracken** are two types of plant that would make a nice soft bed for a tortoise.
9. When farmers **hole up** soil, they turn it over with a tool (called a 'hoe') or a special machine.
10. If metal is **tarnished**, it is not bright or colourful.

'Slowcoach, you have your own box of moss and bracken[8] at home in the shed,' he said. 'That's where you sleep for the winter – not in a damp, cold field where you might be hoed up[9]! Come along!'

Spot went to the hole and sniffed there. Then he began to scrape excitedly at the earth, and in a few moments Jeffery was spattered from head to foot with flying soil.

'Stop, Spot, stop!' he yelled. 'Are you thinking of burying yourself for the winter, too? You're not a tortoise! Don't be silly!'

But Spot wouldn't stop. He went on and on digging – and then a strange thing happened. He pulled hard at a dirty brown rope, and yelped loudly.

Jeffery put the tortoise down and helped Spot. He pulled at the rope – and a sack came slowly up from the earth. Something inside it clinked.

Jeffery undid the rope and looked inside the little sack. Yes – the thief had hurriedly buried them in the middle of the field, meaning to return for them when it was safe. There they all were in the dirty sack, very dull and tarnished[10], and with scratches here and there – but safe!

With Slowcoach in one hand, the sack over his shoulder, and Spot yelping round his feet excitedly, Jeffery rushed home.

'Mother! Mother!' he yelled. 'I've found my twelve silver cups! At least, Slowcoach really found them, and Spot dug them up – but I've got them, I've got them, I've got them!'

Enid Blyton

Comprehension 1

A Choose the correct answers.

1. Jeffery won twelve silver cups for ___________.
   a. running b. swimming c. gardening
2. ___________ stole Jeffery's silver cups.
   a. A burglar b. A tortoise c. The police
3. ___________ called the police.
   a. Jeffery b. Daddy c. Mother
4. Spot is a ___________ and Slowcoach is a ___________.
   a. tortoise, dog b. cat, tortoise c. dog, tortoise
5. Where did Jeffery find Slowcoach?
   a. in the garden b. in the field c. in the sack
6. What was inside the sack?
   a. Jeffery's silver cups b. Slowcoach c. a rope

B Answer the questions.

1. How did Jeffery feel about winning the cups?
2. What happened to Jeffery's cups?
3. What was Slowcoach doing in the field?
4. Where were Jeffery's cups?
5. How did Jeffery feel at the end of the story? Why?

Comprehension 2

Have you ever lost something very special to you? Did you find it? How?

Vocabulary

A Look at the picture and label it with these words.

wire field garden tortoise hole rope sack

B Match the sports with the pictures.

1. football
2. badminton
3. skating
4. cricket
5. cycling
6. swimming

a. 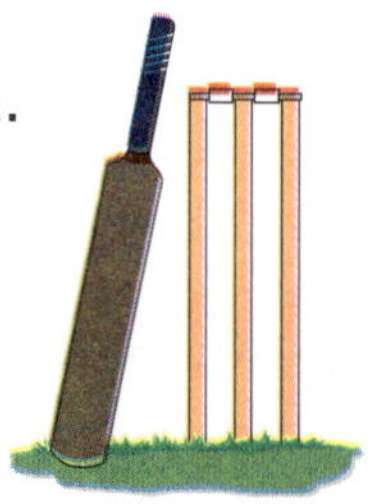

b. 

c. 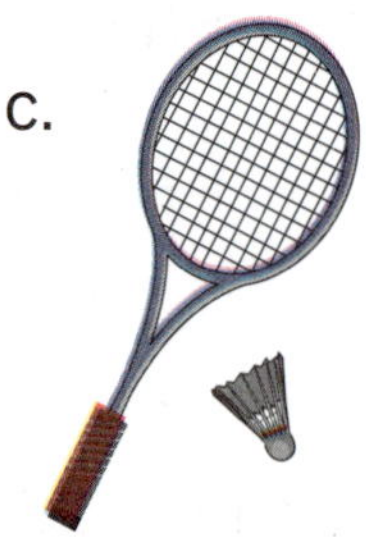

d. 

e. 

f. 

Grammar

Articles: *a*, *an* and *the*

A, ***an*** and ***the*** are articles. Remember:

We use ***an*** before words that begin with vowel sounds: a, e, i, o and u.

We use ***a*** before words that begin with other letters (= consonants).

A, ***an*** or ***the***?

1. Use ***a*** or ***an*** when you talk about something for the first time.

*I need **a** pencil. Can I borrow yours?*

2. Use ***the*** when you mention something again.

*I have a blue pen and a red pen here. I borrowed **the** red pen from Mala.*

We also use ***the*** when the noun is a particular thing.

*Mandip is playing in **the** garden.*

***The** Ganges flows through India.*

A Complete the sentences with articles: *a*, *an* or *the*.

1. Jeffery was ____________ excellent runner. He had twelve silver cups.
2. One night, ____________ burglar stole all ____________ cups.
3. Jeffery couldn't find ____________ cups anywhere.
4. ____________ policeman came to Jeffery's house and asked him some questions.
5. Then, Slowcoach escaped through ____________ hole in ____________ garden fence.
6. Finally, Jeffery found ____________ cups in ____________ sack in ____________ field behind Jeffery's house.

Types of noun

Read the sentences.

1. He already had eleven **cups**.
2. **Jeffery** was a splendid runner.
3. Jeffery found his **collection** of cups in the field.
4. There was a **burglary** at Jeffery's house.

All the **bold** words in the above sentences are **nouns**.

Remember that nouns are naming words for people, places or things.

There are four types of noun:

1. **Common noun:** the name for a person, place or thing: *teacher*, *school*, *cup.*
2. **Proper noun:** the special name that is given to a particular person, place or thing: *Jeffery*, *Mumbai*, *The Red Fort*. Proper nouns always start with a capital letter.
3. **Collective noun:** the name for a collection of people or things: *a crowd of children*, *a collection of cups.*
4. **Abstract noun:** the name for something that we cannot see or touch: *a burglary*, *happiness*.

B Write the type of the underlined nouns. The first one is done for you.

1. My neighbour is very kind. common noun
2. My uncle's name is Ram. ____________
3. A flock of birds flew over the river. ____________
4. We went to Kerala for our holiday. ____________
5. Rahim is a very hardworking student. ____________
6. Everyone knows about Mr Sen's kindness. ____________
7. A herd of cows was standing in the middle of the road. ____________

C **Complete the related abstract noun for these adjectives.**

1.	free	__ __ e e __ o __	2.	angry	a __ __ e __
3.	wise	__ i __ __ o __	4.	honest	__ o __ e __ __ y
5.	sad	__ a __ __ e __ __	6.	happy	__ a __ __ i __ e __ __

Language skills

FA

Ordinal numbers

A **Match the numbers with the words.**

1st 2nd 3rd 4th 5th 6th 7th 8th 9th 10th 11th 12th

ninth	fourth	first	tenth	fifth	seventh
eleventh	eighth	third	twelfth	second	sixth

B **Listen. Write the numbers.**

a. __________ b. __________ c. __________

C **Listen. Which sound do you hear at the end of each number?**

Each number ends in the sound __________.

Listening

FA

Listen and complete the conversation between Jeffery and the police officer.

Policeman: Hello, Jeffery. I understand that your silver cups have been stolen. I have some [1]__________ for you. First of all, where did you keep your cups?

Jeffery: I kept them on the [2]__________ in the living room.

Policeman: Right. When did you last [3]__________ them?

Jeffery: Yesterday [4]__________. I saw them before I went to [5]__________.

Policeman: And what time was that?

Jeffery: Around [6]__________ o'clock.

Policeman: Who went to bed after you?

Jeffery: My mum and dad. I finished my [7]__________ and went straight upstairs.

Policeman: OK. And did you [8]__________ anything odd in the night?

Jeffery: No, I didn't.

Policeman: Hmm... was anything else missing this [9]__________?

Jeffery: No, the [10]__________ didn't steal anything else.

Policeman: Thank you, Jeffery. We will try to find your [11]__________ very soon.

Jeffery: Thank you, Sir.

FA Speaking

Work with a partner.

Student A: Someone has stolen your cycle. Answer Student B's questions.

Student B: You are a police officer. Ask Student A some questions.

Student A:

Someone has stolen my cycle!
It's quite old / new. It's blue / red, etc.
I don't know / I can't remember.
I last used it this morning / yesterday.
No, I didn't / Yes, I did.

Student B:

Let me ask you some questions.
Can you describe it?
When did you last see it?
Where did you leave it?
Did you notice anything odd?

Writing

A Read the last paragraphs of *Twelve Silver Cups* again. Answer the questions.

1. What is in the sack? ______________________________
2. Are the cups new and shiny when Jeffery finds them? Yes / No
3. Does Jeffery go straight home? Yes / No
4. Do you think Jeffery wants to find the thief? Yes / No

B **Write a different ending to the story. You can use these ideas, or you can make up your own ending.**

Jeffery wants to find the thief.

He looks for fingerprints on the sack.

Jeffery and Spot walk across the field to the town centre.

They look for clues.

They see a mysterious man.

Jeffery was very happy to find his silver cups. But who had taken them? And why? Jeffery decided to search for clues. First, he ______________________

____

____

____

____

____

____

____

____

Poem

Did you know that someone follows you around in the day?

Read the poem to find out who it is.

My Shadow

I have a little shadow that goes
in and out with me,
And what can be the use of him
is more than I can see.
He is very, very like me from the
heels up to the head;
And I see him jump before me,
when I jump into my bed.

The funniest thing about him is
the way he likes to grow—
Not at all like proper children,
which is always very slow;
For he sometimes shoots up taller like an india-
rubber ball[1],
And he sometimes gets so little that there's none of
him at all.

He hasn't got a notion[2] of how children ought to play,
And can only make a fool of me in every sort of way.
He stays so close beside me, he's a coward you can
see;
I'd think shame to stick to nursie[3] as that shadow
sticks to me!

One morning, very early, before the sun was up,
I rose and found the shining dew on every buttercup;
But my lazy little shadow, like an arrant[4] sleepy-head,
Had stayed at home behind me and was fast asleep
in bed.

Robert Louis Stevenson

Wordfile

1. An **india-rubber ball** is a small ball that bounces high when it hits a surface.
2. If you **haven't got a notion** about something, you do not know about it.
3. In the past, '**nursie**' was the name for a woman who looked after children in a family.
4. **Arrant** is an old or poetic word meaning 'complete' or 'total'; it is used for making a noun stronger.

Poem appreciation

Read the lines from *My Shadow* and answer the questions.

1. 'For he sometimes shoots up taller like an india-rubber ball,
   And he sometimes gets so little that there's none of him at all.'
   a. Who 'shoots up'?
   b. What does the poet compare him to?
   c. Why do you think he changes his size?

2. 'He stays so close beside me, he's a coward you can see;
   I'd think shame to stick to nursie as that shadow sticks to me!'
   a. Why does the poet call him a coward?
   b. Pick out two rhyming words from the lines above.
   c. Who does the poet refer to as 'nursie'?

Activity

FA

Similes

A simile is a comparison between two different things using 'as' or 'like', to show that they share the same qualities, for example:

***as** fierce **as** a tiger*

***as** black **as** night*

1. Find a simile in the poem. ____________________
2. Make similes with these phrases.
   a. He eats like ____________________
   b. Your skin is as soft as ____________________
   c. The lake was beautiful, like ____________________
   d. My brother is as tall as ____________________
   e. We were working hard, as busy as ____________________

2 The Selfish Sparrow

In this unit, I will...

- learn some words for talking about bird conservation
- practise using pronouns
- think and talk about responsible behaviour
- learn how to use guide words in a dictionary
- practise language for talking about rules

FA Warm-up

Many birds *migrate*. This means that they fly from one place to another place. Birds migrate to find food and better weather.

A These are the birds that migrate. Match their names with the pictures.

a

b

c

1. Cuckoo
2. Siberian Crane
3. Greater Flamingo
4. Comb Duck
5. Kingbird
6. Yellow Wagtail

d

e

f

B Match the sentence halves.

1. Many birds fly along
2. Birds often migrate
3. Birds usually migrate in
4. Some birds migrate in winter to

a. find food in warmer places.
b. large groups, called 'flocks'.
c. the same path every year.
d. with the seasons.

Work with a partner and check your answers.

Reading

Read a story about some hungry birds who went in search of food.

Wordfile

1. A **valley** is a low area of land between two hills, often with a river running through it.
2. If there is **plenty** of something, there is a lot of it.

Wordfile

3. A **cart** is a wooden vehicle, often pulled by an animal.
4. **Pulses** are seeds that can be cooked and eaten.

Then, one cold and windy day...
Oh, it is so windy. This grain keeps flying out of my reach!
Oh... oh... ooohhhhhhhh! I didn't see that cartwheel coming!
I wonder why our friend Sparrow hasn't come home this evening. Where could she be?
Let's go and look for her.
After a long search...
We've looked everywhere.
There's only one place left – the palace road!
But she told us not to go there! She said it was dangerous!
To their relief, Sparrow was still alive.
Oh, look! What has happened to poor Sparrow?
Come, let us take her back!
... They took the sparrow back to King Bird.
Look, she is able to move her wing!

Cheryl Rao

Wordfile

5. If you **mislead** someone, you do not tell them the truth. The past tense of **mislead** is **misled**.

Comprehension 1

A Choose the correct answer: a, b or c.

1. King Bird wanted to find a place where there was __________.
   a. enough food   b. no food   c. a bit of food
2. Sparrow didn't want to __________ the food.
   a. eat   b. hide   c. share
3. Sparrow told Sunbird __________ the palace road.
   a. to go to   b. not to go to   c. to hide near
4. Sparrow was hit by __________.
   a. flying grain   b. a strong wind   c. a cartwheel
5. The other birds __________ Sparrow.
   a. helped   b. hurt   c. hid

B Number the sentences in the correct order (1–5) as they are said in the story.

a. 'I must find a place where there is enough food for all of us!' ____
b. 'I was greedy.' ____
c. 'Look at all the grain in those carts!' ____
d. 'None of you should ever go to that place!' ____
e. 'She told us not to go there! She said it was dangerous!' ____

Comprehension 2

Think and answer the questions.

1. Why did King Bird decide to leave the forest?
2. Give one example from the story to show that the birds were happy at their new home.

3. Why did Sparrow not tell the other birds about the grain? Do you think she was right?
4. Was the Sparrow sorry at the end? How do you know?
5. What do you learn from the story?

Vocabulary

A **Complete the sentences with the correct adjective from the story.**

hungry	greedy	selfish	happy	horrible	dangerous

1. A __________ person doesn't want to share.
2. You smile when you are __________.
3. A __________ person always wants more and more.
4. Something that is __________ is not pleasant at all, and makes you unhappy.
5. When you are __________, it's time to eat.
6. It's __________ to cross the road without looking.

B **All over the world, birds are dying because of pollution, forests being cut down and hunting.**

Read these words related to saving and protecting birds. Match them with their definitions.

1. extinct	a. to make air, water or land dirty
2. poach	b. the natural home of a plant, animal or bird
3. protect	c. not existing any more
4. endangered	d. to hunt without permission
5. habitat	e. needing to be protected
6. pollute	f. to keep something or someone safe

Grammar

Pronouns

A **pronoun** is a word that is used in place of a noun.

1. Read this sentence.

Sparrow *wanted all the grain.* ***Sparrow*** *did not want to share.* ***Sparrow*** *hurt herself. The other birds saved* ***Sparrow****.*

Notice that the name ***Sparrow*** is repeated many times. Instead of repeating Sparrow's name so many times, we can use a **pronoun**.

Sparrow *wanted all the grain.* ***She*** *did not want to share.* ***She*** *hurt herself. The other birds saved* ***her****.*

she is a **subject pronoun**, used instead of the noun *Sparrow*.

her is an **object pronoun**, used instead of the noun *Sparrow*.

2. Now, read these sentences.

Sparrow hurt ***herself****.* *Have you hurt* ***yourself****?*

We use **reflexive pronouns** such as *myself*, *herself* and *yourself* when the object of the sentence is the same person or thing as the subject.

We also use reflexive pronouns to show that someone did something without any help.

Did you eat all the food ***yourself****?* *Look! I made this* ***myself****!*

Here are some more pronouns:

Subject	**Object**	**Reflexive**
I	me	myself
you (sing.)	you	yourself
he/she/it	him/her/it	himself/herself/itself
we	us	ourselves
you (pl.)	you	yourselves
they	them	themselves

A Complete the sentences with subject and object pronouns.

1. King Bird wanted to help the other birds. ____He____ went to look for food.
2. The other birds went to the land of plenty. ________ were very happy.
3. Sparrow found a lot of food. ________ did not want to share it.
4. Asad and I are having problems. Can you help ________?
5. Have you met Yusuf's parents? ________ are very kind.
6. Yes, I met ________ last month at Yusuf's party.
7. Mrs Kapoor is our new teacher. We really like ________.
8. Where is our friend Sparrow? I can't see ________ anywhere.

B Match the sentence halves.

1. The cat jumped over the wall and hurt
2. Please, let me introduce
3. Thank you for inviting us to your party. We really enjoyed
4. All the food is on the table. Please help
5. Be careful with that knife! You could cut
6. My father is trying to teach

a. ourselves.
b. himself Arabic.
c. yourself!
d. myself. My name is Swati Sharma.
e. itself.
f. yourselves.

Language skills

Using a dictionary

The words at the top of a dictionary page are called **guide words**.

These words show the first and last words on a dictionary page. By looking at these words, you will know which words are on that dictionary page.

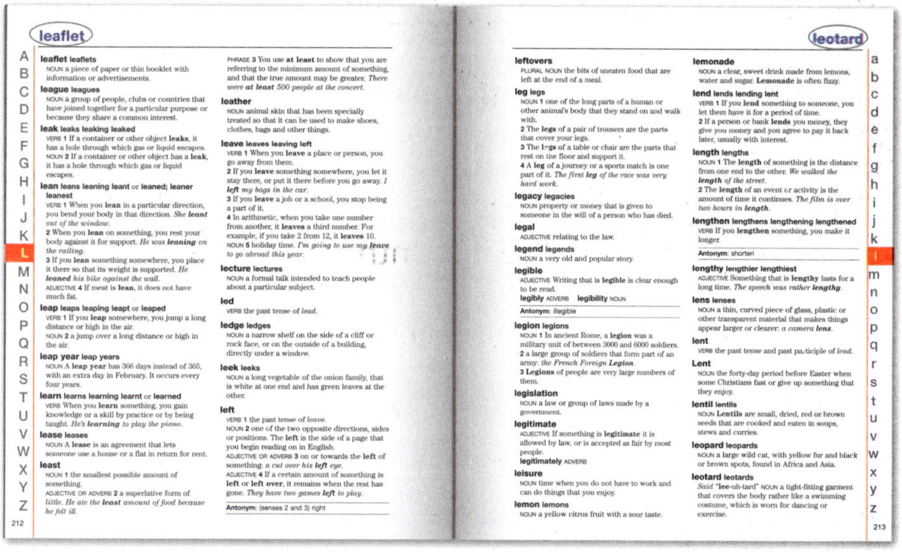

These guide words, taken from a page of the *Collins Primary Illustrated Dictionary*, show that the first word on the left-hand page is *month* and the last word on the right-hand page is *motorcycle*.

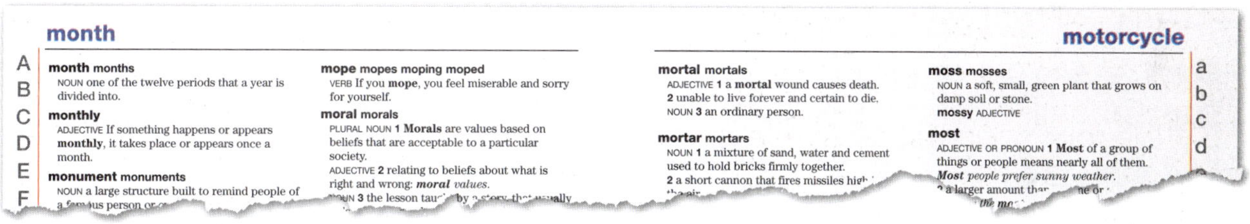

Look at these words. Would you find them on the month–motorcycle dictionary pages shown above? Write Yes or No.

1. month	Yes	2. morning	______
3. mouse	______	4. most	______
5. money	______	6. mobile	______
7. mother	______	8. mosque	______

FA **Listening**

A **Listen to the conversation about World Sparrow Day. Tick [✓] the things that people *should* and *shouldn't* do.**

	People should ...	People shouldn't ...
1. find a solution to help sparrows		
2. think about wildlife		
3. cut down too many trees		
4. destroy birds' nests		
5. ignore the problem		

B **Listen again. Write three things people can do to help sparrows.**

1. People can ____________________
2. People ____________________
3. ____________________

FA **Speaking**

A **Look at the list of tasks and activities. Do you do them yourself, or does someone else help you or do them for you?**

For each task, put a tick [✓] in the column that applies to you.

Task	I do it myself.	Someone else helps me.	Someone else does it for me.
Cleaning my room			
Tidying my room			
Doing my homework			
Making my breakfast			
Waking up in the morning			
Putting my clothes away			

B **Work with a partner.**

Ask and answer questions.

Do you clean your room yourself?

No, my mother does it for me.

C **Now give your partner advice.**

Use *should* and *shouldn't* for telling people about the right way to behave.

sleep late	eat too many chocolates
clean your room yourself	do your homework
be polite to your elders	waste water
put your clothes away yourself	

You shouldn't waste water.

Writing

Work with a partner. Think of ideas to write a story about someone who did not share.

First, answer these questions:

1. Who is the main character? ____________________
2. What did he/she not share? ____________________
3. What happened as a result? ____________________

Write your story. Use these words or your own ideas.

Once upon a time...	They saved their money and bought...
He / She didn't want to share his...	The other children decided to share with him / her.
He / She was selfish / greedy...	He / She felt sorry / thankful / happy...
The other children felt...	Now he / she always shares.
Suddenly, the other children...	

3 Mountain Mona

In this unit, I will...

- learn about the subject and predicate in a sentence
- practise using verbs of movement
- practise hearing and saying the sounds /əʊ/ and /aʊ/
- talk about what I am good at
- write a description of a special event

FA Warm-up

Circle the words in the wordsearch. Then label the pictures.

1. ______________________

R	F	X	S	E	S	O	H	C	A
C	B	B	P	O	T	C	K	A	S
P	U	S	E	W	Z	O	I	I	U
Y	S	Z	C	R	L	H	M	L	N
H	H	F	T	O	Y	L	N	B	F
K	A	K	A	C	L	I	K	P	L
V	Z	R	C	K	R	O	Y	P	O
G	L	K	L	Q	H	N	P	X	W
M	Z	P	E	T	J	U	K	H	E
P	A	B	S	R	G	Q	Z	Y	R

5. ______________________

4. ______________________

2. ______________________

3. ______________________

Reading

What are you good at doing? Is there anything you can't do?

Read the story about a goat that couldn't do things that other goats could do.

Mona was a goat. She lived at the top of a mountain with her brother, her sister and her mother.
Her brother was good at jumping.
Her sister was good at leaping.
Her mother was good at climbing and scrambling[1].

Mona didn't think she was good at ANYTHING... except growing flowers.
Mona grew big yellow sunflowers – huge yellow sunflowers that nodded in the sunshine.
Mona loved them. She fed them and watered them.
She watched them grow... and she smiled.

'Mona,' said her brother, 'goats don't grow flowers. JUMPING is what goats do. If a fierce lion comes along, goats must JUMP out of the way. Jumping is easy peasy[2].
Watch me jump over the bush!' Mona looked round.

'What bush?' she asked.
'THIS bush,' replied her brother.
'Oh,' said Mona. 'I thought it was a rock.'
Mona's brother jumped over the bush.

'There!' he said, 'Now you try!'
Mona tried...
'OW!' she said.
'You should look where you're jumping,' said her brother.

Wordfile

1. To **scramble** means to climb somewhere on all fours
2. Something that is **easy peasy** is very easy.

'I did!' Mona replied, and she went to see her flowers.

'Mona,' said her sister, 'goats don't grow flowers. LEAPING is what goats do. If a fierce lion comes along, goats must LEAP out of the way. Leaping is easy peasy.
Watch me leap from rock to rock!'
Mona looked round.
'What rocks?' she asked.
'THESE rocks,' said her sister.
'Oh,' said Mona. 'I thought they were bushes.'

Mona's sister leapt from rock to rock.
'There!' she said. 'Now you try.'
Mona tried...
'OW!' she said.
'You should look where you're leaping,' said her sister.
'I DID!' replied Mona, and she went to see her sunflowers.

'Mona,' said her mother, 'why don't you try climbing and scrambling?'
Mona sighed a huge sigh.
'All right,' she said 'I'll try.'

Mona began to climb, but she fell on a thistle[3].
She tried to scramble, but she bumped her nose.

'It's no good,' she said, 'I can't do the things other goats can. Besides, I don't LIKE jumping... or leaping ... or climbing... or scrambling.
And I don't care about fierce lions either.
AND I don't like living on top of a mountain.
Mountains make me dizzy[4].'
Mona stomped off[5] down the mountain.

Wordfile

3. A **thistle** is a purple flower with sharp points.
4. If you are **dizzy**, you feel as if everything around you is turning, and you are going to fall.
5. If you **stomp off**, you leave in a bad mood.

At the bottom of the mountain was a lion.
A great big fierce lion.
A great big fierce lion wearing spectacles.
A great big fierce lion wearing spectacles, who opened his mouth WIDE and showed his SHARP teeth.

Mona didn't move. She stood quite still and smiled.
'Excuse me,' said the lion, 'but please don't smile. PLEASE run away. And please do it NOW!'
'Why?' said Mona. 'Because,' said the lion, 'that's what goats do. They run away. Then big fierce lions chase them.'

Mona frowned. 'Are you a lion?'
'YES,' said the lion. 'What did you think I was?'
'Well,' said Mona, 'I thought you were a sunflower.'
'A SUNFLOWER?' The lion looked angry. 'I'm a BIG FIERCE LION!'
Mona looked at the lion more closely.
'I thought you were a BIG sunflower,' she said.

The lion sat down. 'This is terrible,' he said.
'How can I scare anyone if I look like a sunflower?'
Mona thought hard.
'Maybe I'm no good at being scared,' she said, quietly. 'After all, I'm no good at jumping, or leaping or climbing or scrambling. Maybe I'm no good at being scared either.'

'Hmm,' growled the lion. 'But...' He began to look excited. 'What if it's something else? What if you're no good at SEEING things?'
'What do you mean?' asked Mona.
'You thought I was a sunflower, didn't you? Here, try on my spectacles!' 'All right,' said Mona.
She put on the spectacles.

'WOW!' Mona said.
'WOW! I can see for MILES!'
She looked all around.
'WOW! WOW! WOW!'
'Stop saying WOW,' said the lion, 'and look at me.'
Mona looked at the lion.
'WOW' she said, and she sprang in the air. 'You ARE a big fierce lion.'

And Mona jumped...
... and leapt
... and climbed
... and scrambled all the way to the very top of the mountain.

'OI!' roared the lion.
'Bring back my spectacles!'
Mona stood on one leg on the very highest rock.
'You look MUCH fiercer without them!'
she shouted, loudly.
'Oh,' purred the lion. 'DO I'?
And he slipped
... and he staggered[6]
... and he fell over thistles and bushes all the way back down to his cave.

Mona stood on her rock and shouted to her brother, her sister and her mother.
'Look at me!' she said. 'I can jump! And I can leap! And climb! And scramble! I can do all the things goats are meant to do!'
'WOW!' said her brother and sister.
'Good,' said her mother. 'But there's something else you're VERY good at.'
'Is there?' asked Mona. 'What's that?'
'Getting rid of[7] big fierce lions!' said her mother, with a huge smile.

Vivian French and Chris Fisher

Wordfile

6. If you **stagger**, you walk as if you are going to fall.
7. If you **get rid of** something, you make it go away.

Comprehension 1

A Put the sentences in the correct order 1–6.

a. The lion gave Mona his spectacles. ______

b. Mona stomped off down the mountain. ______

c. The lion fell all the way down to his cave. ______

d. Mona tried jumping and leaping but fell. ______

e. Mona loved to grow sunflowers. ______

f. A fierce lion tried to scare Mona. ______

B Complete the sentences. Use these words.

leaping	climbing	scrambling	jumping	growing

1. Mona's brother was good at __________.
2. Mona's sister was good at __________.
3. Mona's mother was good at __________ and __________.
4. Mona was good at __________ sunflowers.

Comprehension 2

A Read this line from the story:

'Jumping is easy peasy. Watch me jump over this bush!'

1. Who says this? ______________________________
2. Who is he talking to? ______________________________
3. Why is he jumping over a bush?______________________________

B **Answer the questions.**

1. Why did Mona have to learn to jump, leap and scramble?

___

2. Was Mona scared of the lion? Why/Why not?

___

3. What happened to the lion at the end?

___

4. Do you think Mona was happy or sad at the end? Why?

___

Vocabulary

A **Circle the correct verb in each sentence.**

1. Watch me **stomp** / **jump** / **scramble** over this bush!
2. Watch me **jump** / **stagger** / **leap** from rock to rock!
3. Why don't you try climbing and **staggering** / **scrambling** / **stomping**?
4. Mona **staggered** / **stomped** / **scrambled** off down the mountain.

B **Match the movement verbs with the pictures.**

a

b

c

d

1. hop
2. wave
3. dig
4. ride
5. kick
6. push
7. skip
8. catch

e

f

g

h

Grammar

Sentence structure: subject-predicate

The **subject** of a sentence is the person or thing that the sentence is about.

A good way to find the subject is to find the verb and then ask the question 'Who...?' or 'What...?'

The **predicate** of a sentence is the part that tells you something about the subject.

For example:

Subject	**Predicate**
Mona	*lived at the top of a mountain.*

Question: Who lived at the top of a mountain?

Answer: **Mona** lived at the top of a mountain.

So in this sentence, *Mona* is the subject and *lived at the top of a mountain* is the predicate.

A Match the subjects with their predicates.

1. Mona	a. was good at leaping.
2. Her brother	b. was wearing spectacles.
3. Her sister	c. loved to grow sunflowers.
4. Her mother	d. fell all the way down to his cave.
5. The lion	e. was good at jumping.
6. He	f. was good at climbing and scrambling.

B Circle the subject and underline the predicate in the following sentences.

1. Daddy gets up early in the morning.
2. Your book is on the table.
3. My brother plays the guitar.
4. A girl from 5th Grade came first in the 100 metre race.
5. The two children helped their mother to clean the house.

C **Add a predicate to these subjects to complete the sentences. Use your own ideas.**

1. Our teacher ____________________
2. This book ____________________
3. My friend ____________________
4. The lion ____________________
5. Goats ____________________

Language skills

Pronunciation: /əʊ/ and /aʊ/

Read these words aloud and put them in the correct column.

/əʊ/	/aʊ/
goat	growl

coal	mouse
clown	owl
goal	towel
comb	foam
bowl	shout

FA

Listening

Raj is choosing people for his team at the school's Annual Day.

Listen to the interview with Samira and Amir.

Tick [✓] the things that they can do and cross [✗] the things that they cannot do.

	Samira	Amir
1.  swimming		
2.  drawing		

3.  cycling		
4.  running		
5. 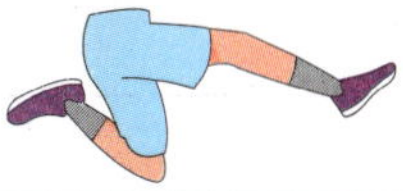 long jump		

Speaking

FA

A **Work with a partner. Ask and answer questions about things that you are good at. Here are some ideas:**

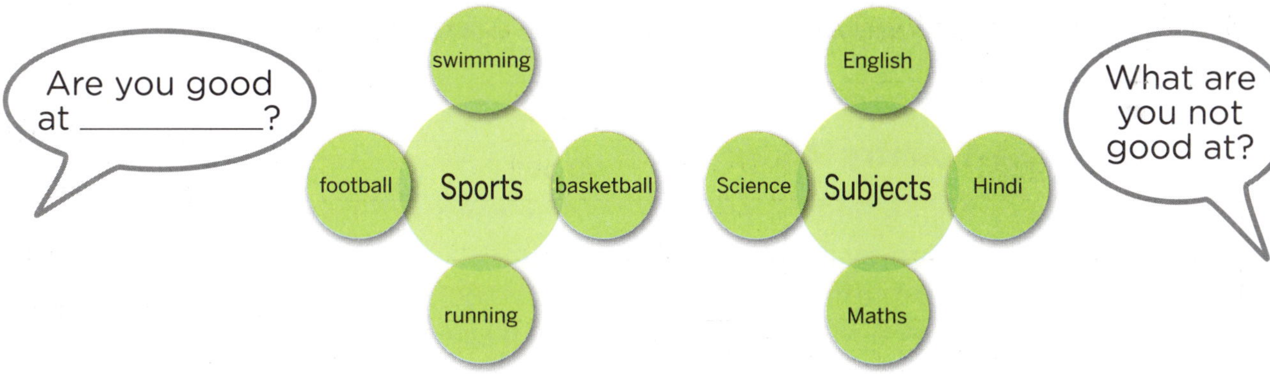

B **Write four activities in the table below.**

Complete the first row for yourself. Use ticks [✓] for 'yes' and crosses [✗] for 'no'.

Complete the table for two classmates.

Name	**Are you good at ...?**				**What are you not good at?**
	______	______	______	______	

Writing

Your school recently celebrated its Annual Day. It was a great day and everyone enjoyed it a lot.

Write a paragraph describing the day. You can write about:

- when and where the event was held
- the special events of the day
- what you participated in
- the main guest

Poem

You are going to read a poem about a town mouse and a country mouse.

Where do you think the town mouse lives?

And where do you think the country mouse lives?

Town Mouse, Country Mouse

You may have read a fable[1] once
Of two mice in country and town
The rural[2] one was happier off
The city one always had a frown.

The country one's life was simple
Frugal[3], basic, rough and tough.
The town one had wealth around
Food and shelter he had enough.

The town one came to country once
And was unable to see the charm
He invited the other one over
'Come see life outside this farm.'

And so the country mouse did scurry[4]
To the city to meet his friend
Where tables lay laden with food
But a broom chased them around
the bend.

The country mouse did choose then
To return to his humble[5] abode[6]
Frightened off by screeches and yells
Such stress being an unbearable load.

Now I wonder if all this
Is as true as made out to be
For in my house I have seven mice
And all do wander here carefree

I feed them myself so often
With bits of food meant for me
Releasing them from our traps
As they look on pleadingly.

My town mice seem happy enough
To put a rural one to shame
Rotund[7] little glistening bods[8]
Twitching whiskers as we play
our game.

Natasha Sharma

Wordfile

1. A **fable** is a short story, usually about animals, that teaches us something.
2. **Rural** things are found in the countryside.
3. A **frugal** life is very simple, and not expensive.
4. If a person or animal **scurries** somewhere, they move there fast with short, quick steps.
5. **Humble** means simple or poor.
6. Someone's **abode** is their home. This is a poetic or old word.
7. **Rotund** means large and plump.
8. **Bod** is short for 'body'.

Poem appreciation

A Answer the questions.

1. According to the poet, who was the happier mouse?
2. What sort of life did the rural mouse lead?
3. Why did the country mouse visit the town mouse? Did he like it there?
4. Why did the town mouse return home?
5. Does the poet believe this story? Give a reason for your answer.

B Match the words with their opposites to describe the life of the two mice.

Country mouse	Town mouse
1. simple	a. unhappy
2. frugal	b. unsafe
3. humble	c. expensive
4. safe	d. difficult
5. happy	e. luxurious

FA **Activity**

Imagine you are a country mouse. Write a paragraph about a day in your life.

Begin like this:

I wake up very early to the sound of the cock's crowing. Then, I...

You can use these phrases to help you.

scurry around the farm	look for food	talk to the animals
sleep on the hay	run away from a snake	drink from the pond
eat fresh vegetables	listen to the birds singing	

A Complete the sentences with the correct words from the box.

lion	invent	buried	share	grain	emperor	field	met

1. In *Twelve Silver Cups,* the thief __________ the cups in a __________.
2. In *The Selfish Sparrow,* the sparrow didn't want to __________ the __________ she found.
3. In *Mountain Mona,* Mona went down the mountain and __________ a fierce __________.

B Complete the names of the sports.

1. Two or four people play this. They use rackets to hit a light object over a net. b__________
2. You do this sport on a bicycle. c__________
3. This is the activity of moving your body through water. s__________
4. In this sport, two teams of eleven players hit a small, hard ball with a long, wooden bat. c__________
5. In this sport, two teams of eleven players try to kick a ball into the other team's goal. f__________
6. This is the activity of moving on ice wearing special boots with metal pieces on the bottom. s__________

C Match these verbs from the story with their descriptions.

1. appear	a. to put your arms around someone because you like them
2. shake your head	b. to put things into a bag, usually to take somewhere
3. scream	c. to suddenly be seen in a place
4. hug	d. to bend your body in a particular direction
5. lean	e. to move your head from side to side, in order to say no or to disagree with someone
6. pack	f. to make a loud, high sound, usually because you are very frightened

D **Complete the sentences with the correct verb of movement. Remember to use the correct form of each verb.**

slip	stomp	hop	scramble	leap	chase

1. The teacher asked the children to __________ on one leg.
2. Ayesha __________ up the rocks on all fours to reach him.
3. He __________ the thief until he caught him.
4. My father __________ on the ice and fell as he was walking to the office.
5. The dog __________ over the gate and ran off.
6. My brother was angry and __________ off to his bedroom.

E **Write about a time when you lost something that you liked very much or were very proud of. Think about the following questions:**

- What did you lose?
- Why was it important to you?
- What was special about it? What did it look like?
- How did you lose it?
- How did you feel?
- Did you get it back?

You can use these phrases to help you, or use your own ideas.

I suddenly noticed/realised that my ... was missing/had gone.
Without realising, I dropped my ....
I looked/searched everywhere, but I couldn't find it.
I couldn't believe it!

____

____

____

____

F **Write a paragraph about what we should do in order to protect the bird population. Use these ideas and any others that you have.**

feed the birds | keep feeding equipment clean | keep cats indoors | plant flowers and bushes that birds like | stop birds flying into windows

G **Write a short paragraph to answer each question.**

1. What things are you good at? (They can be subjects at school or other abilities.)

2. What would you like to be better at? How are you trying to make yourself better?

FA ACTIVITY

A **Look at the pictures and talk about the six differences with a partner.**

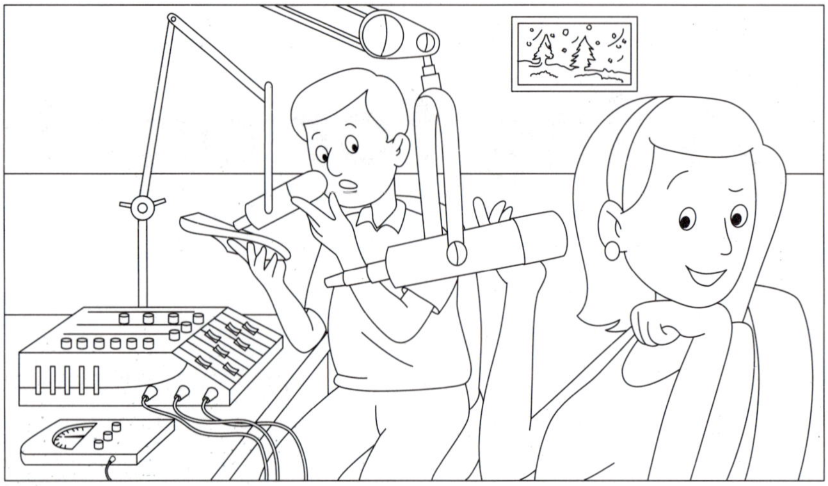

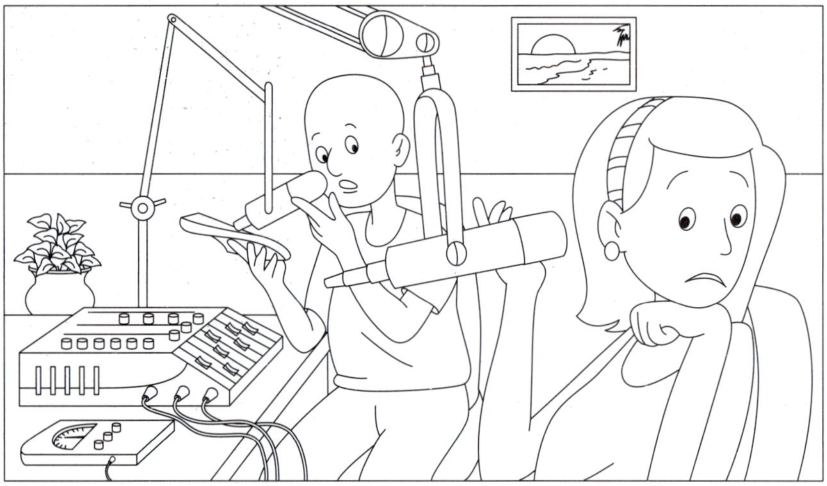

B **Listen and circle the stressed syllables.**

1. spec ta cles
2. lux u ri ous
3. ig nore
4. scram ble
5. min er als
6. pol lu tion
7. en vi ron ment
8. in ven tion
9. snor kel
10. pre da tor

4 Caring for our Planet

In this unit, I will...

- think and talk about different ways of caring for our environment
- practise using the present continuous tense
- learn how to use *should* for giving advice
- practise word stress
- use language for giving opinions in my writing

Warm-up

FA

Work with a partner. Guess whether these statements are true (T) or false (F). Read the text and check your answers.

	T	F
1. Water covers more than half the surface of the Earth.		
2. There are five great oceans on Earth.		
3. Tsunamis are caused by the wind.		
4. A lot of jellyfish die in old plastic bags.		

Reading

Read this excerpt from *Oceans Alive*, a book about life on and under the sea.

Humans and Oceans

Have you ever looked out to sea and wondered what lives within it?

Or how important it is to us, even if we live many miles inland[1]?

We need the sea. It gives us life. It gives us much of the oxygen we breathe and provides us with food and minerals. It provides the water that forms rain, filling our rivers, lakes and reservoirs[2]. We use it to transport people and cargo. We play in it.

Minerals we get from the sea:

We use salt in our food.

Magnesium is used in rockets.

Gas and oil, which people use for fuel, are found under the ocean floor.

Wordfile

1. A place that is **inland** is not near the sea.
2. A **reservoir** is a lake used for storing water.

There are five great oceans on Earth: the Pacific, Atlantic, Indian, Southern and Arctic oceans. They hold 97% of all the water in the world and cover nearly 71% of the Earth's surface. Some oceans are warm, others are icy cold. They are all linked, so what happens to one ocean affects them all.

The Pacific Ocean is the largest ocean in the world. It holds 48% of the world's salt water. The Arctic Ocean is the smallest.

What is a sea? A sea is part of the ocean which has some land surrounding it.

Oceans in Motion

The oceans are never still. Twice a day the tides[3] rise and fall. The wind pushes the water around, making currents. The energy created by tides and waves shapes our coastlines by wearing away the rocks and cliffs.

The sea can give life and take life. Some of the most violent storms begin at sea. Hurricanes or cyclones[4] are revolving[5] storms that form over the ocean. They gather heat and energy from warm water, then speed towards the shore. In 2005, Hurricane Katrina hit the city of New Orleans, USA. Huge floods destroyed everything in their path.

Wordfile

3. The **tide** is the regular rise and fall in the level of the sea.
4. **Hurricanes** and **cyclones** are violent storms.
5. If something **revolves**, it turns in a circle around a central point.

Huge ocean waves caused by underwater earthquakes are called tsunami. They cannot be seen out in the ocean. They gather speed as they get closer to land, travelling up to 800 kilometres per hour. They can push up a wall of water as high as 40 metres. On December 26th, 2004, an earthquake in the Adaman Sea caused a massive tsunami that killed thousands of people. In India, inhabitants of the Andaman and Nicobar islands were badly affected. Many people on these islands were killed or made homeless.

Pollution

Oceans are polluted in many ways: air pollution, sewage[6], chemicals and land rubbish. Would you believe that millions of kilograms of rubbish are thrown into the sea every year?

Old plastic fishing nets and plastic bags are killing hundreds of marine animals. Turtles and other animals try to eat plastic bags, thinking that they are jellyfish. The bags suffocate[7] them, or get stuck in their stomachs.

Fish, crabs, birds and seals become entangled[8] in abandoned fishing nets. They're then unable to get food or defend themselves against predators[9]. For reasons such as these, many sea animals are now on the verge of extinction[10]. The chances of the survival of some species, such as sea turtles, monk seals, sea otters, manatees and orcas, are slim[11].

sea turtle

manatee

Wordfile

6. **Sewage** is liquid waste from people and buildings.
7. If a person or an animal is **suffocated**, they die because they cannot breathe.
8. If a person or animal becomes **entangled** in a net, it gets stuck in it.
9. A **predator** is an animal that kills and eats other animals.
10. If an animal is **on the verge of extinction**, it is dying away, and will probably not exist soon.
11. If you say that the **chances of survival are slim**, you mean that it is not very likely that something will survive.

Oil on the ocean can be extremely harmful. It floats on the surface, covering everything in its path. Spills occur when oil wells[12] leak, or when ships carrying oil have an accident.

Small oil spills farther away from land may be broken up by the waves, or by spraying strong detergents onto them. If the spill is close to land, the chemical in the detergent might harm marine life, so a solution must be found. In 1996, a tanker called the Sea Empress ran into rocks and got stuck near the coast of south Wales. The impact of this was so huge that 72,000 tonnes of crude oil leaked into the sea. It took more than a year to clean up the oil spill.

How can we help?

1. Learn about the oceans

The more we learn about the oceans, the more we will want to look after them. Join a marine studies group or learn how to snorkel[13].

2. Beach clean-ups

Now, thousands of people are joining volunteer groups to help clean up beaches. In a recent clean-up in the UK, volunteers found an average of one piece of litter every 52 centimetres.

3. Plant trees

Trees help to keep our air fresh. They hold the soil in place, so that loose soil doesn't fill our rivers and wash into the sea.

4. Limit your catch

If you go fishing, don't take more fish than you can eat. For our oceans to survive we must preserve them, protect them and prevent further pollution.

Angie and Andy Belcher

Wordfile

12. An **oil well** is a deep hole under the ground or the sea where oil is taken out.
13. To **snorkel** means to swim under the water wearing a special tube that fits in your mouth so that you can breathe.

Comprehension 1

A Complete the sentences with the correct answers: a, b or c.

1. Rainwater comes from ________.
   a. rivers and lakes b. the sea c. reservoirs
2. Salt and magnesium are examples of ________ that we take from the sea.
   a. gas b. cargo c. minerals
3. Hurricanes and cyclones are types of ________.
   a. storm b. flood c. tsunami
4. Tsunami begin ________.
   a. 40 metres high b. 800 kilometres away c. under the sea
5. Plastic objects are a particularly common form of ________.
   a. pollution b. sewage c. rubbish
6. An oil spill is a problem because oil ________ on the sea.
   a. breaks b. floats c. carries

B List the reasons why marine life is in danger.

C State two things that we can do to care for the oceans.

Comprehension 2

A Work with a partner. Ask each other these questions.

1. Have you ever been to the seaside?
2. What did you do there?
3. Was the water clean?
4. Was the beach clean?

Share your ideas with the rest of the class.

B Write three sentences about things we can do to help. Use one of these words in each sentence.

1. We can ______________________________
2. We can ______________________________
3. We can ______________________________

nets
rubbish
oil

Vocabulary

Rearrange the letters in brackets to complete the words in the sentences.

1. We should try harder to protect the envir ___ ___ ___ ent (m o n).
2. Waste from the factory pol ___ ___ ___ es (u t l) the river.
3. These birds are only found in the tropical rai ___ ___ ___ rest (o f n).
4. We have more floods nowadays because of clim ___ ___ ___ (t a e) change.
5. The tiger is an enda ___ ___ ___ red (n e g) species.
6. An animal's hab ___ ___ ___ t (a t i) is the environment it lives in.
7. Air pollu ___ ___ ___ n (i t o) is a problem in the big cities.
8. The rising temperature of the Earth's atmosphere is called glo ___ ___ ___ (b l a) warming.

Grammar

Should and *shouldn't*

Should is a type of verb that we use with another verb to:

1. give advice
2. talk about the right thing to do in a situation.

*People **should** find better ways of dealing with oil spills.*

*We **should** protect endangered sea animals.*

We use **should not** or **shouldn't** to talk about wrong behaviour or actions.

*We **should not** pollute our oceans.*

*Fishermen **shouldn't** leave their nets in the sea.*

A Complete the sentences. Use *should* or *should not*.

1. We ________________ think about how we can care for our planet.
2. We ________________ throw things away if we can use them again.
3. The oceans are important to us. We ________________ keep them clean.
4. We ________________ throw rubbish into the sea.
5. People ________________ hunt animals.
6. Oil companies ________________ transport oil very carefully.
7. People ________________ recycle as much as possible.

B **Rearrange the words to give advice. Add a capital letter and a full stop.**

1. We are not sure where the airport is.

   look at / you / a map / should

   You should look at a map.

2. This piece of music is too difficult for her to play.

   she / more / practise / often / should

   She should ______________________________

3. Rahul is worried that he is not going to pass the English exam.

   harder / study / he / should

   ____

4. My room is very untidy and I can't find anything.

   should / your / you / room / tidy

   ____

5. I love tennis but my friends don't like it at all.

   join / tennis club / should / you / the

   ____

6. Their car is very old and often breaks down.

   buy / a / they / new one / should

   ____

Present continuous tense

We use the **present continuous tense** to talk about what is happening now. Compare it with the simple present tense:

Simple present: *I **go** to school every day.*

Present continuous: *I **am doing** my homework at the moment.*

We form the present continuous with *am/is/are* + verb *-ing*.

If the verb ends in -e, we remove the e and add *-ing*.

make → making *drive → driving*

C Complete the paragraph using the *-ing* form of these verbs.

work plant recycle save use adopt take pollute

Ways of saving our planet

These days everyone is [1] working to save our planet Earth. People are [2] ________ new ways of living which will help to save our natural resources. We are now [3] ________ more trees. People are [4] ________ less; they are [5] ________ public transport instead of private vehicles. Schools and offices are [6] ________ paper. Solar energy panels are being installed. Some communities are also [7] ________ the rain water. People are [8] ________ steps to spread awareness about ways of saving water and natural fuels. It is very encouraging to see so many efforts being made to save our planet.

Language skills

Apostrophe *s* to show belonging

We use an **apostrophe** or **apostrophe *s* ('s)** to show that someone or something belongs or relates to someone or something.

*Mr Sen'**s** house* (= the house that belongs to Mr Sen OR the house where Mr Sen lives)

1. We add apostrophe *s* to the end of:
   a. singular words or personal names
      *a baby'**s** toy* *Mala'**s** book* *the Earth'**s** surface*
   b. plurals that do not end in *s*
      *children'**s** games* *women'**s** clothes* *people'**s** houses*
   c. certain jobs to indicate a place of work
      *Vivek is going to the doctor'**s**.* *Mummy is at the hairdresser'**s**.*
2. We add apostrophe *s* OR apostophe only to names that already end in *s*.
   *James'**s** car* *Mr Bates' garden*
3. We add apostrophe only to plurals that already end in *s*.
   the students' books *the teachers' room*

Tick [✓] the correct option.

1. Sara's father bought her a bicycle. [ ]
   Saras father bought her a bicycle. [ ]
2. Kailas asked for Rheas books. [ ]
   Kailas asked for Rhea's books. [ ]
3. We are going to the Principals' room. [ ]
   We are going to the Principal's room. [ ]
4. How many zeros are there in a lakh? [ ]
   How many zero's are there in a lakh? [ ]
5. The students were all sitting in the girls room. [ ]
   The students were all sitting in the girls' room. [ ]
6. Rohini is going to the dentists for her checkup. [ ]
   Rohini is going to the dentist's for her checkup. [ ]

FA **Listening**

Listen and match the names with suitable advice.

1. Lisa
2. Bela
3. Farida
4. Vijay
5. Samuel
6. Yusuf

a. She should go to see the doctor.
b. He should stop eating so much.
c. She should try waking up early and getting ready on time.
d. She should do her homework more carefully.
e. He should put things safely in his bag.
f. He shouldn't argue with his brother.

FA **Speaking**

Work with a partner. Look at the Listening exercise again.

Say what each person should or shouldn't do and say why. Use 'because'.

Lisa should go to see the doctor because her leg hurts.

Writing

Read these words and their meanings.

Verb	Meaning
reduce	to make something smaller, or less in amount
reuse	to use something again
recycle	to do something to paper, glass, aluminium, etc, so that it can be used again

The words 'reduce, reuse and recycle' are often used to remind people how to care for our environment.

Using these ideas, write three short paragraphs explaining how we can help.

Useful phrases

Introducing paragraphs:
Firstly, ...
Secondly, ...
Thirdly, ... / Lastly, ...

Expressing an opinion:
I think...
In my opinion / view, ...
The best way to... is to...
We can...
We should..., People should...

5 Kaleidoscope

In this unit, I will...

- read a story about funny inventions
- revise words for jobs and the equipment that people use
- learn about comparative adjectives
- practise spelling words ending in *-ful*
- work in a team to make up an invention

Warm-up

FA

An **invention** is something that someone has planned and made for the first time.

An **inventor** sees a problem and finds a solution.

How many new words can you make from the word 'inventions'? Write the new words in the table.

Give yourself points for each word. The more letters there are in a word, the more points you get.

inventions		
2-letter words (1 point)	**3-letter words (2 points)**	**4-letter words (3 points)**
in	tin	nets

Reading

You are going to read a play about an emperor who asked his wise men and women to invent useful things. What sort of things do you think they invented?

Characters

Narrator (Storyteller)
Emperor[1]
Palace sage[2]
Inventor 1
Inventor 2
Inventor 3
Inventor 4
Sign Carrier
Inventors, Wise Men and Women or Palace Attendants

Narrator: It is said that the Great Emperor of all Emperors once called for all his wisest and cleverest people to gather at the royal palace.
(Wise men and women move in and gather around the Emperor.)

(*Trumpet fanfare*[3].)

Emperor: Wise sages, I wish you all to go away for ten years and invent useful things. Whoever invents the most useful thing of all, will win 3,500 chocolate biscuits! *(They all move off enthusiastically talking and making plans. Inventors could act out designing and constructing various inventions.*

Sign Carrier enters with sign: 'Ten Years Later'.)

Narrator: After ten long years, a queue began to gather outside the palace of the Great Emperor of all Emperors. One by one, the people were asked in to show the Emperor their inventions.

Palace Sage: Number two hundred and forty-seven.

Emperor: And what of your invention, old woman?

Wordfile

1. An **emperor** is a ruler of a country, like a king.
2. A **sage** is a very wise and clever person.
3. A **fanfare** is a short piece of music played on a trumpet to announce an important event.

Inventor 1: *(Kneeling at the feet of the Emperor.)* I have invented windscreen wipers for spectacles, Your Highness.

Emperor: Excellent. Very useful for when it is raining. Not a prize winner though, I'm afraid. *(Inventor 1 shuffles off[4].)*

Palace Sage: Number two hundred and forty-eight!

Move along please.

Inventor 2: *(Crouching[5] at the feet of the Emperor.)* Great Emperor, I have invented square tomatoes!

Emperor: Very good, old man. Most useful for putting tomatoes into boxes, but not a prize winner, I'm afraid.

Narrator: The inventions just kept on coming and coming. Ten years had resulted in some very creative thinking indeed.

Palace Sage: Number three hundred and fifty-six!

Inventor 3: *(Holding her invention up for all to see.)* Great Emperor of Emperors, I have invented a pencil that sharpens itself.

Emperor: I like it! Very useful when you are too tired to use a pencil sharpener, but not a prize winner, I'm afraid.

Wordfile

4. If someone **shuffles off**, they walk away slowly.
5. If someone **is crouching**, they are in a position where their body is close to the ground.

Narrator: One man had invented the Kaleidoscope[6]. *(Inventor 4 hands his Kaleidoscope to the Palace Sage, who then hands it on to the Emperor.)*

Emperor: What's this?

Inventor 4: You look through it.

Emperor: It's a telescope, is it? Well I'm afraid that telescopes have already been invented. Hard luck. Goodbye. Next!

Inventor 4: It's not a telescope, but you *do* look through it.

Emperor: What's the point of looking through something that *looks* like a telescope, but isn't a telescope?

Inventor 4: You look through it, then you twist it and move it and before you know what's what, you find yourself saying, Ooh! Or on another day, you might look through it and find yourself saying, Ahhh! And I have to tell you this. Sometimes people find themselves saying Ooh! and Ahhh! all the time.

Emperor: But what's the use of that? I asked for inventions that are useful, not for some stupid little thing that makes you say funny noises all the time. Thank you and goodbye. Next!

Inventor 4: Just try it.

Emperor: *(crossly)* Oh, if I must!

Narrator: So the Emperor picked up the kaleidoscope. He twisted it and turned it, moved it and he looked through it. And when he saw all the colours of the rainbow glowing there and when he saw all those patterns changing over and over again, he said...

Emperor: Ooh!

(Twists the kaleidoscope.)

Ahhh!

(Looking quizzically[7] at the kaleidoscope.)

Yes, it's very nice, but what's it for? Is it useful?

Wordfile

6. A **kaleidoscope** is a tube with coloured pieces inside. When you look into it, you see colourful changing patterns.
7. If you look at someone or something **quizzically**, you look at them in a confused way.

Inventor 4: If you think about it, it's very useful. People travel all over the world to look for things like the Grand Canyon[8] or the Eiffel Tower[9] so that when they see them, they will say Ooh! and Ahhh! With this invention you won't have to move out of your chair. All you have to do is carry the kaleidoscope in your pocket.

Emperor: Very good point indeed. Hmmmm.

Inventor 4: Whenever you feel like a quick Ooh! or a quick Ahhh! you take it out, look through it, twist it around a bit and there you are...

Narrator: But the Great Emperor wasn't listening. He was too busy looking through the world's first kaleidoscope and saying Ooh! and Ahhh!

Later, much later, the man received his promised reward.

(Palace Sage exits and returns with a huge box labelled 3,500 Chocolate Biscuits.)

Palace Sage: There we go. Your prize. It's 3,500 chocolate biscuits. Freshly baked in the Emperor's brand *new*... fan-forced oven[10]!

Mark Carthew

Wordfile

8. The **Grand Canyon** is a very deep valley in the United States of America.
9. The **Eiffel Tower** is a famous structure in Paris, France.
10. A **fan-forced oven** is an oven that cooks food quickly.

Comprehension 1

A **Number the sentences in the order that they are spoken in the play.**

a. Number two hundred and forty-seven. ____

b. It's a telescope, is it? ____

c. Ooh! *(twists the kaleidoscope)* Ahhh! ____

d. Wise sages, I wish you all to go away for ten years and invent useful things. ____

e. Emperor, I have invented square tomatoes! ____

B **Are these sentences true or false? Circle T or F.**

1. The Emperor wanted people to invent the most beautiful thing. T / F
2. The Emperor announced a prize of 350 chocolate biscuits. T / F
3. The Emperor thought the kaleidoscope was a telescope. T / F
4. If you want to be amazed and say 'Ooh' and 'Ahhh', then you look into a telescope. T / F
5. The winning invention was number 356. T / F

C **Answer the questions.**

1. How many years did the Emperor give people to invent a useful thing?
2. Name two of the inventions that people made. Explain how they were useful.
3. What is a kaleidoscope useful for?

Comprehension 2

Answer the questions.

1. Which invention do you find the most useful and why?
2. If you invented something, what would you make?
3. Draw and label your invention and write two sentences to explain what it is.

Vocabulary

A An inventor invents things. Who does these jobs? Complete their names.

1. I do magic tricks: ___ a ___ i ___ i a ___
2. I make things from wood: ___ a ___ ___ e ___ ___ e ___
3. I take care of you when you are ill or hurt: ___ o ___ ___ o ___
4. I fly into space in a spaceship: a ___ ___ ___ o ___ a u ___
5. I work in movies and in plays: a ___ ___ o ___
6. I play cricket: ___ ___ i ___ ___ e ___ e ___

B Match these people with the inventions they use.

1. astronaut	a. 
2. football player	b. 
3. baker	c. 
4. fireman	d. 
5. mason	e. 

Grammar

Adjectives: comparative forms

When we compare two things or people, we use a **comparative** form of the adjective.

*The woman is **tall**.*

*The man is **taller**.*

We can add **than** after the comparative adjective.

*The man is **taller than** the woman.*

To make comparative forms:

1. For short words, add **-er** to the adjective.

   long → long**er**   short → short**er**

   fast → fast**er**   clever → clever**er**

2. When the adjective ends in **-y**, change the **y** to **i** and add **er**.

   pretty → prett**ier**   hungry → hungr**ier**

   silly → sill**ier**   funny → funn**ier**

3. For long words, use **more** in front of the adjective.

   wonderful → **more** wonderful   interesting → **more** interesting

A **Complete the sentences with comparative adjectives.**

1. Arpita is tall. Jasmine is ________.

2. Aadi is small. Hari is ________.

3. The shoes are expensive. The ring is ________ ________.

4. The bag is heavy. The suitcase is ________.

5. The lion is fast. The cheetah is ________.

6. John is happy. Harjit is ________.

B Complete the sentences. Use the comparative form of the adjective in brackets and *than*.

1. Sara is ________________________ Mala. *(small)*
2. My brother is ________________________ me. *(old)*
3. Your car is ________________________ ours. *(new)*
4. My shoes are ________________________ yours. *(dirty)*
5. Saif's school is ________________________ my school. *(near)*
6. It's ________________________ it was yesterday. *(sunny)*

Language skills

Spelling: words ending in *-ful*

You can add ***-ful*** to a noun to make an adjective that describes people or things that have that thing.

use → use**ful** pain → pain**ful**

colour → colour**ful** joy → joy**ful**

When you add ***-ful*** to a noun that ends in a consonant + ***-y***, change the ***y*** to ***i*** and add ***-ful***.

plen**ty** → plent**iful**

A consonant is any letter other than a, e, i, o or u

Make '-ful' adjectives from these nouns.

1. care ______________
2. hope ______________
3. beauty ______________
4. help ______________
5. pain ______________
6. power ______________

FA

Listening

Listen to the description of an invention. Circle the correct words.

This is my new invention. It feeds fish. It is [1]**clever / cleverer** than a normal fish bowl. The fish that live in it will be [2]**bigger / big** than other fish. They will always get fed at the right time. Everyone else's fish will be [3]**hungrier / hungry** than the fish living in your fishbowl!

And no more dirty fishbowls. All your friends' fishbowls will be [4]**dirty / dirtier** than yours. This fishbowl cleans itself. Your fish will always live in a [5]**cleaner / clean** fish bowl.

Speaking

FA

Work with a partner. Look around you at the people in your classroom.

Make two comparative sentences about a person.

Use *He...* or *She....* Do not say the person's name. For example:

She is smaller than Alka.

Your partner must guess who or what you are talking about.

Use comparative forms of these adjectives.

young tall fast thin short old small light heavy

She is taller than me.

She is smaller than Swati.

Is it Parveen?

Writing

A Work with a partner or a small group. You are going to plan an invention.

1. Think of a boring or time-consuming task.
2. Imagine an invention which could do that task for you.
3. Draw and label a picture of your invention.

B Write a paragraph describing your invention.

1. Describe how you thought up your invention.
2. Describe why this invention is useful. Who would use it?

Useful phrases

We invented this machine because...
Our invention is useful because it can...
This invention will help...
People can use this invention when...
This invention works by... [verb + *-ing*]
We use this because it is...

Poem

'Fabulous' things exist only in stories. This poem is about a 'fabulous beast'.

What do you think a fabulous beast might look like?

Fabulous Beast

for Maahir

There's a fabulous beast in my neighbourhood –
It's called the Garbage Truck.
It arrives every morning and gobbles up[1]
Everything that *we* call yuck[2]!

Its mouth is in its rear-end[3]
And it's always gaping[4] wide.
In its head it's got a human
Who takes it for a ride.

When it's done its rounds you'll see
Stuck between its pointy teeth
Curls of peel and plastic bags
Fish bones and shreds[5] of meat.

And when it's full, it spits it out –
Wack-thhoo – onto a garbage dump.
And that's why this monstrous[6] beast
Never gets fat or even plump!

Sampurna Chattarji

Wordfile

1. To **gobble** something **up** means to eat something very quickly.
2. We say **'Yuck!'** when we see, taste or smell something horrible.
3. The **rear-end** of something is the part that is at the back.
4. If something **is gaping**, it is open wide.
5. **Shreds** are small thin pieces of something that has been used or destroyed.
6. **Monstrous** means very big, like a monster.

Poem appreciation

1. What is the fabulous beast? Where is it?
2. What does it look like?
3. Who takes the beast for a ride?
4. Read these lines from the poem:

> And when it's full, it spits it out –
> *Wack-thhoo* – onto a garbage dump.

   a. What is being talked about here?
   b. What does the poet call it? Why?
   c. What is it full of?

5. The words 'truck' and 'yuck' end with the same sound. When words end with the same sound, we say that they **rhyme**.

   Find two more pairs of words in the poem that **rhyme**.

   ________ rhymes with ________.

   ________ rhymes with ________.

Activity

FA

Draw a 'fabulous beast' of your own. Write a sentence explaining why it is fabulous.

It could be a thing, an animal or even a bird.

FA REVISION 2

A Complete the sentences with the correct words.

emperor protect invent oceans

1. In Caring for the Planet, we learnt about things we can do to ____________ our ____________.
2. 2. In Kaleidoscope, the ____________ wanted his people to ____________ things.

B Match the beginning of each sentence with its ending.

1. Most scientists now agree that human activity is causing climate
2. The rise in temperatures around the world is usually known as global
3. By cutting down trees, we are destroying many animals' natural
4. Unfortunately, the mountain gorilla is now an endangered
5. The traffic in cities is causing terrible air
6. A wide variety of animals live in the tropical

a. species.
b. rainforests.
c. pollution.
d. habitats.
e. change.
f. warming.

C Find a word in the story Kaleidoscope that means:

1. to arrive at a place after a long journey (verb) ____________
2. a person whose job is to protect someone (noun) ____________
3. wanting more of something than is fair (adjective) ____________
4. to say to someone that you will definitely do something (verb) ____________
5. to make someone suffer in some way because they have done something wrong (verb) ____________
6. to suddenly begin laughing or crying loudly (verb) ____________

D **Create a leaflet explaining what children at your school should do in order to protect the environment. Use the words 'should' and 'shouldn't'. Explain why these things are important. Here are some ideas you could include in your leaflet.**

lights paper litter reduce trees
reuse water recycle save

We should write on both sides of any paper that we use. Why should we do this?

- to save paper
- to protect trees
- to save other resources

FA

REVISION 2

E **Which of these inventions do you think is the most useful? Write a paragraph about why you consider this invention to be the most useful.**

electric light | freezer | bicycle | spaceship | telescope | garbage truck | oven | mobile phone

A **Look at the three topics. Choose one and talk about it for two minutes. You have five minutes to make notes.**

1. Why is it important to have good friends?
2. What can we do to take care of the environment?
3. Talk about three interesting inventions.

B **Listen and tick (✓) the correct answer.**

1. Which sport do the boys decide to watch on TV?

a. ☐

b. ☐

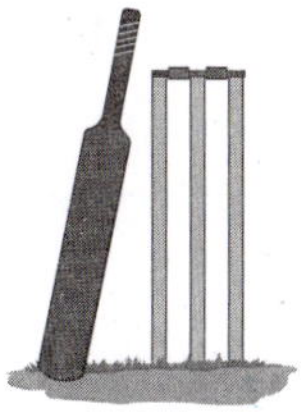

c. ☐

2. Which bird is in the zoo?

a. ☐

b. ☐

c. ☐

3. What is Sanjit doing?

a. ☐

b. ☐

c. ☐

FA ACTIVITY

FA

GRAMMAR PRACTISE

Unit 1: Twelve Silver Cups

A Circle the correct word to complete the sentences.

1. Look up at *the / a* sky!
2. Have you got *a / an* umbrella that I could borrow, please?
3. We must do all we can to protect *a / the* environment.
4. We all sat down on *the / a* ground.
5. I can't cook at all, but my sister is *the / a* fantastic cook.
6. My mother bought me a skirt and a dress. Unfortunately, *the / a* dress was too small.
7. *The / A* Nile is the longest river in the world.

B Complete the table by putting these nouns in the correct place.

love Varanasi badminton herd ambulance team the Taj Mahal group honesty child Sara ambition Sachin Tendulkar anger laptop gang

Common noun	Proper noun	Collective noun	Abstract noun

Unit 2: The Selfish Sparrow

A Complete the sentences with the correct word. You will need one word twice.

her she him he himself

My older brother, Ravi, had an accident the other day while my mother was out at my aunt's house. [1]__________ was preparing the vegetables for the evening meal and accidentally cut [2]__________ on a sharp knife. He called my mother at my aunt's house and told [3]__________ what had happened. [4]__________ drove home immediately and took [5]__________ to the hospital in the next town.

Luckily the cut wasn't deep and Ravi was fine. A nurse just put a bandage on the cut and told [6]__________ to be more careful next time he was using a knife!

B Put the words in the correct order to make sentences. Use capital letters and full stops wherever needed.

1. to the other / myself / I introduced / guests

   ____

2. dried / their towels / after swimming they / themselves on

   ____

3. my father / himself to play / is teaching / the guitar

   ____

4. the party / enjoyed / we really / ourselves at

   ____

5. that sharp knife / not to cut / be careful / yourself with

   ____

6. herself / the ice / she slipped on / and hurt

   ____

FA GRAMMAR PRACTISE

Unit 3: Mountain Mona

A Look at the <u>underlined</u> part of these sentences. Write S if the <u>underlined</u> part is a subject and P if it is a predicate.

1. <u>My father</u> was a very good athlete when he was younger. ______
2. My sister <u>studies very hard</u>. ______
3. <u>Most of my friends</u> are good at sports. ______
4. My bicycle <u>needs mending</u>. ______
5. <u>My uncle's car</u> broke down last week. ______
6. <u>My best friend's mother</u> is always baking delicious cakes. ______

B Which part of these sentences is missing? Write S if the subject is missing and write P if the predicate is missing. Then complete the sentence using your own idea.

1. My first teacher ____________________. ______
2. ____________________ was a great success. ______
3. ____________________ is my favourite piece of clothing. ______
4. My neighbour's house ____________________. ______
5. My favourite food ____________________. ______
6. ____________________ is really good fun. ______

Unit 4: Caring for our Planet

A <u>Underline</u> the correct word to complete these sentences about the right thing to do.

1. We *should / shouldn't* walk or cycle to places rather than go by car.
2. We *should / shouldn't* remember to turn the light off when we leave a room.
3. We *should / shouldn't* leave electrical equipment on when we are not using it.

4. We *should / shouldn't* reuse things rather than keep buying new things.
5. We *should / shouldn't* buy more food than we need.
6. We *should / shouldn't* throw litter on the ground where it may cause problems for wildlife.
7. We *should / shouldn't* plant trees to make our air fresher.
8. We *should / shouldn't* take more fish from the sea than we need.

B Tick (✓) the correct sentence in each pair.

1. a. I leave the house at seven-thirty every morning. ☐
   b. I am leaving the house at seven-thirty every morning. ☐
2. a. I'm reading a really good book at the moment. ☐
   b. I read a really good book at the moment. ☐
3. a. The phone rings. Can you answer it? ☐
   b. The phone is ringing. Can you answer it? ☐
4. a. Could you be quiet, please? The baby is sleeping! ☐
   b. Could you be quiet, please? The baby sleeps! ☐
5. a. We are having the same lunch every day! ☐
   b. We have the same lunch every day! ☐
6. a. My sister has long hair. ☐
   b. My sister is having long hair. ☐

C Compete the paragraph with the correct form of the verb in brackets.

I __________ [1] (live) by the sea. I __________ [2] (go) diving every weekend. I usually, __________ [3] (dive) with my father and my sister, but today, I __________ [4] (dive) with my uncle. We __________ [5] (leave) the house early because we __________ [6] (go) quite far out on his boat and dive down to a coral reef. Unfortunately, lots of tourists have come to the reef and damaged it, so today we __________ [7] (try) to clean the reef by removing any rubbish. Lots of people __________ [8] (join) us. It is going to be a good day!

FA GRAMMAR PRACTISE

Unit 5: Kaleidoscope

A Write the comparative form of these words.

1. tall ______________
2. easy ______________
3. cheap ______________
4. beautiful ______________
5. pretty ______________
6. nice ______________
7. fast ______________
8. clever ______________
9. interesting ______________
10. funny ______________
11. short ______________
12. thin ______________
13. dirty ______________
14. boring ______________
15. silly ______________
16. clean ______________

B Match the sentences and complete the second sentence with the comparative form of the adjective in brackets.

1. Bela's room is quite small.
2. Bela's bag is quite light.
3. Bela's tennis racket was quite cheap.
4. Bela's exam was quite easy.
5. Bela's house is quite old.
6. Bela's grandmother is quite young.

a. Yours is much ______________. (heavy)

b. Yours is much ______________. (modern)

c. Yours was much ______________. (difficult)

d. Yours is quite a lot ______________. (big)

e. Yours is a bit ______________. (old)

f. Yours was much ______________. (expensive)

Comparing city life with village life

What do you think the differences and similarities are between life in the city and life in a village?

Find a person who was brought up in the city and someone who was brought up in a village. You may need to look outside your class. Ask them the questions below. Think of two more questions and add them to the questionnaire.

Questionnaire

1. Is there a school? If 'yes', does it have a proper building and good facilities?
2. How far is the nearest school from your home?
3. How do the children get to the school?
4. Is there a library nearby where people can get books to read?
5. Is there regular electricity and a water supply?
6. What do people do in their free time?
7. What are the children's favourite games?
8. Where do people usually go for holidays?
9. Are there movie theatres nearby?
10. Do the people celebrate festivals with their immediate family or with local people?
11. What do most adults do for a living?
12. Do you prefer village life or city life?

Fill in the comparison table with the answers you get.

Country life	Village life

Keeping the environment clean

A In Unit 4, we read about how important it is to keep the environment clean.

Tick the things we must all do to keep our environment clean and healthy.

1. Plant trees, and water them from time to time. ☐
2. Throw garbage on the roads. ☐
3. Recycle waste water and other waste materials. ☐
4. Get vehicles checked for pollution regularly. ☐
5. Organize and participate in cleanliness drives from time to time. ☐
6. Use paper bags. Avoid using plastic bags. ☐

B Do you try to keep the environment clean for yourself and for others? What sort of things do you do?

Write a diary entry about your daily routine, pointing out things that you do to preserve our environment.

Unit 1: Twelve Silver Cups

Language skills

B. a first
b second
c third

C. fourth, fifth, sixth, seventh, eighth, ninth, tenth, eleventh, twelfth]

Listening

Policeman: Hello, Jeffery. I understand that your silver cups have been stolen. I have some questions for you. ... First of all, where did you keep your cups?

Jeffery: I kept them on the shelf in the living room.

Policeman: Right. When did you last see them?

Jeffery: Yesterday evening. I saw them before I went to bed.
Policeman: And what time was that?

Jeffery: Around nine o'clock.

Policeman: Who went to bed after you?

Jeffery: My mum and dad. I finished my homework and went straight upstairs.
Policeman: OK. And did you hear anything odd in the night?

Jeffery: No, I didn't.
Policeman: Hmm... was anything else missing this morning?

Jeffery: No, the burglar didn't take anything else.

Policeman: Thank you, Jeffery. We will try to find your cups very soon.

Jeffery: Thank you, Sir.

Unit 2: The Selfish Sparrow

Listening

A: Did you know that World Sparrow Day is in March?
B: No, what is that?
A: Well, there are fewer sparrows around the world now, which is a big problem. So, World Sparrow Day is a day for telling people about this problem. This is not someone else's problem. We should find a solution to this problem ourselves.
B: Oh, I see! I love sparrows. But why are their numbers falling?
A: No one really knows why it's happening. But some people think the sparrow's habitat is being destroyed. People should think about wildlife when they build new houses and offices. People shouldn't cut down so many trees!
B: Oh, I didn't know about this. I'd like to get involved. What can I do?
A: Well, there are lots of things you can do, and you can really enjoy yourself at the same time. You can set out a bird feeder with grain and water or make a nest box for sparrows. When you go for a picnic, you should leave crumbs and grain on the grass! Or you can introduce yourself to your local community wildlife group that plants bushes and shrubs in parks and neighbourhoods.
B: That sounds great. We shouldn't ignore this problem!

Unit 3: Mountain Mona

Listening

Raj: Hello, Amir and Samira
Amir and Samira: Hello, Raj.
Raj: I'm choosing my team for the Annual Day. Could you please answer a few questions?
Samira: Yes, of course.
Amir: Sure.
Raj: Are you good at swimming?
Samira: Yes, I'm quite good.
Amir: No, I'm not a very good swimmer.
Raj: Are you good at drawing?
Samira: No! I'm terrible!
Amir: Sorry, I can't draw either!
Raj: Are you good at cycling?
Samira: Not really.
Amir: Oh yes; it's my favourite sport!
Raj: Are you good at running?
Samira: Yes.

Amir: Me too!

Raj: One last question. Are you good at long jump?

Samira: No, I can't do it at all.

Amir: Yes, I came first in long jump last year.

Raj: Thank you, Samira and Amir. That was very helpful.

Unit 4: Caring for our Planet

Listening

1. Lisa hurt her leg playing tennis.
2. Bela got three out of ten for this exercise.
3. Farida is late for school every day.
4. Vijay lost the note from his teacher.
5. Samuel is arguing with his brother, Jacob.
6. Yusuf is getting fat because he loves eating chocolate.

Unit 5: Kaleidoscope

Listening

This is my new invention. It feeds the fish. It is cleverer than a normal fish bowl. The fish that live in it will be bigger than other fish. They will always get fed at the right time. Everyone else's fish will be hungrier than the fish living in this fishbowl!

And no more dirty fishbowls. All your friends' fishbowls will be dirtier than yours. This fishbowl cleans itself. Your fish will always live in a cleaner fish bowl.

Activity 1

Listening

A. One: **spec**tacles
Two: lux**u**rious
Three: ig**nore**
Four: **scram**ble
Five: **min**erals
Six: pol**lu**tion
Seven: en**vi**ronment
Eight: in**ven**tion
Nine: **snor**kel
Ten: **pre**dator

Activity 2

Listening

B. One

Boy 1: Is there a cricket match on today?

Boy 2: No. No, cricket, but there is some ice skating.

Boy 1: That's boring.

Boy 2: OK, let's watch the football match.

Two

Adult: Wow! That's a beautiful bird.

Child: I like the long neck. It is called a crane, right?

Adult: No. This is a flamingo. Look at the long legs.

Child: Oh, that's right. And where is the king bird?

Adult: Sorry, they do not have those here.

Three

Man: Look at Sanjit. He is working hard.

Woman: Yes. He is digging holes for the new goal posts.

Man: He really loves playing football, that boy.

Woman: Just like a rabbit loves hopping.

Four

Woman: Have you heard the terrible news?

Man: It is not another tsunami, is it?

Woman: No. There has been a terrible oil spill.

Man: What happened?

Woman: The ship was caught in a hurricane.

Five

Man: I need to go to the store.

Woman: Oh, we need to buy Manik a toy fire engine for his birthday.

Man: Well, I just need to buy a new hammer, so no birthday shopping today.

Woman: It is OK. I can buy the fire engine later. And maybe a rocket, too.

MATHEMATICS

1 Place Value of Larger Numbers

Learning Objectives

- To read, write and expand 5-digit and 6-digit numbers
- To round off numbers to the nearest 10, 100, 1000 and 10,000

Let's Get Started

We have studied about numbers from 1 to 9999 in earlier classes. Let us recall some important concepts.

Place Value: It is the value of digits in different places (ones, tens, hundreds and thousands) of a number.

Example: Consider the number 7286.

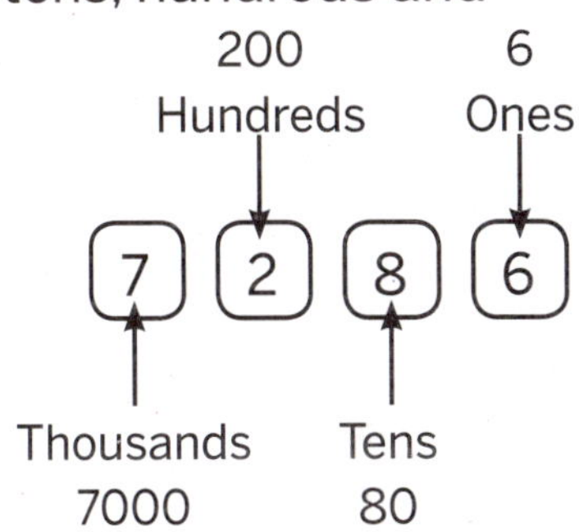

The place value of 6 in the ones place is 6.
The place value of 8 in the tens place is 80.
The place value of 2 in the hundreds place is 200.
The place value of 7 in the thousands place is 7000.

Expanded Form: It is the way in which a number is written to show the sum of the values of its digits. For example: 7286 = 7000 + 200 + 80 + 6

Number Name: It is the name of a number when written based on its place value. For example: Seven thousand two hundred eighty-six

Comparison of numbers: Two numbers can be compared by comparing the digits at different places of the numbers. For example, when we compare the numbers 825 and 2701, we find that 2701 is bigger than 825 as 2701 has 2 thousands whereas 825 has no thousands.

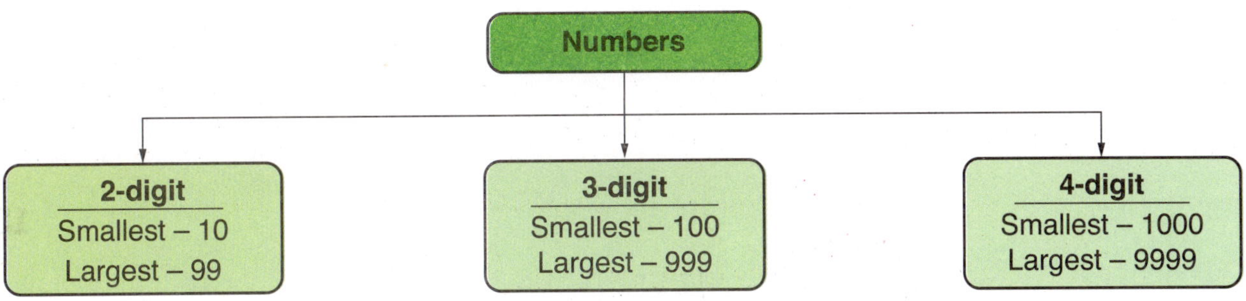

5-DIGIT NUMBERS

Read the following statements and recognize the numbers.

- India attained independence on 15 August 1947.
- Sachin Tendulkar scored 18,426 runs in 463 one-day internationals.
- The Indian government has awarded 2,678 Padma Shri Awards to the citizens of India as of 2014.
- Goa is the state with the least area of 3,702 square kilometres, followed by Sikkim (7,096) and then Tripura (10,492).
- The population of Lakshadweep as of 2013 is 64,429.

Could you read all the numbers?

The numbers 18,426, 10,492 and 64,429 are the numbers which have more than four digits.

We know that 9999 is the largest 4-digit number. On adding 1 to it, you will get the next number, that is, 10,000. Recall that adding 1 to a number will give its successor. Therefore, 10,000 is the successor of 9999. In other words, 9999 is the predecessor of 10,000. This number has five digits and the new place added is known as **ten thousands** place.

Th	H	T	O
9	9	9	9

	Th	H	T	O
1	0	0	0	0

→

TTh	Th	H	T	O
1	0	0	0	0

This place is known as **ten thousand** and it is written as **TTh**.

The numbers with five place values—ones, tens, hundreds, thousands and ten thousands—, are known as 5-digit numbers.

Reading a 5-digit Numbers

In order to make the reading easy, the digits are grouped into periods. The ones digit, the tens digit and the hundreds digits are grouped to form the ONES period. The thousands digit and the ten thousands digit are grouped to form the THOUSANDS period.

Thousands period

TTh Th H T O

Ones period

In order to read a number:

Step 1: Read the THOUSANDS period together.

Step 2: Then, read the digits in the ONES period.

Use of Commas in Writing 5-digit Numbers

Commas are used to distinguish the periods in a number. A comma is placed after the THOUSANDS period to distinguish it from the ONES period. In the number 18426, a comma has to be placed after 18, so the number is written as 18,426.

Examples:

64429 – 64,429 10350 – 10,350 45608 – 45,608 10001 – 10,001

Place Value and Expanded Form

The place value of the ten thousands digit is 10,000. The place values of other digits of 5-digit numbers can be written in the same way as written for the 4-digit numbers. Consider the example give below.

TTh	Th	H	T	O
1	2	5	4	8
↓	↓	↓	↓	↓
10,000	2000	500	40	8

Number: **12,548**

Number name: Twelve thousand five hundred forty-eight

Expanded form: 10,000 + 2,000 + 500 + 40 + 8

Commas can also be used to write 4-digit numbers. For example, 2458 is written as 2,458

Consider some more examples of writing the place values of different digits and also the expanded form.

TTh	Th	H	T	O
4	8	1	2	9
↓	↓	↓	↓	↓
40,000	8000	100	20	9

Number: **48,129**

Number name: Forty-eight thousand one hundred twenty-nine

Expanded form: 40,000 + 8,000 + 100 + 20 + 9

TTh	Th	H	T	O
9	0	0	0	9
↓	↓	↓	↓	↓
90,000	0	0	0	9

Number: **90,009**

Number name: Ninety thousand nine

Expanded form: 90,000 + 9

6-DIGIT NUMBERS

The largest 5-digit number is 99,999.
What number would you get if you add 1 to it?

99,999 + 1 = ?

9 + 1 = 10

99 + 1 = 100

999 + 1 = 1000

9999 + 1 = 10,000

99,999 + 1 = ________

Look at the addition pattern and try to find the sum of 99,999 + 1.

On adding 1 to 99,999, you get the number **100000**.

Note that the number has six digits. It is read as **One lakh**.

The new place is known as the **lakhs** place and it is denoted by **L**.

The lakhs place is a new period.

A comma is used after the lakhs digit to distinguish the digit from other periods.

Example: 1,00,000 – One lakh

1,15,264 – One lakh fifteen thousand two hundred sixty-four
4,81,731 – Four lakh eighty-one thousand seven hundred thirty-one
7,06,990 – Seven lakh six thousand nine hundred ninety
2,00,008 – Two lakh eight
9,99,999 – Nine lakh ninety-nine thousand nine hundred ninety-nine

Thousands period
L TTh Th H T O
Lakhs period **Ones period**

Place Value and Expanded Form

Consider the examples given below.

L	TTh	Th	H	T	O
3	4	8	1	2	9
↓	↓	↓	↓	↓	↓
3,00,000	40,000	8000	100	20	9

Number: **3,48,129**

Number name: Three lakh forty-eight thousand one hundred twenty-nine

Expanded form: 3,00,000 + 40,000 + 8,000 + 100 + 20 + 9

L	TTh	Th	H	T	O
4	1	0	0	8	6
↓	↓	↓	↓	↓	↓
4,00,000	10,000	0	0	80	6

Number: **4,10,086**

Number name: Four lakh ten thousand eighty-six

Expanded form: 4,00,000 + 10,000 + 80 + 6

L	TTh	Th	H	T	O
9	9	9	9	9	9
↓	↓	↓	↓	↓	↓
9,00,000	90,000	9000	900	90	9

Number: **9,99,999**

Number name: Nine lakh ninety-nine thousand nine hundred ninety-nine

Expanded form: 9,00,000 + 90,000 + 9,000 + 900 + 90 + 9

Fun Project

Make a spike abacus with six spokes and represent different 5-digit and 6-digit numbers on it.

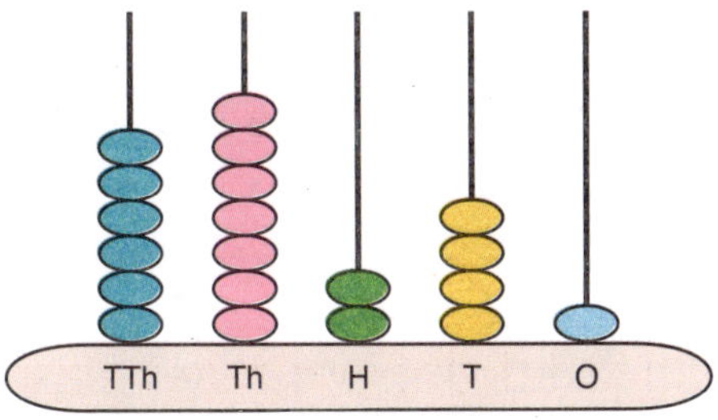

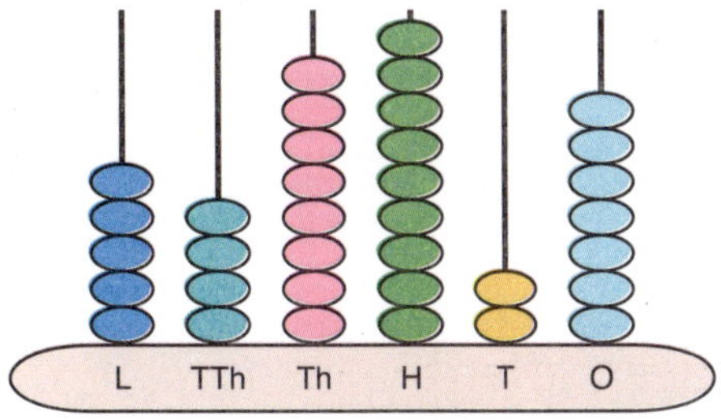

Did You Know?

The Postal Index Number (PIN) of different places is a 6-digit number. The PIN code helps the postal department to categorize the parcels region wise, state wise and district wise.

Cross-curriculum Link: Find out the postal code of your area. Interact with a postman to know how the postal codes are useful in their work. Also, find out if all the countries have 6-digit postal codes or not.

Exercise 1.1

1 **Write the numbers represented on the spike abacus and also write their number names.**

(a)

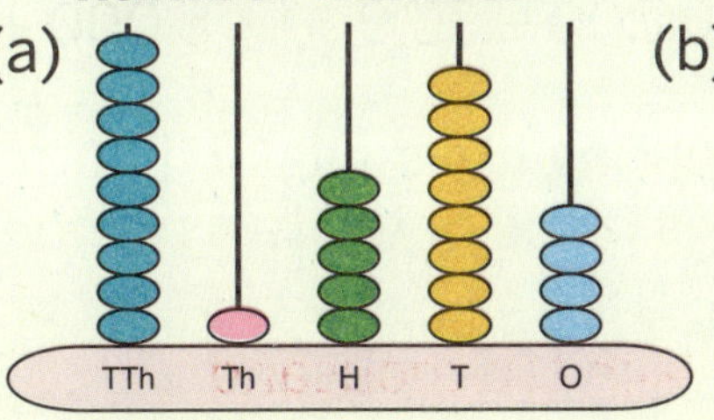

Number: ________

Number name: ________

(b)

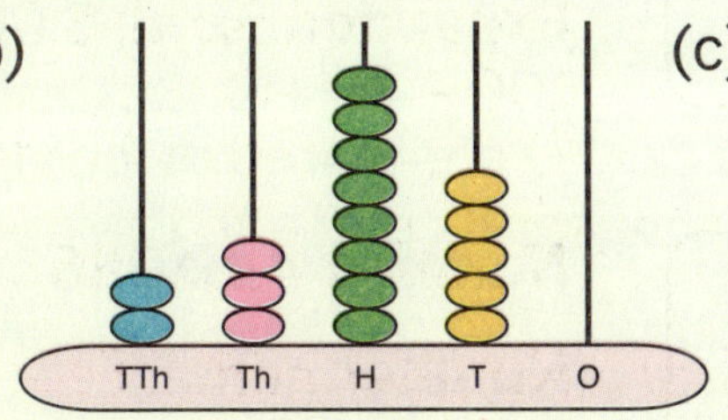

Number: ________

Number name: ________

(c)

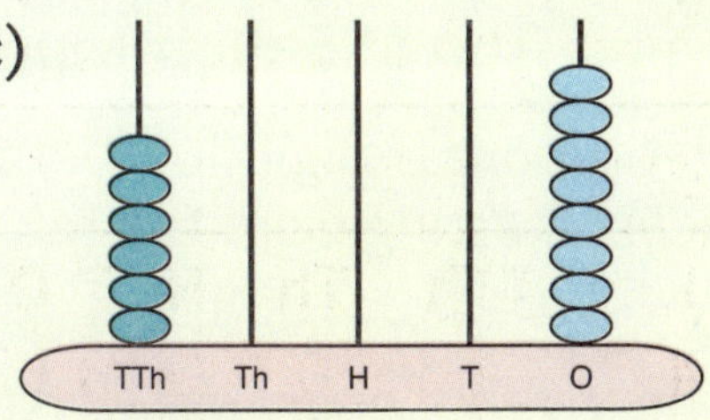

Number: ________

Number name: ________

2 **Represent the following numbers on the coresponding spike abacus.**

(a) Forty-three thousand three hundred twenty-one (b) 4,12,045 (c) 9,09,890

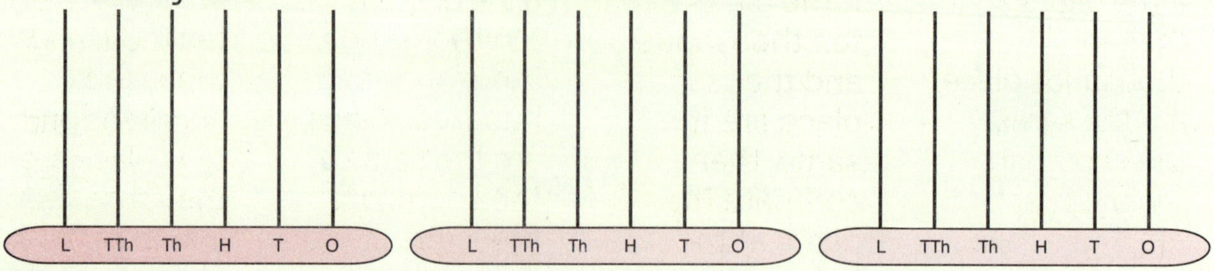

3 **Write the numbers corresponding to the given number names and expanded form.**

(a) Forty-five thousand six hundred ninety-five = ____________

(b) 1,00,000 + 200 + 10 + 9 = ____________

(c) Two lakh sixty thousand eighty-two = ____________

(d) 80,000 + 6000 + 500 + 40 + 2 = ____________

4 **Write the place value of the underlined digits.**

(a) 40,93**6** ________ (c) **7**,10,581 ________ (e) 1,27,3**5**5 ________

(b) 9,**2**1,456 ________ (d) 8,12,**7**35 ________ (f) 4,0**9**,453 ________

5 **Fill in the blanks.**

(a) 80,000 + ______ + 300 + 20 + 5 = __ 4 __ __ __

(b) 5,00,000 + 10,000 + 1000 + _____ + 20 + __ = __ __ __ 8 __ 4

(c) 70,000 + 4000 + _____ + ____ + 2 = __ __ 8 4 __

(d) _________ + ________ + 7000 + _____ + _____ + __ = 67 __ 477

COMPARISON OF NUMBERS

Comparison of 5-digit Numbers

Two or more 5-digit numbers can be compared by comparing the digits at different places, starting from the ten thousands place to the ones place of the two numbers.

The balance in the savings account of Appu and Achu are ₹17,895 and ₹21,435 respectively. Let us find who has more money.

TTh	Th	H	T	O
1	7	8	9	5

TTh	Th	H	T	O
2	1	4	3	5

1 < 2

First, compare the digits at ten thousands place in both the numbers. 17,895 has one ten thousand whereas 21,435 has two ten thousands. Therefore, 21,435 is greater than the 17,895. So, Achu has more money in his account.

If the digits at the ten thousands place are the same, then compare the digits at the thousands place.

TTh	Th	H	T	O
4	5	2	9	5

5 < 8

TTh	Th	H	T	O
4	8	4	3	5

45,295 < 48,435

If the digits at ten thousands and thousands place are the same, then compare the digits at the hundreds place.

TTh	Th	H	T	O
7	6	4	0	5

4 > 1

TTh	Th	H	T	O
7	6	1	8	2

76,405 > 76,182

If the digits at the ten thousands, thousands and hundreds place are the same, then compare the digits at the tens place.

TTh	Th	H	T	O
3	4	6	8	1

8 > 2

TTh	Th	H	T	O
3	4	6	2	9

34,681 > 34,629

If the digits at the ten thousands, thousands, hundreds and tens place are the same, then compare the digits at the ones place.

TTh	Th	H	T	O
9	3	7	8	4

4 < 6

TTh	Th	H	T	O
9	3	7	8	6

93,784 < 93,786

Comparison of 6-digit Numbers

Consider the examples given below.

The number with the greater digit at the lakhs place is greater than the other number.

284351 507258

2 < **5**

2,84,351 < 5,07,258

If the digits at lakhs place are the same in both the numbers, then compare the digits at the ten thousands place.

474056 438451

7 > **3**

4,74,056 > 4,38,451

If the digits at the lakhs and ten thousands place are the same in both the numbers, then compare the digits at the thousands place.

362859 368754

2 < **8**

3,62,859 < 3,68,754

If the digits at the lakhs, ten thousands and thousands place are the same in both the numbers, then compare the digits at the hundreds place.

172952 172450

9 > 4

1,72,952 > 1,72,450

If the digits at the lakhs, ten thousands, thousands and hundreds place are the same in both the numbers, then compare the digits at the tens place.

904762 904738

6 > 3

9,04,762 > 9,04,738

If the digits at the lakhs, ten thousands, thousands, hundreds and tens place are the same in both the numbers, then compare the digits at the ones place.

700002 700008

2 < 8

7,00,002 < 7,00,008

Exercise 1.2

1 Compare the numbers and put the appropriate symbol (>/</=).

(a) 45,251 ____ 6,81,320

(b) 10,024 ____ 10,204

(c) 8,00,756 ____ 7,84,245

(d) 92,475 ____ 85,784

(e) 6,87,999 ____ 1000

(f) 34,251 ____ 34,208

2 State whether the following are true (T) or false (F).

(a) 2,00,812 > Two lakh eight hundred two ☐

(b) 10,000 + 4000 + 20 + 1 < 10,000 + 400 + 90 + 8 ☐

(c) 4,00,000 + 50,000 + 3000 + 3 > 4,00,000 + 80,000 + 3000 + 30 + 3 ☐

(d) 6,00,000 + 600 + 30 + 7 < 6,00,000 + 6000 + 30 + 4 ☐

(e) 20,000 + 2000 + 1 > 20,000 + 200 + 10 ☐

ASCENDING AND DESCENDING ORDER

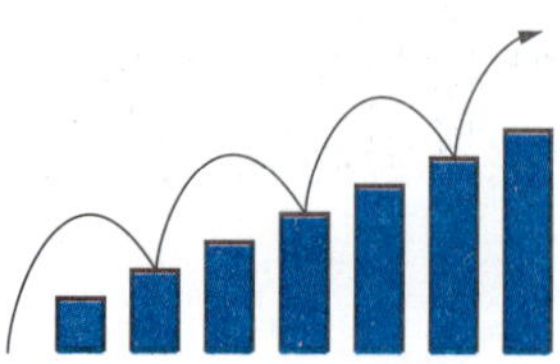

Ascending Order

Numbers when arranged from the smallest to the greatest are said to be in the ascending order

Numbers when arranged from the greatest to the smallest are said to be in the descending order.

Descending Order

The numbers given below are arranged in either ascending or descending order.

Ascending order – 10,245 17,405 17,845 38,712 72,125 72,807

Descending order – 8,14,545 6,54,747 4,05,751 4,05,324 2,09,007

GREATEST AND SMALLEST NUMBERS

There are a total of 90,000 5-digit numbers!

There are a total of 9,00,000 6-digit numbers!

Given a certain number of digits, they can be arranged in different ways to form 5-digit and 6-digit numbers.

For example, using the digits 1, 5, 7, 6 and 2 only once, you can form 120 different 5-digit numbers. Some of them are 15,762, 12,756, 67,512, 26,517 and so on.

How can you find the smallest and greatest among these 120 possible numbers?

Arrange the digits in increasing order to get the smallest number. For example, by using the digits 1, 5, 7, 6 and 2 only once, the smallest number that can be formed is 12,567.

Arrange the digits in decreasing order to get the greatest number. For example, by using the digits 1, 5, 7, 6 and 2 only once, the greatest number that can be formed is 76,521.

Study the example given in the table. Also, fill in the empty boxes.

Digits	Smallest Number	Greatest Number
8, 3, 6, 7, 9	36,789	98,763
2, 1, 8, 4, 5		

Note: If one of the digits is 0, then the smallest 5-digit number is obtained by first writing them in ascending order and then interchanging the digits at the ten thousands and thousands places.

Example: If the digits are 4, 8, 2, 0 and 3, then by arranging them in ascending order you get 02348. Interchange the positions of 0 and 2 such that the number we get is 20348. Therefore, 20,348 is the smallest 5-digit number that can be formed with the digits 4, 8, 2, 0 and 3.

The greatest 5-digit number can be obtained by writing the same numbers in descending order, that is, 84,320.

Try These!

Digits	Smallest Number	Greatest Number
7, 4, 8, 0, 5		
6, 1, 9, 2, 0		

The steps to form the smallest 6-digit number from the given digits are the same as that of 5-digits numbers, that is, write the digits in ascending order. For example, the smallest 6-digit number that can be formed using the digits 5, 8, 9, 2, 4 and 1 is 1,24,589.

The greatest number is obtained by writing the digits in descending order, that is, 9,85,421.

Study the example given below and fill in the empty boxes.

Digits	Smallest Number	Greatest Number
8, 3, 6, 7, 9, 1	1,36,789	9,87,631
2, 1, 8, 4, 5, 7		
9, 5, 8, 7, 4, 6		
3, 7, 2, 4, 1, 5		

Note: If one of the digits is 0, then the smallest 6-digit number is obtained by first writing them in ascending order and then interchanging the digits in lakhs and ten thousands places.

Example: If the digits are 7, 4, 8, 2, 0 and 3, then by arranging them in ascending order, you get 023478. Interchange the positions of 0 and 2 such that the number becomes 203478. Therefore, 2,03,478 is the smallest 6-digit number that can be formed with the digits 7, 4, 8, 2, 0 and 3.

The greatest 6-digit number can be obtained by writing the same numbers in descending order, that is, 8,74,320.

Try These!

Digits	Smallest Number	Greatest Number
7, 4, 8, 0, 5, 6		
6, 1, 9, 2, 0, 3		

SUCCESSORS AND PREDECESSORS

The successor of a number is the number we get by adding 1 to the given number.

For example, if the number is 8,74,320, then the successor of the number will be: 8,74,320 + 1 = 8,74,321.

The predecessor of a number is the number we get by subtracting 1 from the number.

For example, if the number is 8,74,320, then the predecessor of the number will be: 8,74,320 – 1 = 8,74,319.

Exercise 1.3

1 Arrange the following numbers in ascending order.

(a) 12,054, 30,458, 20,105, 40,306 ____________

(b) 2,41,475, 4,30,490, 4,13,281, 4,30,087 ____________

(c) 75,802, 7,50,806, 7,50,608, 75,871 ____________

2 Tick (✓) the group of numbers in descending order.

(a) 8,51,407, 62,405, 30,112, 1845, 1001 ☐

(b) 72,924, 72,356, 89,425, 10,658, 10,012 ☐

(c) 6,75,852, 5,67,514, 4,06,489, 4,02,257, 2,56,200 ☐

3 Write the greatest number that can be formed using all the digits only once.

(a) 4, 5, 2, 3, 0, 8 ____________

(b) 6, 9, 4, 7, 2, 8 ____________

(c) 8, 1, 5, 2, 7 ____________

(d) 0, 6, 4, 3, 8 ____________

4 Write the successors and the predecessors of the following numbers.

(a) ________, 59768, ________

(b) ________, 23875, ________

(c) ________, 65793, ________

(d) ________, 35987, ________

ROUNDING OFF NUMBERS

Rounding off numbers to the nearest 10

Recall the method of rounding off numbers to the nearest 10. Consider the numbers as marked on a number line; find the nearest multiple of 10 on both sides of the number.

(a) If the ones digit of a number is less than five, then it is rounded off to the ten to its left on then number line..

(b) If the ones digit is greater than or equal to 5, then it is rounded off to the ten to its right on the number line..

Example: The number 17 is rounded off to 20, whereas the number 12 will be rounded off to 10.

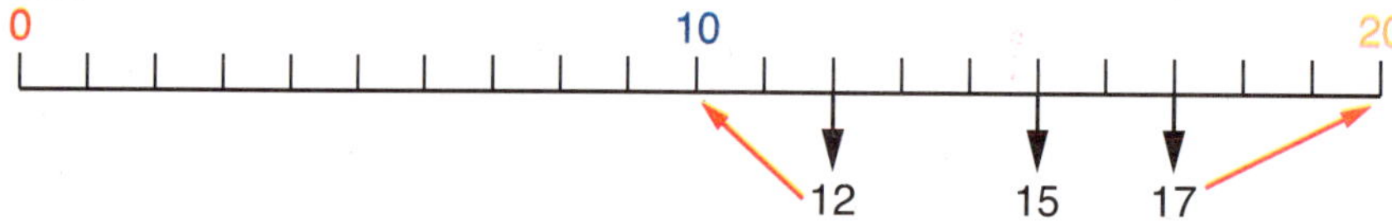

Consider some more examples.

Number	Rounded off to 10
352	350
37,861	37,860

Number	Rounded off to 10
95,789	95,790
63,981	63,980

Number	Rounded off to 10
1,35,245	1,35,250
9,37,868	9,37,870

Rounding off numbers to the nearest 100

Rule: If the last two digits of a number read together is less than 50, then round it off to the hundred to its left. If the last two digits of a number read together is greater than or equal to 50, then round it off to the hundred to its right.

Consider the example 365. Note that 65 is greater than 50. Therefore, 365 will be rounded off to 400. Similarly, 321 will be rounded off to 300 since 21 is less than 50.

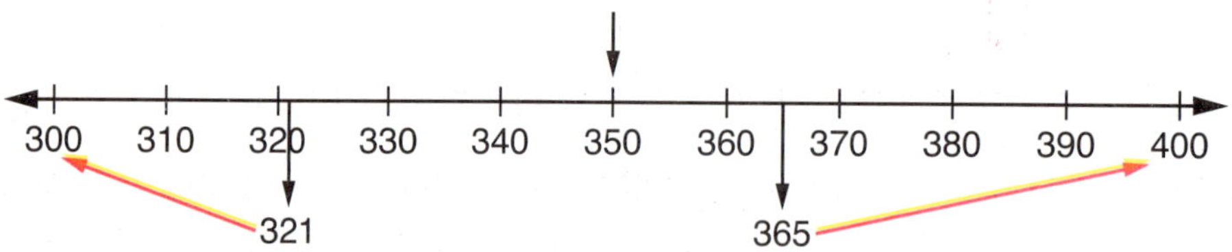

Consider some more examples.

Number	Rounded off to 100
850	900
37,861	37,900

Number	Rounded off to 100
95,789	95,800
63,250	63,300

Number	Rounded off to 100
1,35,245	1,35,200
9,37,868	9,37,900

Rounding off numbers to the nearest 1000

Rule: If the last three digits of a number read together is less than 500, then round it off to the thousand to its left. If the last three digits of a number read together is greater than or equal to 500, then round it off to the thousand to its right.

Consider the example 5,198. Note that 198 is less than 500. Therefore, it will be rounded off to 5000, whereas 5,712 will be rounded off to 6000 since 712 is greater than 500.

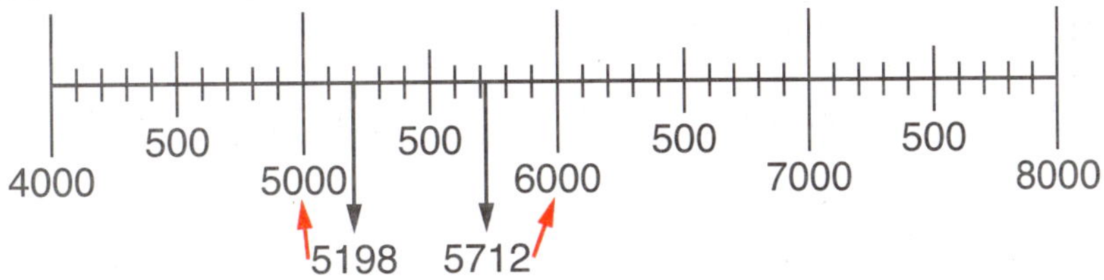

Consider some more examples.

Number	Rounded off to 1000
1850	2000
37,861	38,000

Number	Rounded off to 1000
95,789	96,000
63,250	63,000

Number	Rounded off to 1000
1,35,245	1,35,000
9,37,500	9,38,000

Rounding off numbers to the nearest 10,000

Rule: If the last four digits of a number read together is less than 5000, then round it off to the ten thousand to its left. If the last four digits of a number read together is greater than or equal to 5000, then round it off to the ten thousand to its right.

Example: 15,821 will be rounded off to 20,000 as 5821 is greater than 5000. 71,540 will be rounded off to 70,000 as 1540 is less than 5000.

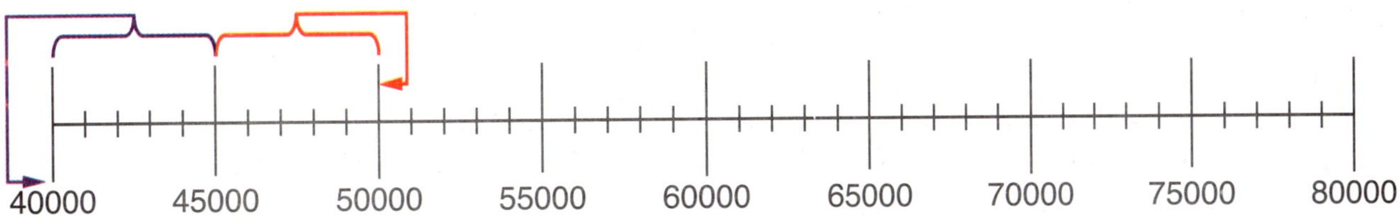

Consider some more examples.

Number	Rounded off to 10,000
18,500	20,000
70,028	70,000

Number	Rounded off to 10,000
55,789	60,000
22,135	20,000

Number	Rounded off to 10,000
4,85,245	4,90,000
5,18,528	5,20,000

Exercise 1.4

1 **Round off the following numbers to the nearest 1000.**

(a) 78,124 ________ (c) 80,945 ________ (e) 1,55,201 ________

(b) 8,12,874 ________ (d) 30,540 ________ (f) 1,71,500 ________

2 **The numbers are rounded off to the nearest 10,000. Tick (✓) the correct option out of the three options given.**

(a) 18,136 —	10,000	☐	19,000	☐	20,000	☐
(b) 5,47,801 —	5,40,000	☐	5,50,000	☐	5,00,000	☐
(c) 53,851 —	53,000	☐	50,000	☐	60,000	☐
(d) 3,64,999 —	3,60,000	☐	3,80,000	☐	3,70,000	☐

3 **Round off the numbers to the nearest 100.**

(a) 51,202 ________ (c) 82,500 ________ (e) 6,71,012 ________

(b) 4,60,150 ________ (d) 1,94,878 ________ (f) 2,47,109 ________

4 **Round off the numbers in the following sentences to the nearest 10,000 and rewrite the sentences. The first one has been done for you.**

(a) In a stadium, there are 43,512 spectators.

In a stadium there are about 40,000 spectators.

(b) The population of a city is 4,24,540.

(c) The distance from the planet Earth to Moon is 3,84,400 km.

ROMAN NUMERALS

Look at the wall clock. How do you read time in the wall clock?

Are the numbers familiar to you?

Note that the numbers used in the wall clock are different from the numbers that we use, which are, 0, 1, 2, 3, 4, 5, 6, 7, 8 and 9.

The numbers used in the clock are given below.

I, II, III, IV, V, VI, VII, VIII, IX, X

Roman Numerals

These numbers are known as **Roman Numerals**. This way of writing numbers was used during the ancient Roman period. Let us see the differences between Hindu-Arabic numbers and Roman numerals.

Hindu-Arabic Numbers	Roman Numerals
These numbers were invented by Indian mathematicians and extensively used during the period of the Arabs.	These numbers were invented and used in ancient Rome.
The basic numbers are: 0, 1, 2, 3, 4, 5, 6, 7, 8 and 9.	The basic numerals are: I, V, X, L, C, D, M Note: The Roman numeral system does not have 0.

Roman numerals can be written in Hindu-Arabic numbers. The following table gives the basic symbols of Roman numerals and their value in Hindu-Arabic numbers.

There are certain rules to be followed in order to write different numbers using the basic symbols of Roman numerals.

Symbol	I	V	X	L	C	D	M
Value in Hindu-Arabic Number System	1	5	10	50	100	500	1000

Rules:

1

If a symbol is repeated, then its value is added as many times as it occurs.

Examples

III = 1 + 1 + 1 = 3

XX = 10 + 10 = 20

✗ IIII = 1 + 1 + 1 + 1 = 4 **Wrong!**

Note: However, a symbol is not repeated more than three times.

2

Symbol of Smaller Value

- To the left of a number → Subtracted from the Number
  - IV = 5 – 1 = 4
  - IX = 10 – 1 = 9
- To the right of a number → Added to the Number
  - VI = 5 + 1 = 6
  - VIII = 5 + 1 + 1 + 1 = 8

Explanation: If a smaller number is written to the left of a bigger number, then it has to be subtracted from the bigger number. For example, in IV, I is the smaller number and it is written to the left of V. V represents 5 and I represent 1. Therefore, IV = 5 – 1 = 4

Similarly, IX = 10 – 1 = 9

Explanation: If a smaller number is written to the right of a bigger number, then it has to be added to the bigger number. For example, in VI, I is the smaller number and it is written to the right of V. V represents 5 and I represent 1. Therefore, VI = 5 + 1 = 6

✗ VX = 10 – 5 = 5 **Wrong!**

Note: The symbol I can only be written to the left of V and X. Also, V is never written to the left of a bigger number.

XI = 10 + 1 = 11 | XV = 10 + 5 = 15 | XVI = 10 + 5 + 1 = 16

Roman Number Representation of Hindu-arabic Numbers

Follow the rules to write the Roman numeral corresponding to the numbers from 1 to 39. Expand the given number into tens and ones and then form its Roman numeral.

Examples:

14 = 10 + 4 = X + IV = XIV

19 = 10 + 9 = X + IX = XIX

37 = 10 + 10 + 10 + 7 = X + X + X + VII = XXXVII

Forming Hindu-Arabic numbers from Roman Numbers

Examples:

XXI = X + X + I = 10 + 10 + 1 = 21

XXXIV = X + X + X + IV = 10 + 10 + 10 + 4 = 34

XXIX = X + X + IX = 10 + 10 + 9 = 29

XVI = X + V + I = 10 + 5 + 1 = 16

XXIII = X + X + I + I + I = 10 + 10 + 1 + 1 + 1 = 23

XXV = X + X + V = 10 + 10 + 5 = 25

Roman Numerals from 1 to 39

Write the missing Roman numerals.

Number System Table				
1 – I	9 – IX	17 – XVII	25 – XXV	33 – ______
2 – II	10 – X	18 – XVIII	26 – XXVI	34 – ______
3 – III	11 – XI	19 – ______	27 – ______	35 – ______
4 – IV	12 – ______	20 – XX	28 – XXVIII	36 – ______
5 – V	13 – XIII	21 – XXI	29 – ______	37 – ______
6 – VI	14 – ______	22 – ______	30 – XXX	38 – ______
7 – VII	15 – XV	23 – XXIII	31 – XXXI	39 – ______
8 – VIII	16 – XVI	24 – ______	32 – ______	

Revision Exercise

1 Write the numbers corresponding to the number names. Also, write the expanded form.

(a) Forty-three thousand two hundred fifty-seven = ________

Expanded form: ____________________

(b) Six lakh seventy-four thousand six hundred thirty-five = ________

Expanded form: ____________________

(c) Ninety nine thousand twenty-nine = ________

Expanded form: ____________________

(d) One lakh five thousand sixty-one = ________

Expanded form: ____________________

(e) Eight lakh forty thousand four hundred ninety-nine = ________

Expanded form: ____________________

(f) Twenty-two thousand nine = ________

Expanded form: ____________________

2 Write the numbers in expanded form and also write the number names.

(a) 84,852 = ____________

Number name: ____________

(b) 52,901 = ____________

Number name: ____________

(c) 61,509 = ____________

Number name: ____________

(d) 3,17,656 = ____________

Number name: ____________

(e) 7,01,025 = ____________

Number name: ____________

(f) 9,93,100 = ____________

Number name: ____________

3 Write the place value of the underlined digits in the numbers.

(a) 5**6**,253 = ____________

(b) **4**5,069 = ____________

(c) 13,**7**07 = ____________

(d) 2,10,5**8**4 = ____________

(e) 9,**1**5,024 = ____________

(f) **2**,68,009 = ____________

4 **Write the smallest number and the greatest number that can be formed using the given digits only once.**

Digits	Smallest Number	Greatest Number
3, 9, 1, 7, 8		
2, 8, 5, 4, 0, 6		
6, 1, 4, 2, 5, 3		

5 **Compare the numbers and place the appropriate symbol (</>/=).**

(a) 50,825 ____ 50,809

(b) 83,687 ____ 87,256

(c) 4,21,045 ____ 5,21,036

(d) 79,891 ____ 79,897

(e) 2,14,523 ____ 2,57,025

(f) 6012 ____ 76,009

(g) 40,000 ____ 4,00,000

(h) 6,75,036 ____ 6,75,031

6 **Fill in the blanks.**

(a) Round off 10,593 to the nearest 100 = __________

(b) Round off 7,53,126 to the nearest 10,000 = __________

(c) Round off 21,846 to the nearest 1000 = __________

(d) Round off 4, 17,605 to the nearest 10 = __________

7 **Write the missing numbers.**

(a) 18 = XVIII

(b) 12 = __________

(c) XXVI = __________

(d) 23 = __________

(e) 39 = __________

(f) IX = __________

(g) 30 = __________

(h) XXXIV = __________

(i) XV = __________

FA

HOTS (Higher Order Thinking Skills)

Identify the wrong notations of Roman numerals. Also, correct them.

IIII = 4	XIX = 19	VX = 5	XXXIIIV = 38	XX = 20
XI = 11	XXXVIV = 39	VII = 7	IIX = 8	IX = 9
XIIIX = 17	XXIX = 29	XIXI = 22	VI = 6	

2 Adding and Subtracting Large Numbers

Learning Objectives

- To add 5-digit and 6-digit numbers
- To subtract 5-digit and 6-digit numbers
- To solve word problems on addition and subtraction

Let's Get Started

Addition of two or more numbers can be carried out by adding the digits at different places and carrying them forward, if required. Add the ones first, then the tens, then the hundreds and then the thousands.

Example: *Find out the total weight of the two bags of rice weighing 1,255 kg and 3,785 kg respectively.*

Total weight = 1,255 + 3,785

	Th	H	T	O
	[1] 1	[1] 2	[1] 5	5
+	3	7	8	5
	5	0	4	0

There are a total of 10 ones and they are regrouped into 1 ten. 1 is taken to the tens place. Similarly, 1 hundred and 1 thousand are carried forward.

Therefore, the total weight of the two bags of rice is 5,040 kg.

ADDITION OF 5-DIGIT NUMBERS

Steps to add 5-digit numbers:

1. Add ones. Regroup the ones to tens, if required, and carry it forward to the tens place.

NUMBER FACTS

1 ten = 10 ones
1 hundred = 10 tens = 100 ones
1 thousand = 10 hundreds
1 ten thousand = 10 thousands
1 lakh = 10 ten thousands

2. Add tens. Regroup the tens to hundreds, if required, and carry it forward to the hundreds place.
3. Add hundreds. Regroup the hundreds to thousands, if required, and carry it forward to the thousands place.
4. Add thousands. Regroup the thousands to ten thousands, if required, and carry it forward to the ten thousands place.

Example:

The cost of a television is ₹12,750 and that of a refrigerator is ₹14,999. Find out the total cost.

The total cost = 12,750 + 14,999

		1	1		
	1	2	7	5	0
+	1	4	9	9	9
	2	7	7	4	9

Solution: *Therefore, the total cost is ₹27,749.*

Examples:

	1				
	4	9	1	4	3
+	3	4	2	5	4
	8	3	3	9	7

			1	1	
	1	2	1	3	6
+	3	4	2	9	4
	4	6	4	3	0

	1	1	1		
	1	6	8	5	3
+	1	4	6	5	4
	3	1	5	0	7

	1	1	1	1	
	2	9	9	9	9
+	6	0	2	0	1
	9	0	2	0	0

ADDITION OF 6-DIGIT NUMBERS

The same procedure of adding 5-digit numbers can be extended to 6-digit numbers too. Here, you have digits in lakhs position also.

NUMBER FACTS

1 lakh = 10 ten thousands
1 ten lakhs = 10 lakhs

Example: *A businessman earned ₹1,25,300 in the first week and ₹1,54,850 in the second week. Find out the total amount he earned in two weeks.*

Total amount = 1,25,300 + 1,54,850

		1	1			
	1	2	5	3	0	0
+	1	5	4	8	5	0
	2	8	0	1	5	0

12 hundreds = 1 thousand + 2 hundreds
10 thousands = 1 ten thousand

Therefore, the amount he earned in two weeks is ₹2,80,150.

Example: *A farmer borrowed money from a bank worth ₹1,78,975 and ₹1,56,306 from another bank. Find out the total amount borrowed by him.*

Total amount = 1,78,975 + 1,56,306

$$\begin{array}{rcccccc} & {}^{1} & {}^{1} & {}^{1} & & {}^{1} & \\ & 1 & 7 & 8 & 9 & 7 & 5 \\ + & 1 & 5 & 6 & 3 & 0 & 6 \\ \hline & 3 & 3 & 5 & 2 & 8 & 1 \\ \hline \end{array}$$

Therefore, the total loan amount is ₹3,35,281.

Consider some more examples on the addition of 6-digit numbers.

$$\begin{array}{rcccccc} & {}^{1} & & {}^{1} & {}^{1} & {}^{1} & \\ & 4 & 3 & 6 & 2 & 8 & 6 \\ + & 3 & 9 & 1 & 9 & 5 & 7 \\ \hline & 8 & 2 & 8 & 2 & 4 & 3 \\ \hline \end{array} \qquad \begin{array}{rcccccc} & & {}^{1} & {}^{1} & {}^{1} & {}^{1} & \\ & 5 & 0 & 8 & 9 & 9 & 9 \\ + & 1 & 5 & 9 & 8 & 0 & 4 \\ \hline & 6 & 6 & 8 & 8 & 0 & 3 \\ \hline \end{array} \qquad \begin{array}{rcccccc} & {}^{1} & {}^{1} & {}^{1} & {}^{1} & & \\ & 3 & 7 & 8 & 3 & 4 & 2 \\ + & 1 & 6 & 5 & 6 & 7 & 5 \\ \hline & 5 & 4 & 4 & 0 & 1 & 7 \\ \hline \end{array} \qquad \begin{array}{rcccccc} & {}^{1} & {}^{1} & {}^{1} & {}^{1} & {}^{1} & \\ & 5 & 3 & 9 & 2 & 8 & 9 \\ + & 2 & 9 & 6 & 8 & 5 & 7 \\ \hline & 8 & 3 & 6 & 1 & 4 & 6 \\ \hline \end{array}$$

WORD PROBLEMS

Example: *The savings of Preeti for two years are ₹58,750 and ₹69,950 respectively. Find her total savings.*

Amount saved in the first year = ₹

Amount saved in the second year = ₹

Therefore, the total amount saved by Preeti is ₹1,28,700.

$$\begin{array}{rcccccc} & & {}^{1} & {}^{1} & {}^{1} & & \\ & & 5 & 8 & 7 & 5 & 0 \\ + & & 6 & 9 & 9 & 5 & 0 \\ \hline & 1 & 2 & 8 & 7 & 0 & 0 \\ \hline \end{array}$$

Example: *A small water reservoir had 1,62,915 litres of water. If 2,47,624 litres of water was added into the reservoir due to heavy rain, find the total amount of water in the reservoir.*

Total amount of water
= 162915 + 247624

$$\begin{array}{rcccccc} & {}^{1} & {}^{1} & {}^{1} & & & \\ & 1 & 6 & 2 & 9 & 1 & 5 \\ + & 2 & 4 & 7 & 6 & 2 & 4 \\ \hline & 4 & 1 & 0 & 5 & 3 & 9 \\ \hline \end{array}$$

Therefore, total amount of water is 4,10,539 litres.

Exercise 2.1

1 Add the following 5-digit numbers and write the answer.

(a) 15,245 + 22,829 = ____________ (d) 20,001 + 39,090 = ____________

(b) 54,826 + 18,194 = __________ (e) 36,148 + 47,845 = __________

(c) 87,354 + 12,389 = __________ (f) 67,657 + 54,379 = __________

2 **Add the following 6-digit numbers and write the answer.**

(a) 2,05,245 + 1,82,829 = __________ (d) 4,45,781 + 2,39,090 = __________

(b) 1,54,826 + 6,18,194 = __________ (e) 3,82,187 + 4,07,205 = __________

(c) 5,22,584 + 3,48,452 = __________ (f) 3,25,999 + 4,75,101 = __________

3 **Add the numbers and write the missing digits.**

(a) 15,750 + 1,21,825 = 1__7__7__ (d) 87,486 + 98,254 = __857__ __

(b) 2,05,197 + 8,999 = 21__ __9__ (e) 4,46,870 + 3,24,502 = 77__ __72

(c) 99,999 + 1,99,999 = __999__ __ (f) 10,000 + 1,00,000 = 1__00__0

4 **Solve the following word problems.**

(a) A bicycle company sold 75,890 bicycles in May and 63,458 bicycles in June. Find out the total number of bicycles sold in the two months.

(b) A man sold his two houses for ₹4,58,000 and ₹3,75,000 respectively. Find out the total amount of money he got.

(c) One water tank has the capacity of 42,812 litres and the other water tank has the capacity of 2,14,560 litres. Find out the total capacity of the two tanks.

(d) The weight of one truck is 15,450 kg and the weight of the other truck is 38,658 kg. Find the weight of the two trucks.

Mental Maths

Observe the patterns and complete them.

10 + 89 = 99	10 + 1 = 11	1 + 9 = 10
100 + 899 = 999	100 + 11 = 111	1 + 99 = 100
1,000 + 8,999 = 9,999	1,000 + 111 = 1,111	1 + 999 = 1,000

10,000 + 89,999 = ______   10,000 + 1,111 = ______   1 + 9,999 = ______

1,00,000 + 8,99,999 = ______   1,00,000 + 11,111 = ______   1 + 99,999 = ______

SUBTRACTION

Subtraction of two numbers involves finding the difference between them. In order to subtract two numbers, follow the steps given below.

1. Write the smaller number below the bigger number and subtract the ones. Borrow a ten from the tens place if there are not sufficient ones to subtract.
2. Subtract tens. Borrow a hundred from the hundreds place if there are not sufficient tens to subtract.
3. Subtract hundreds. Borrow a thousand from the thousands place if there are not sufficient hundreds to subtract.

Example:

There are 1584 students in a school, out of which 695 are boys. Find out the number of girls.

The total number of students = 1584

The total number of boys = 695

Therefore, the number of girls = 1584 – 695

(1)

	1	5	8	4
–		6	9	5

(2)

	1	5 (→4)	8 (→7→17)	4 (→14)
–		6	9	5
			8	9

(3)

	1 (→0)	5 (→4→14)	8 (→7→17)	4 (→14)
–		6	9	5
		8	8	9

Therefore, there are 889 girls in the school.

SUBTRACTION OF 5-DIGIT NUMBERS

Two 5-digit numbers can be subtracted by the same method as we followed for subtracting 4-digit numbers. The steps are:

1. Subtract ones. Borrow a ten from the tens place, if required.
2. Subtract tens. Borrow a hundred from the hundreds place, if required.

	8	7	3	5	7
–	4	5	2	0	5
	4	2	1	5	2

3. Subtract hundreds. Borrow a thousand from the thousands place, if required.
4. Subtract thousands. Borrow a ten thousand from the ten thousands place, if required.
5. Subtract ten thousands.

Example:

In a stadium, there are 27,587 people out of which 12,478 are males. Let us find out the number of females in the stadium.

The total number of people =

The number of males =

Therefore, the number of females = 27,587 – 12,478

```
      7 17
2 7 5 8̸ 7̸
-1 2 4 7 8
----------
 1 5 1 0 9
```

Borrow one ten as there are not sufficient ones

Therefore, there are 15,109 females in the stadium.

Verification: The answer can be checked by adding the total number of males and females and verifying whether the sum gives the total number of people or not.

```
      1
 1 5 1 0 9
+1 2 4 7 8
----------
 2 7 5 8 7
```

Consider some more examples. Observe that the numbers are borrowed from different places.

```
 3 12 6 14              11 13                 4 11 10 17            2 12 17 10 10
 4̸ 2̸ 7̸ 4̸ 5          8 9̸ 1̸ 2̸ 3̸ 7 4          7 5̸ 2̸ 1̸ 0̸ 7̸           3̸ 3̸ 8̸ 1̸ 0̸ 1̸ 0̸
-2 7 0 6 1           -6 4 5 4 3            -4 1 5 6 9            -1 9 8 2 4
----------           ----------            ----------            ----------
 1 5 6 8 4            2 7 8 3 1             3 3 6 4 8             1 3 9 8 6
```

The sum of two numbers is 47,500 and one number is 24,351. Find the other number.

The second number = 47500 – 24351

```
 4 7 5 0 0
-2 4 3 5 1
----------

----------
```

As there are not sufficient ones in the ones place, borrow one ten from the tens place. But, here, there are no tens. So, borrow one hundred from the hundreds place to the tens place first. Now, you will have 10 tens in the tens place.

Now, carry out the subtraction.

```
     4 10                   4 9 10
 4 7 5̸ 0̸ 0             4 7 5̸ 0̸ 0̸
-2 4 3 5 1    ---->    -2 4 3 5 1
----------             ----------
                        2 3 1 4 9
----------             ----------
```

SUBTRACTION OF 6-DIGIT NUMBERS

In order to subtract two 6-digit numbers, subtract the ones, tens, hundreds, thousands, ten thousands and lakhs digits of both the numbers respectively. Borrow the numbers, if required.

Example: *If ₹4,75,356 is withdrawn from a savings bank account having ₹7,96,487, then find the balance amount in the account.*

The total amount in the account =	7 9 6 4 8 7
The amount withdrawn =	− 4 7 5 3 5 6
The balance amount =	3 2 1 1 3 1

3 2 1 1 3 1
+ 4 7 5 3 5 6
7 9 6 4 8 7

Therefore, the balance in the account in the bank is ₹3,21,131.

Verification: The amount withdrawn and the balance amount together should be equal to the total amount.

Consider some more examples. Observe the borrowing of numbers from different places while subtracting.

3 4 2 7 5 4	9 8 4 6 8 7	7 5 6 2 4 3	4 2 3 5 3 1
− 1 2 9 6 3 5	− 5 9 6 2 9 1	− 4 1 8 5 7 8	− 1 3 7 8 4 5
2 1 3 1 1 9	3 8 8 3 9 6	3 3 7 6 6 5	2 8 5 6 8 6

Subtraction of Numbers with Zeroes

If the population of a town is 5,75,000 and out of them 3,42,321 are females, then find out the number of males.

Carry out the subtraction.

5 7 5 0 0 0		5 7 5 0 0 0		5 7 5 0 0 0		5 7 5 0 0 0
− 3 4 2 3 2 1	→	− 3 4 2 3 2 1	→	− 3 4 2 3 2 1	→	− 3 4 2 3 2 1
						2 3 2 6 7 9

Therefore, there are a total of 2,32,679 males in the city.

WORD PROBLEMS

(a) *The capacity of a water tank is 88,245 litres. If 42,983 litres of water is taken out, then how much water will be left in the tank?*

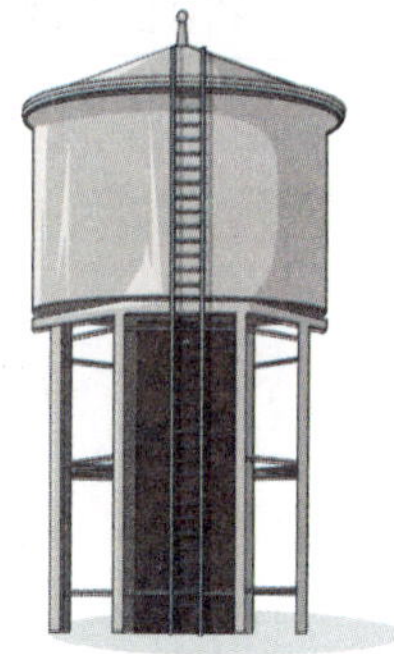

The capacity of water tank =	8	$\overset{7}{\cancel{8}}$	$\overset{11}{\overset{1}{\cancel{2}}}$	$\overset{14}{\cancel{4}}$	5
Amount of water taken out =	− 4	2	9	8	3
Remaining water = 88,245 − 42,983	4	5	2	6	2

Therefore, 45,262 litres of water will be left in the tank.

(b) *How much should be subtracted from 5,24,698 to get 3,40,897?*

Subtract 3,40,897 from 5,24,698 to get the answer.

Greater number =	$\overset{4}{\cancel{5}}$	$\overset{12}{\cancel{2}}$	$\overset{3}{\cancel{4}}$	$\overset{16}{\cancel{6}}$	9	8
Smaller number =	− 3	4	0	8	9	7
Therefore, the answer is 1,83,801.	1	8	3	8	0	1

Exercise 2.2

1 Subtract the following and write the missing digits.

(a) 28,786 − 14,547 = 14__3__

(b) 2,80,560 − 1,76,410 = 1__4__5__

(c) 4,05,009 − 3,09,007 = 96__ __ __

(d) 94,312 − 76,400 = 1__9__2

(e) 7,19,876 − 4,45,948 = __7__9__ __

(f) 45,280 − 17,571 = 2__7__9

2 Solve the following word problems.

(a) In an election, Candidate A secured 58,625 votes and Candidate B secured 34,970 votes. Find out by how many votes did Candidate A win the election.

(b) If the sum of two numbers is 1,67,410 and one of the numbers is 90,980, then find the other number.

(c) A car manufacturing company produced 8,75,134 cars during a month and sold 7,89,052 cars. Find out the number of cars left unsold.

Revision Exercise

1 Solve the given addition and subtraction problems. There could be more than one correct answer.

(a) 31,190 (i) 20,900 + 10,290 (iii) 47,820 – 10,630

(ii) 17,408 + 13,782 (iv) 1,45,741 – 1,14,634

(b) 27,344 (i) 56,124 – 28,080 (iii) 56,124 – 27,780

(ii) 1,17,287 – 89,943 (iv) 56,124 – 28,780

(c) 4,25,000 (i) 2,17,150 + 2,07,750 (iii) 2,07,150 + 2,07,750

(ii) 2,17,150 + 2,07,850 (iv) 3,52,100 + 1,25,000

(d) 2,89,145 (i) 6,24,990 – 3,35,845 (iii) 7,24,990 – 3,35,845

(ii) 5,24,990 – 3,35,845 (iv) 3,52,100 – 1,25,000

2 Choose the appropriate operation symbol (+/–) to get the given answer.

(a) 47,890 _____ 21,850 = 26,040

(b) 1,11,111 _____ 99,999 = 2,11,110

(c) 4,05,312 _____ 3,15,874 = 7,21,186

(d) 54,287 _____ 87,320 = 1,41,607

(e) 15,987 _____ 32,205 = 48,192

(f) 3,00,009 _____ 2,99,991 = 6,00,000

3 Solve the following word problems.

(a) A person withdrew ₹51,280 and ₹1,18,750 from his account. How much amount has he withdrawn in all?

(b) An auto driver had to pay an amount of ₹1,50,875 to a bank. He has already paid ₹34,680 to the bank. How much of loan amount does he still have to pay?

(c) Two tanks were filled with water. One tank has the capacity of 35,879 litres while the other tank has the capacity of 42,008 litres. Find out the total capacity of the two tanks.

(d) In an election, a candidate got 3,75,421 votes and his opponent won by 28,328 votes. Find out the two number of votes secured by the opponent.

(e) The weight of two containers is 4,56,789 kg and 3,05,314 kg. Find out their total weight.

(f) The odometer readings in two passenger cars are 75,862 km and 62,994 km. Find out the difference in the readings.

3 Multiplication of Numbers

Learning Objectives

- To multiply a 3-digit number by a 3-digit number
- To solve word problems on the multiplication of numbers

Let's Get Started

In multiplication, two numbers are multiplied to get a product. The two numbers are known as **factors**.

$18 \times 12 = 216$

Factors (18 and 12) → *Product* (216)

1. Multiply the following numbers and find their products.

(a) 65×37

(b) 246×74

(c) 134×21

(d) 781×58

(e) 475×27

(f) 341×93

MULTIPLICATION OF A 4-DIGIT NUMBER BY A SINGLE-DIGIT NUMBER

With regrouping

A ceiling fan costs ₹1,325. Find the cost of three such fans.

The cost of 1 fan = ₹1,325

The cost of 3 fans = ₹1,325 × 3

Recall the method of multiplying a 4-digit number by a single-digit number. Multiply the ones, the tens, the hundreds and the thousands digits by the single digit.

Step 1: Multiply the ones and carry forward.

			1	
	1	3	2	5
×				3
				5

Step 2: Multiply the tens and add the 1.

			1	
	1	3	2	5
×				3
			7	5

Step 3: Multiply the hundreds.

			1	
	1	3	2	5
×				3
		9	7	5

Step 4: Multiply the thousands.

			1	
	1	3	2	5
×				3
	3	9	7	5

Therefore, the cost of 3 fans = ₹3,975.

Find out the cost of four such fans.

The cost of 4 fans = ₹1,325 × 4

Multiply each digit by 4 and carry forward the numbers, if any.

		1	1	2
	1	3	2	5
×				4
	5	3	0	0

Therefore, the cost of 4 fans = ₹5,300.

MULTIPLICATION OF A 3-DIGIT NUMBER BY A 3-DIGIT NUMBER

Recall the steps followed to multiply a 3-digit number by a 2-digit number. Multiply 215 × 18

Step 1: Multiply the 3-digit number by the ones digit of the 2-digit number, that is, 215 × 8 = 1,720

Step 2: Multiply the 3-digit number by the tens digit of the 2-digit number, that is, 215 × 10 = 2,150

Step 3: Add the numbers obtained in Step 1 and Step 2, that is, 1,720 + 2,150 = 3,870

The same steps can be followed for the multiplication of a 3-digit number by a 3-digit number. Consider the example: 245 × 124

Step 1: Multiply by ones.

245 × 4 = 980

			1	2	
			2	4	5
		×	1	2	(4)
			9	8	0
+					

Step 2: Multiply by tens.

245 × 20 = 4,900

				1	
			2	4	5
		×	1	(2)	4
			9	8	0
		4	9	0	0
+					

Step 3: Multiply by hundreds.

245 × 100 = 24,500

			2	4	5
		×	(1)	2	4
			9	8	0
		4	9	0	0
+	2	4	5	0	0

Step 4: Add the products.

			2	4	5
		×	1	2	4
			9	8	0
		4	9	0	0
+	2	4	5	0	0
	3	0	3	8	0

(carries: 2 above the thousands column, 1 above the ten thousands column)

Therefore, 245 × 124 = 30,380

Note: During the multiplication process of 245 × 124, we got three numbers: 980, 4,900 and 24,500. These numbers are known as **partial products**. Their sum will give the product of the numbers 245 and 124.

Consider another example: 845 × 475

Step 1: Multiply by ones.

845 × 5 = 4,225

				2	2	
				8	4	5
			×	4	7	(5)
			4	2	2	5
+						

Step 2: Multiply by tens.

845 × 70 = 59,150

				3	3	
				8	4	5
			×	4	(7)	5
			4	2	2	5
		5	9	1	5	0
+						

Step 3: Multiply by hundreds.

845 × 400 = 3,38,000

$$\begin{array}{rrrrrrr} & & & & ^{1} & ^{2} & \\ & & & & 8 & 4 & 5 \\ & & & \times & ④ & 7 & 5 \\ \hline & & & 4 & 2 & 2 & 5 \\ & & 5 & 9 & 1 & 5 & 0 \\ + & 3 & 3 & 8 & 0 & 0 & 0 \\ \hline & \square & \square & \square & \square & \square & \square \end{array}$$

Step 4: Add the products.

$$\begin{array}{rrrrrrr} & & & & 8 & 4 & 5 \\ & & & \times & 4 & 7 & 5 \\ \hline & & & 4 & 2 & 2 & 5 \\ & & ^{2}5 & 9 & 1 & 5 & 0 \\ + & ^{1}3 & 3 & 8 & 0 & 0 & 0 \\ \hline & 4 & 0 & 1 & 3 & 7 & 5 \end{array}$$

Therefore, 845 × 475 = 4,01,375

Multiplication of Numbers with One of the Digits as Zero

If one of the digits of a factor being multiplied is 0, that is, either in the ones or in the tens place, then the multiplication with that number can be avoided, as any number multiplied by zero is always 0. Consider the examples given below.

The ones digit is 0

$$\begin{array}{rrrrrr} & & & 5 & 4 & 8 \\ & & \times & 1 & 2 & 0 \\ \hline & & & 0 & 0 & 0 \\ & 1 & 0 & 9 & 6 & 0 \\ + & 5 & 4 & 8 & 0 & 0 \\ \hline & 6 & 5 & 7 & 6 & 0 \end{array}$$

This step can be skipped.

The tens digit is 0

$$\begin{array}{rrrrrrr} & & & & 4 & 5 & 3 \\ & & & \times & 8 & 0 & 5 \\ \hline & & & 2 & 2 & 6 & 5 \\ & & 0 & 0 & 0 & 0 & 0 \\ + & 3 & 6 & 2 & 4 & 0 & 0 \\ \hline & 3 & 6 & 4 & 6 & 6 & 5 \end{array}$$

This step can be skipped.

The ones digit and the tens digit is 0

$$\begin{array}{rrrrrrr} & & & & 8 & 4 & 5 \\ & & & \times & 4 & 0 & 0 \\ \hline & & & 0 & 0 & 0 & 0 \\ & & 0 & 0 & 0 & 0 & 0 \\ + & 3 & 3 & 8 & 0 & 0 & 0 \\ \hline & 3 & 3 & 8 & 0 & 0 & 0 \end{array}$$

Both these steps can be skipped.

Try These!

(a) 367 × 408 = ____________

(b) 298 × 840 = ____________

(c) 912 × 806 = ____________

(d) 267 × 300= ____________

(e) 875 × 600 = ____________

(f) 401 × 200 = ____________

Exercise 3.1

1 Match the correct answer.

(a) 241 × 124	(i) 1,75,032
(b) 468 × 374	(ii) 88,072
(c) 101 × 872	(iii) 29,884
(d) 456 × 470	(iv) 3,06,030
(e) 100 × 943	(v) 2,14,320
(f) 606 × 505	(vi) 94,300

2 Fill in the missing digits.

(a) 300 × 248 = __4__00

(b) 628 × 378 = 2__ __3__4

(c) 18__ × 612 = 1,12,608

(d) 450 × 293 = 1__18__ __

MULTIPLICATION - EXPANDED FORM OF A NUMBER

```
     4 2
   × 1 4
   1 6 8
 + 4 2 0
   5 8 8
```

Consider the multiplication methods given below for each multiplication fact.

In this method, one of the numbers is split up into tens and ones. Here, 14 is written as 10 + 4. The number 10 is multiplied by 42 and the number 4 is multiplied by 42. Their partial products are added to get the answer. 42 × 14 = (42 × 10) + (42 × 4)

×	10	4
42	420	168

→

```
  420
+ 168
  588
```

Note that in both the methods, the product is the same, that is, 42 × 14 = (42 × 10) + (42 × 4) = 588.

Consider another example: 57 × 46

```
      5 7
    × 4 6
    3 4 2
+ 2 2 8 0
  2 6 2 2
```

Here, 46 is written as 40 + 6. The number 40 is multiplied by 57 and the number 6 is multiplied by 57. Their partial products are added to get the answer.

×	40	6
57	2280	342

→

```
   1
  2280
+  342
  2622
```

57 × 46 = (57 × 40) + (57 × 6) = 2,622

Multiplication Techniques

Let us look at some of the techniques which can be used to multiply 2-digit numbers. Consider the example 35 × 42

Step 1: Multiply the digits at the ones place of both the numbers. Carry forward 1 and write 0 in the answer.

$$\begin{array}{r} 3\ 5 \\ \times \\ 4\ 2 \\ \hline 0 \end{array}$$

Step 2: Multiply the digits of both the numbers crosswise. Add the products. Also, add the 1 which was carried forward.

$$\begin{array}{r} 3\ 5 \\ 4\ 2 \\ \hline 7\ 0 \end{array}$$

(2 × 3) + (4 × 5) = 26

26 + 1 = 27. Write 7 in the answer as shown and carry forward 2.

Step 3: Multiply the digits at the tens place and add the number carried forward. You get the answer.

3 × 4 = 12

12 + 2 = 14

$$\begin{array}{r} 3\ 5 \\ \times \\ 4\ 2 \\ \hline 1\ 4\ 7\ 0 \end{array}$$

Try These!

(a) 34 × 28 = ______________________ (b) 18 × 46 = ______________________

Multiplication Technique

The following technique can be used when both the numbers have the same digit at the tens place and the sum of the digits at the ones place of both the numbers is 10. For example, in 57 × 53, here, the tens digits of both the numbers is the same, that is, 5. Also, the sum of the digits at the ones place is 10, that is, 3 + 7 = 10.

Step 1: Multiply the ones digits and write the answer. Here, 7 × 3 = 21 ⟶

$$\begin{array}{r} 5\ 7 \\ \times\ 5\ 3 \\ \hline 2\ 1 \end{array}$$

Step 2: Multiply the tens digit by its next number, that is, 5 × 6 = 30. ⟶

$$\begin{array}{r} 5\ 7 \\ \times\ 5\ 3 \\ \hline 3\ 0\ 2\ 1 \end{array}$$

Therefore, 57 × 53 = 3,021

Some more examples are given below.

24 × 26	51 × 59	38 × 32	73 × 77
= _____24 = 624	= _____09 = 3,009	= _____16 = 1,216	= _____21 = 5,621
↓	↓	↓	↓
2 × 3 = 6	5 × 6 = 30	3 × 4 = 12	7 × 8 = 56

45 × 45	65 × 65	85 × 85	15 × 15
= _____25 = 2,025	= _____25 = 4,225	= _____25 = 7,225	= _____25 = 225
↓	↓	↓	↓
4 × 5 = 20	6 × 7 = 42	8 × 9 = 72	1 × 2 = 2

Note: If the product of the digits at the ones place is a single digit, then write it under the units place of the answer and 0 in the tens place. For example, in the problem, 51 × 59, the product is 9. So, write 9 in the units place and 0 in the tens place.

Note: If the sum of the digits at the ones place is not 10, then one of the numbers can be split such that the sum is 10 and then the multiplication can be carried out. For example, in 38 × 37, 8 + 7 = 15, so 38 × (32 + 5) = (38 × 32) + (38 × 5) = 1216 + 190 = 1,406.

ESTIMATION OF PRODUCTS

Estimation is the method of finding an approximate value but not the exact value. It can be done by rounding off the digits to either the nearest tens or the hundreds.

(a) *If a box has 145 apples, then find out roughly how many apples will be there in 12 boxes.*

The total number of apples in 12 boxes = 145 × 12

145 can be rounded off to the ones place, which will make it 150.
Therefore, 150 × 12 = 1,800

Therefore, there are roughly about 1,800 apples in 12 boxes.

(b) *If a ticket costs ₹389, then estimate the cost of 17 tickets.*

Round off 389 to the hundreds place, which will be ₹400. Estimate the cost of 17 tickets, which will make it ₹400 × 17 = ₹6,800.

Therefore, 17 tickets will cost roughly about ₹6,800.

Try These!

(a) 284 × 14 = __________ (b) 84 × 26 = __________ (c) 408 × 92 = __________

NUMBER PATTERNS - MULTIPLICATION

Consider the following number patterns.

(a) 2, 4, 6, 8, 10, 12, 14, 16

Rule: Products of multiplication tables of 2, starting with 2 × 1 = 2

(b) 6, 18, 30, 42, 54, 66, 78

Rule: Multiplication factors of 6 alternatively starting from 6

(c) 50, 100, 150, 200, 250

Rule: Multiplication of the number 10 by 5, 10, 15, 20, 25 and so on.

(d) 1, 4, 9, 16, 25, 36

Rule: Multiplication of a number by itself, that is, 1 × 1 = 1, 2 × 2 = 4, 3 × 3 = 9, 4 × 4 = 16 and so on.

PROBLEM SOLVING

In real life, we come across many problems for which we need to find solutions. In order to solve problems, one needs to understand the problem and try to find out ways to solve the problem. So, it is important to develop problem-solving skills by being systematic.

Read the problem and understand it. → Identify the known and unknowns. → Identify the operation to be performed. → Carry out the calculations. → Check the answer.

Example: *A train ticket from Bangalore to Chennai costs ₹225. If there are 582 passengers, then find out the total fare collected from them.*

$$\begin{array}{rrrrrrr} & & & & 5 & 8 & 2 \\ & & & \times & 2 & 2 & 5 \\ \hline & & & 2 & 9 & 1 & 0 \\ & & 1 & 1 & 6 & 4 & 0 \\ + & 1 & 1 & 6 & 4 & 0 & 0 \\ \hline & 1 & 3 & 0 & 9 & 5 & 0 \end{array}$$

The cost of one ticket from Bangalore to Chennai = ₹225.

The total number of passengers on the train = 582

The total amount collected = 225 × 582

Therefore, the total fare collected = ₹1,30,950.

Example: *If a 10 kg rice packet costs ₹850, then find out the cost of 150 such packets.*

$$\begin{array}{rrrrrr} & & & 8 & 5 & 0 \\ & & \times & 1 & 5 & 0 \\ \hline & 4 & 2 & 5 & 0 & 0 \\ & 8 & 5 & 0 & 0 & 0 \\ \hline 1 & 2 & 7 & 5 & 0 & 0 \end{array}$$

The cost of one packet of rice = ₹850

The cost of 150 such packets = ₹850 × 150

Therefore, the total cost of rice packets = ₹1,27,500.

Revision Exercise

1 **Multiply the following numbers using the standard multiplication method and write their products.**

(a) 135 × 281 = ___________

(b) 424 × 356 = ___________

(c) 485 × 278 = ___________

(d) 815 × 100 = ___________

(e) 414 × 612 = ___________

(f) 386 × 254 = ___________

(g) 232 × 304 = ___________

(h) 198 × 110 = ___________

(i) 214 × 546 = ___________

(j) 727 × 304 = ___________

2 **Fill in the missing digits.**

(a) 898 × 214 = 1___2___72

(b) 124 × 151 = 1___ ___ ___ ___

(c) 485 × 179 = 86___ ___5

(d) 614 × 257 = 15___ ___ ___8

(e) 186 × 204 = ___7___4___

(f) 432 × 283 = 1___22___6

(g) 298 × 101 = 3___0___8

(h) 210 × 180 = 37___0___

3 **Solve the following word problems.**

(a) In a town, there are 145 elderly people. The government gives ₹500 per month as pension to each one of them. Find out the total amount of money received as pension by these elderly people in a month.

(b) If a school charges ₹1285 as bus fees for 1 month, then find out the amount for 3 months, 6 months and 9 months.

4 **Tick (✓) the best estimate.**

(a) 147 × 30	4,500	45,000	70,000
(b) 291 × 19	7,000	6,000	3,000
(c) 605 × 308	2,00,000	1,80,000	3,00,000
(d) 198 × 103	20,000	20,000	2,00,000

4 Division

Learning Objectives

- To divide 2-digit, 3-digit and 4-digit numbers by a 2-digit number
- To solve word problems on division of numbers

Let's Get Started

Division is equal sharing or equal grouping.

Terms used in division:
Dividend: The number that is being divided
Divisor: The number which divides the dividend
Quotient: The number of times the divisor will go into the dividend
Remainder: The left over number after long division, which is less than the divisor

Quotient → 154

Divisor ← 3) 464 → Dividend

```
     154
3 ) 464
   -3
   ---
    16
   -15
   ---
     14
     12
    ---
      2   → Remainder
```

Dividend = (Divisor × Quotient) + Remainder

464 = (3 × 154) + 2

DIVISION OF A 2-DIGIT NUMBER BY A 2-DIGIT NUMBER

12 times table

1 × 12 = 12
2 × 12 = 24
3 × 12 = 36
4 × 12 = 48
5 × 12 = 60
6 × 12 = 72
7 × 12 = 84
8 × 12 = 96
9 × 12 = 108
10 × 12 = 120

When the Remainder is Zero

1. *A crayon box can contain only 12 crayons. If there are 84 crayons, then find out the number of boxes required to pack them.*

In a box, 12 crayons can be packed.

It is given that 84 crayons are to be packed in boxes.

So, the number of boxes required to pack 84 crayons = 84 ÷ 12

Find how many times the divisor 12 can go into the dividend 84.

$$\begin{array}{r} 7 \\ 12\overline{)\,84} \\ -84 \\ \hline 0 \end{array}$$

Therefore, the number of boxes required to pack 84 crayons is 7.

Try These!

(a) 33 ÷ 11 = ____ (b) 56 ÷ 14 = ____ (c) 78 ÷ 26 = ____ (d) 99 ÷ 33 = ____

When the Remainder is Other Than Zero

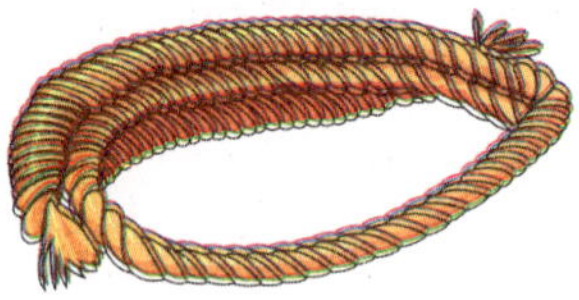

If a rope of length 94 metres is cut into 13 equal parts, then find the length of each part. Will there be some extra piece of rope left?

13 × 6 = 78
13 × 7 = 91
13 × 8 = 104

A rope of length 94 metres is cut into 13 equal parts.
So, the length of each part is 94 ÷ 13

Note: List the multiplication facts of 13 until the product crosses 94. Then, choose the one immediately before 94. Here, it is 13 × 7 = 91.

Note that 7 times 13 is 91 whereas 8 times 13 is 104.

So, write 7 in the quotient and subtract 91 from 94.

Therefore, the length of each part is 7 metres and 3 metres of rope is left.

Common Error!

$$\begin{array}{r} 61 \\ 13\overline{)\,94} \\ -78 \\ \hline 16 \\ -13 \\ \hline 3 \end{array}$$

Exercise 4.1

Divide the following in your notebook.

(a) 75 ÷ 16 (b) 90 ÷ 15 (c) 96 ÷ 32 (d) 45 ÷ 18 (e) 63 ÷ 19 (f) 88 ÷ 36

DIVISION OF 3-DIGIT NUMBER BY A 2-DIGIT NUMBER

When the Remainder is Zero

If a sack of rice weighs 25 kg, then how many such sacks can be made from 525 kg of rice?

Quantity of rice in one sack = 25 kg

So, the number of sacks that can be made from 525 kg of rice = 525 ÷ 25

Step 1: Note that the digit 5 at the hundreds place of the dividend is less than 25. So it can't be divided by 25. Now, take the hundreds and tens digits together, that is, 52. Note that 52 is greater than 25. So, it can be divided by 25. It goes 2 times, leaving 2 as the remainder.

$$\begin{array}{r} 2 \\ 25\overline{)525} \\ -50 \\ \hline 2 \end{array}$$

Step 2: Now, 2 is smaller than 25. So, bring down the digit 5. Now, you have 25. It goes 1 time, leaving 0 as the remainder.

$$\begin{array}{r} 21 \\ 25\overline{)525} \\ -50\downarrow \\ \hline 25 \\ -\ 25 \\ \hline 0 \end{array}$$

Therefore, 21 sacks can be made out of 525 kg of rice such that each sack has 25 kg of rice.

Consider some more examples.

$$\begin{array}{r} 34 \\ 14\overline{)476} \\ -42\downarrow \\ \hline 56 \\ -\ 56 \\ \hline 0 \end{array} \qquad \begin{array}{r} 48 \\ 15\overline{)720} \\ -60\downarrow \\ \hline 120 \\ -120 \\ \hline 0 \end{array} \qquad \begin{array}{r} 18 \\ 36\overline{)648} \\ -36\downarrow \\ \hline 288 \\ -288 \\ \hline 0 \end{array}$$

When the Remainder is Other Than Zero

In the long division method, if the remainder is less than the divisor, then further division can't be carried out. For example, let us see what happens when 876 is divided by 35.

Step 1: The digit 8 at the hundreds place is less than 35. So, it can't be divided by 35. Now, take the hundreds and tens digits together, that is, 87. Note that 87 is greater than 35. So, it can be divided by 35. It goes 2 times, leaving 17 as the remainder. Note that 35 × 3 = 105, which is more than 87.

$$\begin{array}{r} 2 \\ 35\overline{)876} \\ -70 \\ \hline 17 \end{array}$$

Step 2: The number 17 is smaller than 35. So, bring down the number 6. Now, you have 176. It goes 5 times, leaving 1 as the remainder. Here, 1 is smaller than the divisor.

$$\begin{array}{r} 25 \\ 35\overline{)876} \\ -70\downarrow \\ \hline 176 \\ -\ 175 \\ \hline 1 \end{array}$$

Therefore, the quotient of this division is 25 and the remainder is 1.

Some more examples are given below.

```
     31             26             20
12)376         27)720         43)896
  -36↓           -54↓           -86↓
    16            180             36
  - 12           -162           -  0
     4             18             36
```

Exercise 4.2

Divide the following in your notebook.

(a) 875 ÷ 24 (c) 925 ÷ 37 (e) 276 ÷ 16

(b) 741 ÷ 54 (d) 832 ÷ 64 (f) 563 ÷ 12

DIVISION OF A 4-DIGIT NUMBER BY A 2-DIGIT NUMBER

When the Remainder is Zero

If an amount of ₹4,410 is to be distributed equally among 15 workers, then find out the amount each worker would get.

Total amount to be distributed among workers = ₹4,410

Number of workers = 15

So, the amount of money that each one would get = ₹4,410 ÷ 15

Step 1: Take the thousands digit, that is, 4. Note that 4 is less than 15. So, it can not be divided by 15. Now, take the thousands and the hundreds digits together, that is, 44. Note that 44 is greater than 15. So, it can be divided by 15. It goes 2 times, leaving 14 as the remainder.

```
      2
15)4410
  -30
   14
```

Step 2: Bring down 1 from the tens place. The new dividend is 141. It goes 9 times with 15, leaving 6 as the remainder.

```
      29
15)4410
  -30↓
   141
  -135
     6
```

Step 3: Now, bring down 0 from the ones place. The new dividend is 60. It goes 4 times with 15, leaving 0 as the remainder.

```
      294
15)4410
  -30↓
   141
  -135↓
     60
  -  60
      0
```

Therefore, each worker would get ₹294.

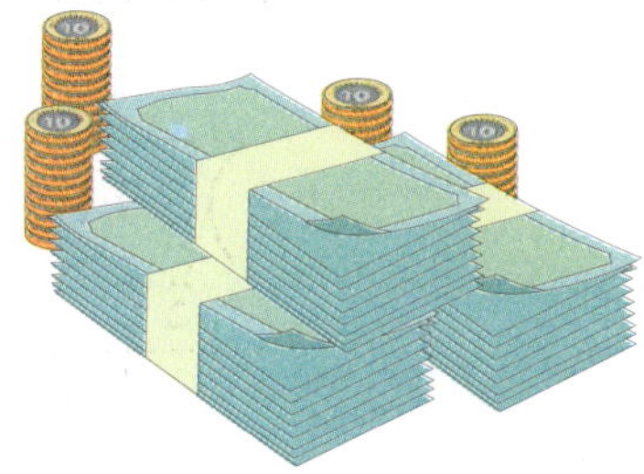

If an amount of ₹1,632 is to be shared equally among 24 workers, then find out the amount that each one would get.

Total amount to be shared = ₹1,632

Number of workers = 24

The amount that each worker would get = ₹1,632 ÷ 24

Step 1: Here, note that the thousands and hundreds digits together, that is, 16 is less than 24. So, take the tens digit along with the thousands and the hundreds digits, that is, 163. Now, 163 is greater than 24 and it goes 6 times, leaving 19 as the remainder.

Step 2: Bring down the 2 from the ones place. Now, the new dividend is 192 and it goes with 8, leaving 0 as the remainder.

```
       68
24)1632
  -144↓
    192
  - 192
      0
```

Therefore, each worker would get ₹68.

When the Remainder is Other Than Zero

Consider some examples where the remainder is not 0.

```
      154               94
17)2627          32)3020
  - 17↓             -288↓
    92               140
  - 85↓            - 128
    77                12
  - 68
     9
```

Exercise 4.3

Divide the following in your notebook.

(a) 2487 ÷ 42 (c) 5608 ÷ 24 (e) 7490 ÷ 35

(b) 8916 ÷ 73 (d) 8075 ÷ 19 (f) 8382 ÷ 64

DIVISION FACTS FOR A GIVEN MULTIPLICATION FACT

Recall that you can write two division facts for a given multiplication fact.

The division concept can be used to find missing factors in a multiplication fact.

Example:

```
       46
   ┌────
12 ) 552
   - 48↓
   ────
      72
   -  72
   ────
       0
```

12 × _____ = 552

Here, the other factor can be found by dividing 552 by 12.

Therefore, the other factor is 46, that is, 12 × 46 = 552.

Try These!

(a) _____ × 18 = 648 (b) 24 × _____ = 4,440 (c) _____ × 74 = 3,552

Common Errors!

```
          41                 401
     ┌──────           ┌──────
  15 ) 6019         15 ) 6019
✗    - 60↓↓            - 60↓↓        ✓
     ──────            ──────
          19                19
     -    15           -    15
     ──────            ──────
           4                 4
```

Here, digits 1 and 9 are brought down one after the other. If two digits are brought down simultaneously, then you should place 0 in the quotient before dividing further.

Note that, (15 × 41) + 4 = 619 whereas (15 × 401) + 4 = 6,019 which is not equal to the dividend.

Exercise 4.4

1 **Calculate and fill in the missing numbers.**

(a) divisor = 13; dividend = 585; remainder = ______; quotient = ______

(b) divisor = 56; dividend = 1512; remainder = ______; quotient = ______

(c) divisor = 19; dividend = 584; remainder = ______; quotient = ______

(d) divisor = 26; dividend = 637; remainder = ______; quotient = ______

(e) divisor = 67; dividend = 8308; remainder = ______; quotient = ______

(f) divisor = 81; dividend = 9704; remainder = ______; quotient = ______

(g) divisor = 37; dividend = 7696; remainder = ______; quotient = ______

(h) divisor = 21; dividend = 1470; remainder = ______; quotient = ______

2 **Calculate and fill in the missing numbers.**

(a) _____ × 11 = 858 (d) 49 × _____ = 7,448 (g) _____ × 64 = 2,368

(b) 25 × _____ = 2,000　　(e) 14 × _____ = 1,414　　(h) _____ × 74 = 6,068

(c) _____ × 26 = 8,970　　(f) _____ × 99 = 6,237　　(i) 39 × _____ = 4,641

3 The answers of the above question have been used to make the following decoding puzzle. Decode the messages given below.

A	B	C	D	E	F	G	H	I	J	K	L	M	N	O	P	Y	R	S
78	152	37	101	80	82	345	63	45	27	14	30	24	13	124	119	65	28	70

Message 1: I am one among the 29 capital cities of the states in India. I belong to the period of Nizams.

63 65 D 80 28 A 152 78 101 __________

Message 2: I am known as 'The City of Dreams'. I am also the 'Commercial Capital' of India. I used to be known as

152 124 24 B 78 65 __________

Also, create a decoding message of your own.

WORD PROBLEMS

1. *A class of 27 students went for a picnic, and the total expenditure of the trip came out to be ₹4,968. Find out the amount to be paid by each student.*

Number of students that went for the picnic = 27

Total expenditure = ₹4,968

The amount to be paid by each student = ₹4968 ÷ 27

Therefore, each student would have to pay ₹184.

```
      184
27 ) 4968
   - 27
     226
   - 216
     108
   - 108
       0
```

2. What is the least number that should be subtracted from 5,974 to make it exactly divisible by 71?

```
       84
71 ) 5974
   - 568
      294
   -  284
       10
```

In order to find the answer, first divide 5,974 by 71.

The remainder is 10. In order to make 5,974 completely divisible by 71, you need to subtract 10 from 5,974.

So, 5,964 ÷ 71 = 84.

DIVISION BY 10, 100 AND 1000

Division by 10

Observe the quotients and the remainders of numbers when divided by 10. Can you see a relation between the digits at different places of the given number and its quotient and remainder?

Number	Quotient	Remainder
35	3	5
370	37	0
547	54	7
7,009	700	9

Note that when we divide a number by 10, the remainder is the digit at the ones place of the number. The rest of the digits forms the quotient. For example, in 124 ÷ 10, 4 is the remainder and 12 is the quotient.

Division by 100

Can you extend the above method while dividing a number by 100?

Observe the remainders and the quotients of numbers when divided by 100. Look at the relation of digits with the quotient and the remainder.

Number	Quotient	Remainder
135	1	35
718	7	18
1,182	11	82
4,370	43	70
5,047	50	47

The digit at the ones and the tens place form the remainder, while the rest of the digits form the quotient. For example, in 718 ÷ 100, 18 is the remainder and 7 is the quotient.

Division by 1,000

Number	Quotient	Remainder
1,835	1	835
9,718	9	718
10,182	10	182
49,370	49	370
95,047	95	47

If we divide a number by 1,000, then the digits at the ones, tens and hundreds place form the remainder while the rest of the digits form the quotient.

ESTIMATION OF QUOTIENTS

In some cases, you may have to roughly estimate the quotient in order to get an idea of the quantity.

If for a birthday party you are charged ₹5,934 for 23 people, then by estimating the quotient, you can get to know the cost of food for one person.

Estimation can be done by rounding off the dividend and divisor. For example,

In 5,934 ÷ 23, 5,934 can be rounded off to 6,000 and 23 can be rounded off to 20.

6,000 ÷ 20 gives the estimated quotient, that is, 300. So, the food for one person roughly costs ₹300.

Example 1: *If 18 T-shirts cost ₹2,810, then estimate the cost of each T-shirt.*

2,810 can be rounded off to 3,000 and 18 can be rounded off to 20.

In 3,000 ÷ 20, the quotient is 150.

So, a T-shirt will roughly cost ₹150 each.

Example 2: *If the weight of 14 bags is 976 kg, then estimate the weight of each bag.*

In 976 ÷ 14, 976 can be rounded off to 1,000 and 14 can be rounded off to 10.

So, in 1,000 ÷ 10, the quotient is 100.

Therefore, each bag roughly weighs 100 kg.

Do you think this skill of estimation is useful? Find out its applications at home, in shops, etc.

Cross-curriculum Link:
Find the synonyms of the word 'estimation'.

PROBLEM SOLVING

In order to solve word problems, you first need to read the given information and identify the unknown values. Then, you need to identify the operation to be used in order to find the unknowns. Finally, you need to verify your answer. The four basic operations are addition (+), subtraction (−), multiplication (×) and division (÷).

− + × ÷

Steps to solve the word problems

Read the problem carefully.
↓
Identify what is to be found.
↓
Identify the operation.
↓
Solve the problem.
↓
Verify the answer.

PROBLEM SOLVING USING MULTIPLE OPERATIONS

Sometimes you may have to use more than one operation in order to solve a given problem. In such cases, identify both the operations and solve the problem.

Consider the following example.

Rahul bought 8 eggs, 6 bananas and 5 kg of rice from a shop. He gave ₹300 to the shopkeeper. Find out the bill amount and also find out the balance amount that Rahul should get back.

Item	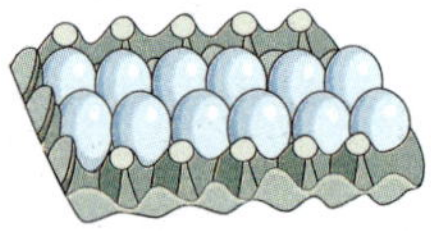		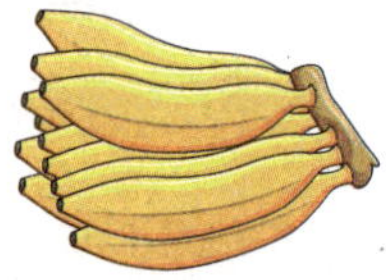
Price (₹)	1 dozen eggs (12 eggs) = ₹48	1 kg of rice = ₹35	1 dozen bananas = ₹36

In this problem, you need to find out the cost of individual items first.

The cost of 12 eggs = ₹48

Hence, the cost of 1 egg = 48 ÷ 12 = ₹4

Therefore, the cost of 8 eggs = 8 × 4 = ₹32

The cost of 12 bananas = ₹36

Hence, the cost of 1 banana = 36 ÷ 12 = ₹3

Therefore, the cost of 6 bananas = 6 × 3 = ₹18

Item	**Price (₹)**
8 eggs	32
6 bananas	18
5 kg of rice	175

The cost of 1 kg of rice = ₹35

Therefore, the cost of 5 kg of rice =35 × 5 = ₹175

Therefore, the total cost of all the items = 32 + 18 + 175 = ₹225.

Rahul paid ₹300, and the bill amounted to ₹225.

Therefore, the amount that Rahul should get back = 300 – 225 = ₹75.

Revision Exercise

1 **Divide the numbers by long division method and find out the quotient and the remainder.**

(a) divisor = 14; dividend = 364; remainder = ______; quotient = ______

(b) divisor = 31; dividend = 2,697; remainder = ______; quotient = ______

(c) divisor = 19; dividend = 6,560; remainder = ______; quotient = ______

(d) divisor = 72; dividend = 6,269; remainder = ______; quotient = ______

(e) divisor = 26; dividend = 2,050; remainder = ______; quotient = ______

2 **Calculate and write the missing numbers.**

(a) ________ × 12 = 216

(b) 61 × ________ = 5,185

(c) 93 × ________ = 2,232

(d) ________ × 34 = 3,434

(e) ________ × 15 = 6,075

(f) 45 × ________ = 3,105

3 **Tick (✓) the problems wherein the remainder is not 0.**

(a) 978 ÷ 18

(b) 6,048 ÷ 28

(c) 8,643 ÷ 43

(d) 896 ÷ 10

(e) 5,602 ÷ 100

(f) 4,970 ÷ 10

4 **Estimate the quotients.**

(a) 7,170 ÷ 15 (b) 8,124 ÷ 22 (c) 3,645 ÷ 81 (d) 9,089 ÷ 89 (e) 415 ÷ 12

5 **Solve the following word problems.**

(a) If 25 kg of rice cost ₹1,125, then find out the cost of 14 kg of rice

(b) A train covers a distance of 2,340 km in 36 hours. Find out the distance covered by the train in the first 15 hours. Assume that the train runs with the same speed.

(c) A gift coupon of ₹ 9,250 was given to all the 37 employees of a company to be shared equally. Calculate how much amount did each employee get.

(d) What number should be subtracted from 3,700 in order to make it exactly divisible by 24?

(e) The product of the age of two persons is 2,438 years. If one of them is 46 years old, then find out the age of the other person.

(f) Find out the cost of fencing 50 m if fencing 72 m costs ₹9,000.

5 Factors and Multiples

Learning Objectives

- To apply the tests of divisibility by 10, 5, 2, 3 and 9
- To find the common factors and the common multiples of given numbers

Let's Get Started

Solve and classify the following division problems into two categories, one where the remainder is 0 and the other where the remainder is not 0.

(a) 84 ÷ 3 = _____, quotient = _____, remainder = _____

(b) 72 ÷ 8 = _____, quotient = _____, remainder = _____

(c) 124 ÷ 4 = _____, quotient = _____, remainder = _____

(d) 145 ÷ 6 = _____, quotient = _____, remainder = _____

(e) 350 ÷ 5 = _____, quotient = _____, remainder = _____

(f) 100 ÷ 10 = _____, quotient = _____, remainder = _____

Problems Where Remainder Is 0	Problems Where Remainder Is Not 0

Note: In a division problem, the number to be divided is called the *dividend* and the number that divides it is called the *divisor*. When a number is divided by another number and the remainder is 0, then the number is said to be *completely divisible* by the divisor.

Examples: The number 84 is completely divisible by 12.

The number 96 is completely divisible by 24.

$$\begin{array}{r} 7 \\ 12\overline{)84} \\ -84 \\ \hline 0 \end{array} \qquad \begin{array}{r} 4 \\ 24\overline{)96} \\ -96 \\ \hline 0 \end{array}$$

DIVISIBILITY RULES

Is it possible for you to say whether a given number is divisible by another number without doing actual division?

Divisibility Rule by 10

Consider the examples of division by 10.

Divide the following numbers and fill in the table.

Division problem	Is It completely divisible?
20 ÷ 10	Yes
160 ÷ 10	
2,050 ÷ 10	

Division problem	Is it completely divisible?
84 ÷ 10	No
491 ÷ 10	
5,036 ÷ 10	

Observe that the numbers which are divisible by 10 have 0 in the ones place. Also, if the digit is not 0, then the number is not completely divisible by 10.

Think of some numbers with 0 in the ones place and check their divisibility by 10. Also, take some numbers with digits other than 0 in the ones place and check their divisibility by 10.

Divisibility Rule by 10: A number is divisible by 10 only if it has 0 in its ones place.

Divisibility Rule by 5

Activity: Take some numbers and divide them by 5. Write the numbers which are divisible by 5 and observe the digits in the ones place.

Note that the digit in the ones place of the numbers divisible by 5 is either 0 or 5.

Divisibility Rule by 5: A number is divisible by 5 only if it has 5 or 0 in its ones place.

Note: The process of checking whether a number is divisible by a given number or not without actual division is known as the *test of divisibility*.

Divisibility Rule by 2

Activity: Take some numbers and divide them by 2. Write the numbers which are divisible by 2 and observe the digits in ones place.

You will note that the numbers which are divisible by 2 have 0, 2, 4, 6 or 8 in their ones place. Numbers with 1, 3, 5, 7 or 9 in their ones place are not divisible by 2.

Divisibility Rule by 2: A number is divisible by 2 only if the digit in its ones place is 0, 2, 4, 6, or 8.

Divisibility Rule by 3

Activity: Take some numbers and divide them by 3. Write the numbers which are divisible by 3 and observe the sum of the digits.

Divisibility Rule by 3: If the sum of the digits of a number is divisible by 3, then the number is also divisible by 3, otherwise it is not.

Divisibility Rule by 9

Activity: Take some numbers and divide them by 9. Write the numbers which are divisible by 9 and observe the sum of the digits.

Divisibility Rule by 9: If the sum of the digits of a number is divisible by 9, then the number is also divisible by 9, otherwise it is not.

Exercise 5.1

1 Write 'yes' or 'no' under the divisibility of each number.

Number	Divisible by 2	Divisible by 5	Divisible by 10	Divisible by 3	Divisible by 9
24					
1,025					
876					
9,122					
1,000					

2 Write three examples each of the numbers which are not divisible by 5, 2, 10, 3 and 9 in your notebook.

FACTORS

Raj has 10 potted plants. He wants to arrange the flower pots in a rectangular flower bed with the same number of plants in each row. Help Raj to find the different possibilities.

Let us discuss the different possibilities.

Arrangement 1: All the ten flower pots in one row, that is, $1 \times 10 = 10$

Arrangement 2: Five flower pots each in two rows, that is, $2 \times 5 = 10$

Arrangement 3: Two flower pots each in five rows, that is, $5 \times 2 = 10$

Arrangement 4: Ten rows and one flower pot in each row, that is, $10 \times 1 = 10$

Multiplication facts representing the four arrangements are:

$1 \times 10 = 10$; $2 \times 5 = 10$; $5 \times 2 = 10$; $10 \times 1 = 10$

In each multiplication fact, there are two multiplicands and they divide their product exactly. For example, in $2 \times 5 = 10$, both 2 and 5 divide 10 exactly. The numbers which divide a number exactly are known as *factors*. Here, 2 and 5 are factors of 10. Similarly, 1 and 10 are factors of 10.

Therefore, the factors of 10 are 1, 2, 5 and 10.

A number is said to be a factor of another number if one number divides the other number completely.

6 is not a factor of 10 since it does not divide it completely.

Similarly, 5 is not a factor of 21.

$$\begin{array}{r} 1 \\ 6\overline{)10} \\ -\ 6 \\ \hline 4 \end{array} \qquad \begin{array}{r} 4 \\ 5\overline{)21} \\ -20 \\ \hline 1 \end{array}$$

Let us consider another example of finding out the factors of 18.

$18 = 1 \times 18$; $18 = 2 \times 9$; $18 = 3 \times 6$ So, the factors of 18 are 1, 2, 3, 6, 9 and 18.

Method of finding the factors of a given number: Write all the possible multiplication facts for the given number and then list the factors of a given number.

Example: Find the factors of 30.

The factors of 30 are 1, 2, 3, 5, 6, 10, 15 and 30.

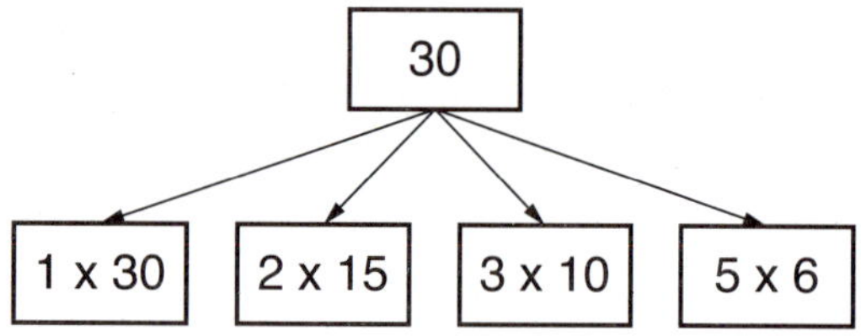

Try These!

Find out the factors of 12 and 24.

PROPERTIES OF FACTORS

Write the factors of the following numbers and answer the questions.

Number	Factors
6	
8	
16	
20	
24	
22	
36	

1. Is 1 a factor of every number?
2. Is every number a factor of itself?
3. Count the number of factors of each number. Are they countable?
4. Is every factor less than or equal to the given number?
5. Is every factor an exact divisor of the given number?

Fact 1: It can be observed that 1 is a factor of every number since it divides the number exactly.

For example, $10 \div 1 = 10$ $\quad 14 \div 1 = 14$ $\quad 27 \div 1 = 27$

Fact 2: It can also be noted that every number is a factor of itself since the number divides itself exactly.

$$\begin{array}{r} 1 \\ 10\overline{)10} \\ -10 \\ \hline 0 \end{array}$$

For example, $10 \div 10 = 1$ $\quad 14 \div 14 = 1$ $\quad 27 \div 27 = 1$

Fact 3: The number of factors of a number is countable. For example, the factors of 6 are 1, 2, 3 and 6, that is, 6 has four factors.

Fact 4: Every factor of a number is less than or equal to the given number. For example, the factors of 6 are 1, 2, 3 and 6. Note that, the factors are either less than or equal to 6.

Fact 5: Every factor is an exact divisor of the given number. For example, the factors of 6 are 1, 2, 3 and 6. Note that each one divides 6 completely.

CHALLENGE

Can a number have odd number of factors? Why or why not?

MULTIPLES

Read the sentences given below and find the meaning of the word 'multiple'.

- A juice company sells its products in quantities of 250 ml, 500 ml, 750 ml, 1 litre and in multiples of 2 litres.
- The total number of books that fit in a box completely is always a multiple of five.

The word 'multiples' means a mathematical product. It is obtained by multiplying two numbers. For example, in $6 \times 2 = 12$, 12 is a multiple of 6 and also a multiple of 2.

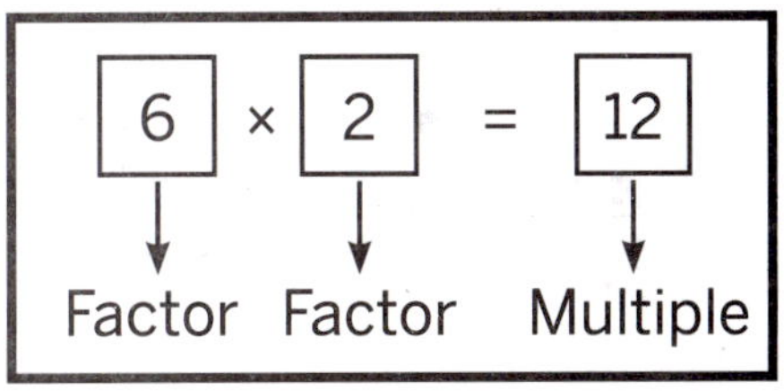

The numbers 6 and 2 are known as factors and the number 12 is known as multiple.

Note that 12 is a multiple of 6 since 6 divides 12 completely. Similarly, 12 is a multiple of 2 since 2 divides 12 completely.

12 is not a multiple of 5 since 5 does not divide 12 completely.

```
   2
5)12
 -10
   2
```

A number is said to be a multiple of another number if it is divided by the other number completely. That is , the second number divides the multiple completely.

Try These!

Ring the number whose multiple is 20.

3 7 5 8 9

THE METHOD OF FINDING THE MULTIPLES OF A NUMBER

Let us study the method of writing the multiples of a number, say 2. Multiply the number 2 by 1 to get 2. So, 2 is a multiple of 2. Then, again, multiply it by 2 to get 4. So, 4 is the second multiple. Similarly, multiply 2 by 3, 4, 5, 6 and so on to get different multiples of number 2.

Therefore, the multiples of 2 are 2, 4, 6, 8, 10, 12, 14, 16, 18, 20, 22, 24, 26, 28 and so on.

In order to write the multiples of a number, multiply the number by 1, 2, 3, 4 and so on. The products are the multiples of a given number.

Try These!

(a) Mention the first 7 multiples of 5.

(b) Mention the first 6 multiples of 9.

PROPERTIES OF MULTIPLES

Observe the table with multiples of different numbers.

Number	Multiples
3	3, 6, 9, 12, 15, 18, 21, 24, 27, 30, 33, 36, 39, 42, 45 ...
4	4, 8, 12, 16, 20, 24, 28, 32, 36, 40, 44, 48, 52, 56, 60 ...
6	6, 12, 18, 24, 30, 36, 42, 48, 54, 60, 66, 72, 78, 84, 90 ...
7	7, 14, 21, 28, 35, 42, 49, 56, 63, 70, 77, 84, 91, 98, 105 ...

Note that 3 is a multiple of 3; 4 is a multiple of 4; 6 is a multiple of 6. It can be observed that every number is a multiple of itself.

Fact 1: Every number is a multiple of itself.

Also, note from the table that the multiples of 3 start with 3 and the rest of the numbers are greater than 3. Similarly, the multiples of 4 start with 4 and the rest of the numbers are greater than 4. So, any multiple of a number is greater than or equal to that number.

Fact 2: Every multiple of a number is greater than or equal to that number.

Note that you can write as many multiples as you can think of. There is no end to the list of multiples of a number. So, the number of multiples of a number is infinite.

Fact 3: The number of multiples of a given number is infinite.

Cross-curricular Link: Find the meaning of the word 'infinite' and make some sentences with the word.

Exercise 5.2

1 **Write all the factors of the following numbers.**

Number	Factors
27	
4	
45	
19	

Number	Factors
14	
9	
30	
15	

2 **Write the first five multiples of the following numbers.**

Number	First Five Multiples
7	
8	
1	
3	
9	

Number	First Five Multiples
10	
2	
12	
6	
5	

3 **Tick (✓) the factor(s) of the given numbers.**

(a) **42** 4 7 8 10 (d) **24** 8 5 6 13 (g) **25** 2 3 5 10

(b) **16** 5 2 8 15 (e) **19** 6 4 8 19 (h) **22** 1 7 11 2

(c) **55** 5 10 4 11 (f) **13** 1 15 10 13 (i) **45** 6 9 2 3

4 **Tick (✓) the multiple(s) of the given numbers.**

(a) **7** 56 77 14 24 (d) **3** 81 18 22 13 (g) **5** 60 41 12 55

(b) **11** 11 12 88 48 (e) **10** 5 100 150 200 (h) **6** 22 33 66 55

(c) **8** 14 80 26 32 (f) **9** 72 63 21 27 (i) **15** 45 30 60 70

COMMON FACTORS

The factors which are common to two or more numbers are known as *common factors.* Let us take an example of two numbers 12 and 15.

Look at the factors which are common to both the numbers as shown.

Factors of 12	1, 2, 3, 4, 6, 12
Factors of 15	1, 3, 5, 15

Therefore, the common factors of 12 and 15 are 1 and 3.

The same can be represented using a different representation.

Write the common factors in the intersection area of both the circles and the rest in their respective circles.

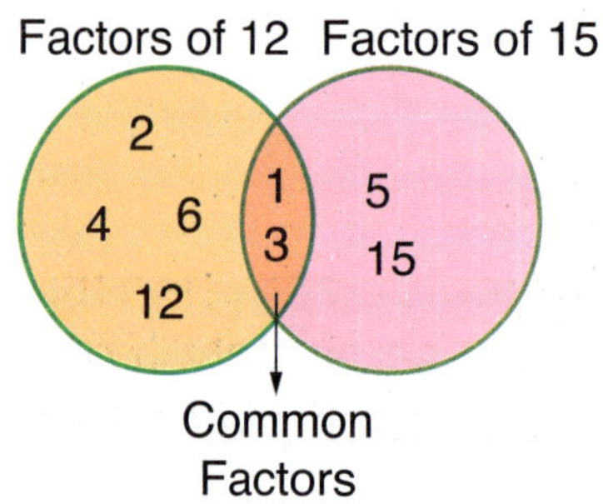

Let us take another example of two numbers 24 and 18.

Factors of 24	1, 2, 3, 4, 6, 8, 12, 24
Factors of 18	1, 2, 3, 6, 9, 18

Therefore, the common factors of 24 and 18 are 1, 2, 3 and 6.

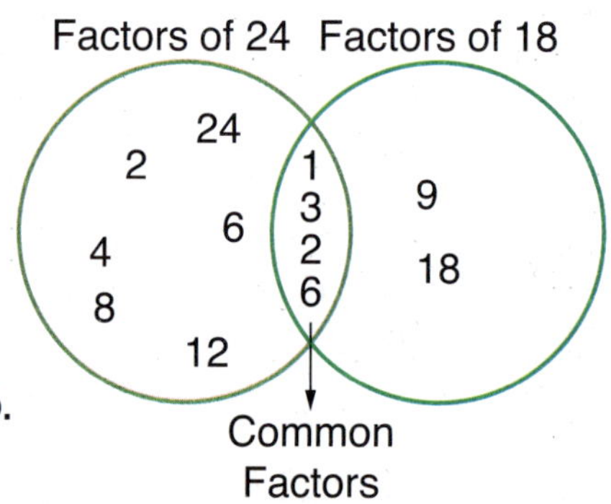

(a) 1 is always a common factor of any two given numbers. Hence, it is sufficient to write the common factors other than 1. For example, the common factors of 24 and 18 are 2, 3 and 6.

(b) Sometimes, two numbers may not have common factors. For example, 12 and 17 do not have any common factors other than 1.

COMMON MULTIPLES

The multiples which are common to two or more numbers are known as *common multiples.* Let us take an example of two numbers 3 and 5.

Look at the multiples which are common to both the numbers as shown.

Multiples of 3	3, 6, 9, 12, 15, 18, 21, 24, 27, 30
Multiples of 5	5, 10, 15, 20, 25, 30, 35, 40, 45, 50

Therefore, in the first ten common multiples of 3 and 5 two common multiples are 15 and 30. If you write the next ten multiples, you will get some more common multiples.

Try These!

Find out the first three common multiples of 2 and 3.

To Check Whether a Given Number Is a Common Multiple or Not

To find out whether a given number is a common multiple of two numbers, divide the given number by both the numbers separately. If both the numbers divide it completely, then the given number is a common multiple of the two numbers, otherwise it is not.

Example 1: Check whether 120 is a common multiple of 2 and 3.

Step 1: 120 ÷ 2 = 60 **Step 2**: 120 ÷ 3 = 40

Therefore, 120 is a common multiple of 2 and 3.

Example 2: Check whether 243 is a common multiple of 2 and 3.

Step 1: 243 ÷ 3 = 81 **Step 2**: 243 ÷ 2 = ? We find that 243 is not completely divisible by 2.

Therefore, 243 is not a common multiple of 2 and 3.

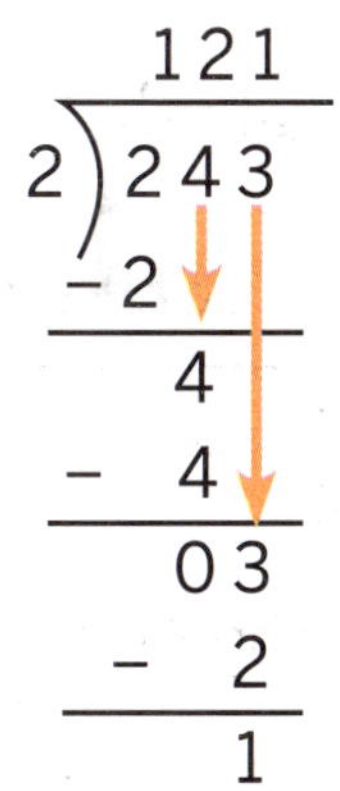

Note: You can also divide the given number by the product of the two numbers. If it divides completely, then it is a common multiple, otherwise it is not. This is applicable if two numbers have no common factors. For example, 16 is a common multiple of 4 and 8, but 16 is not divisible by 4 × 8 = 32 as 4 and 8 have common factors.

Revision Exercise

1 **Find all the factors of the following pairs of numbers. Also, find their common factors.**

(a) 10, 15 (b) 12, 16 (c) 18, 24 (d) 16, 18 (e) 14, 35

2 **Write the first ten multiples of the following numbers. Also, find their common multiples.**

(a) 3, 7 (b) 2, 6 (c) 8, 3 (d) 5, 2 (e) 4, 3

3 **Match the following.**

(a) A factor of 16	(i) 5
(b) A multiple of 3	(ii) 8
(c) A common factor of 10, 40	(iii) 63
(d) A common multiple of 9, 7	(iv) 7
(e) A factor of 42	(v) 36

4 **Tick (✓) the common factor(s) of the given numbers.**

(a) 18, 10 8 2 9 3
(b) 9, 18 2 6 3 9
(c) 15, 30 5 2 6 3
(d) 12, 14 5 7 6 4
(e) 11, 22 1 6 9 11
(f) 16, 4 2 4 8 5

5 **Tick (✓) the common multiple(s) of the given numbers.**

(a) 2, 7 56 77 14 24
(b) 6, 2 6 12 18 26
(c) 4, 2 90 16 48 25
(d) 3, 4 20 12 18 36
(e) 5, 10 25 15 50 100
(f) 3, 5 35 30 60 90

6 **Write 'yes' or 'no' under the divisibility of each number.**

Number	Divisible by 2	Divisible by 5	Divisible by 10
120			
35			
5,872			

HOTS (Higher Order Thinking Skills)

FA

1. Are all the factors of a number a multiple of it? Justify your answer.
2. If Q is divisible by P, then which of the following is correct? Tick the right answer(s).

   (a) P is a factor of Q. ☐

   (b) Q is a factor of P. ☐

   (c) P is a multiple of Q. ☐

   (d) Q is a multiple of P ☐

6 Fractions

Learning Objectives

- To understand the concept of equivalent fractions
- To understand the types of fractions and compare fractions
- To add and subtract like fractions

Let's Get Started

The word 'fraction' means a part of the whole object.

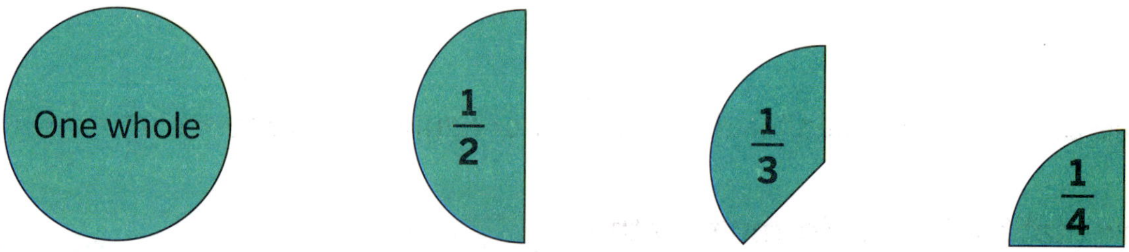

$$\text{Fraction} = \frac{\text{Numerator}}{\text{Denominator}}$$

Numerator: It tells you the number of equal parts which have been shaded.

Denominator: It tells you the number of equal parts into which the whole has been divided.

EQUIVALENT FRACTIONS

Look at all these representations of fractions.

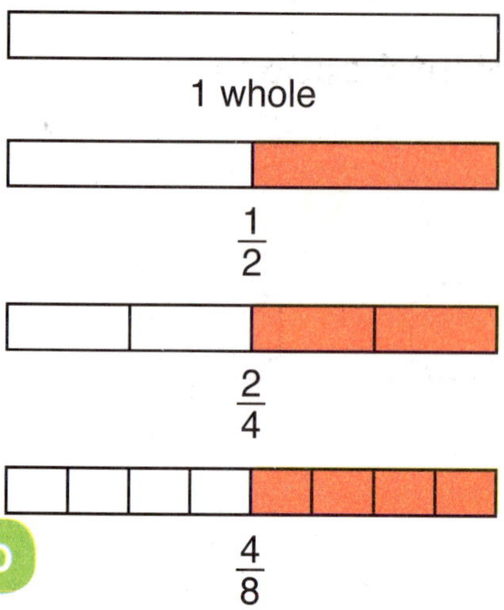

These fractions are $\frac{1}{2}, \frac{2}{4}, \frac{4}{8}$ and they represent the parts taken from the total number of parts. If you compare the pictorial representation of these fractions when placed one over the other, you will find them to be equal. These are called *equivalent fractions*.

Therefore, these are written as $\frac{1}{2} = \frac{2}{4} = \frac{4}{8}$.

Equivalent fractions are two or more fractions which have the same value.

Finding Equivalent Fractions

To find an equivalent fraction, you need to multiply the numerator and the denominator by the same number.

Example 1: Write two equivalent fractions of $\frac{2}{4}$.

Multiply the numerator and the denominator by 2.

That is, $\frac{2}{4} = \frac{2 \times 2}{4 \times 2} = \frac{4}{8}$

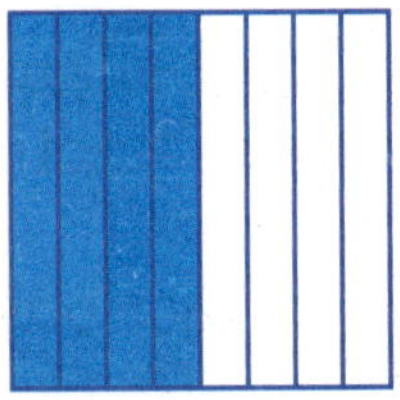

Multiply the numerator and the denominator by 3.

That is, $\frac{2}{4} = \frac{2 \times 3}{4 \times 3} = \frac{6}{12}$

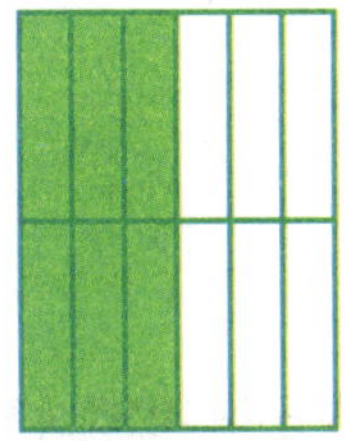

Therefore, the equivalent fractions of $\frac{2}{4}$ are $\frac{4}{8}$ and $\frac{6}{12}$.

Example 2: Fill in the boxes for the given set of equivalent fractions $\frac{2}{5} = \frac{[\,]}{10} = \frac{6}{[\,]}$

We know that 5 × 2 = 10. So, multiply the numerator and the denominator by 2.

That is, $\frac{2}{5} = \frac{2 \times 2}{5 \times 2} = \frac{4}{10}$

We know that 2 × 3 = 6. So, multiply the numerator and the denominator by 3.

That is, $\frac{2}{5} = \frac{2 \times 3}{5 \times 3} = \frac{6}{15}$

Therefore, $\frac{2}{5} = \frac{4}{10} = \frac{6}{15}$ are the required equivalent fractions.

Exercise 6.1

1 Write the fractions and identify the pairs of equivalent fractions.

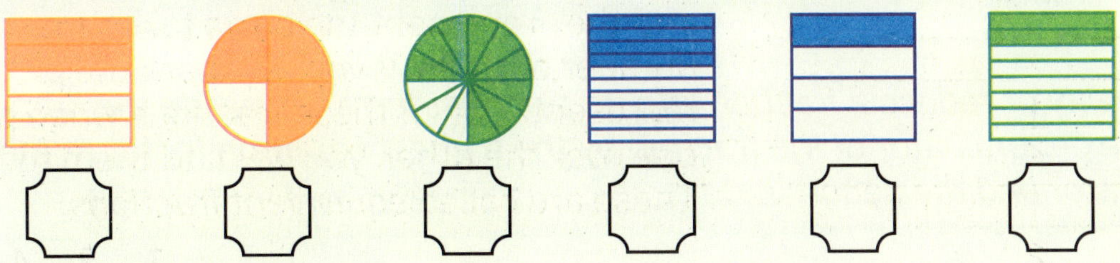

Pairs of equivalent fractions: ______________

2 **Fill in the boxes for the given set of equivalent fractions.**

(a) $\frac{2}{3} = \frac{4}{[\ ]} = \frac{6}{[\ ]} = \frac{[\ ]}{12} = \frac{[\ ]}{[\ ]}$

(b) $\frac{1}{7} = \frac{2}{[\ ]} = \frac{[\ ]}{21} = \frac{4}{[\ ]} = \frac{[\ ]}{[\ ]}$

(c) $\frac{3}{5} = \frac{6}{[\ ]} = \frac{[\ ]}{15} = \frac{12}{[\ ]} = \frac{[\ ]}{[\ ]}$

(d) $\frac{1}{4} = \frac{3}{[\ ]} = \frac{[\ ]}{16} = \frac{6}{[\ ]} = \frac{[\ ]}{[\ ]}$

The Simplest Form of a Fraction

A fraction is said to be in the simplest form if its numerator and denominator have no common factor other than 1.

Example 1:

Consider the fraction $\frac{1}{2}$

Common factors of 1: 1
Common factors of 2: 1 and 2

Here, the numerator and the denominator have no common factors other than 1.

Therefore, the fraction $\frac{1}{2}$ *is in its simplest form.*

Example 2:

Consider the fraction $\frac{9}{27}$

How do you convert it into its simplest form?

Is the given fraction in the simplest form? No.

Divide the numerator and the denominator by the same number until they have no common factors other than 1.

That is, $\frac{9 \div 9}{27 \div 9} = \frac{1}{3}$

Now, 1 and 3 have no common factor other than 1. Hence, the fraction $\frac{1}{3}$ is in its simplest form.

FACT

To simplify or reduce a fraction into its simplest form, we divide the numerator and the denominator of the fraction by the highest common factor of the numerator and the denominator.

Exercise 6.2

Reduce the following fractions into their simplest forms.

(a) $\frac{64}{72}$ (c) $\frac{28}{56}$ (e) $\frac{48}{96}$ (g) $\frac{9}{63}$

(b) $\frac{27}{81}$ (d) $\frac{110}{550}$ (f) $\frac{75}{225}$ (h) $\frac{64}{216}$

Checking the Equivalence of Two Fractions

To check whether the given two fractions are equivalent or not, you need to find out whether the given fractions are in their simplest forms or not.

Example 1:

Check if $\frac{1}{2}$ and $\frac{2}{4}$ are equivalent fractions.

The simplest form of $\frac{1}{2}$ is $\frac{1}{2}$.

The simplest form of $\frac{2}{4}$ is $\frac{\cancel{2}^{1}}{\cancel{4}_{2}} = \frac{1}{2}$.

Therefore, $\frac{1}{2}$ and $\frac{2}{4}$ are equivalent fractions.

Example 2:

Check if $\frac{3}{4}$ and $\frac{6}{8}$ are equivalent fractions.

The simplest form of $\frac{3}{4}$ is $\frac{3}{4}$.

The simplest form of $\frac{6}{8}$ is $\frac{\cancel{6}^{3}}{\cancel{8}_{4}} = \frac{3}{4}$.

Therefore, $\frac{3}{4}$ and $\frac{6}{8}$ are equivalent fractions.

Did You Know?

We can check whether the two fractions are equivalent or not by the method of cross-multiplying.

Example: Are $\frac{1}{3}$ and $\frac{3}{9}$ equivalent fractions?

We cross multiply them. $\frac{1}{3} \times \frac{3}{9}$

That is, $3\times3 = 1\times9$

$9 = 9$

Hence, we can say that the two fractions are equivalent.

Exercise 6.3

1 Check whether the given fractions are equivalent or not.

(a) $\frac{4}{5}$ and $\frac{8}{10}$ (c) $\frac{1}{7}$ and $\frac{2}{14}$ (e) $\frac{5}{6}$ and $\frac{10}{12}$ (g) $\frac{4}{9}$ and $\frac{16}{38}$

(b) $\frac{1}{3}$ and $\frac{8}{24}$ (d) $\frac{3}{7}$ and $\frac{9}{14}$ (f) $\frac{3}{5}$ and $\frac{2}{3}$ (h) $\frac{1}{4}$ and $\frac{6}{7}$

LIKE AND UNLIKE FRACTIONS

What do you observe from the following sets of figures?

$\frac{1}{4}$ $\frac{2}{4}$ $\frac{3}{4}$ $\frac{1}{5}$ $\frac{2}{5}$ $\frac{3}{5}$

The two sets of figures have common denominators in their fractions.

Fractions with the same denominator are called *like fractions*.

$\frac{4}{6}, \frac{5}{6}, \frac{3}{6}$ are like fractions since they have a common denominator 6.

Fractions which have different denominators are called *unlike fractions*.

Examples:

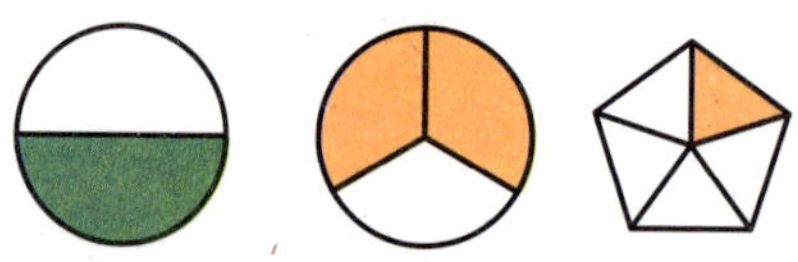

$\frac{1}{2}$ $\frac{2}{3}$ $\frac{1}{5}$

$\frac{32}{64}, \frac{8}{16}, \frac{2}{4}$ are unlike fractions since they have different denominators.

Did You Know?

The fractions with one as numerator are known as *unit fractions*. For Example, $\frac{1}{2}$ and $\frac{1}{23}$

Exercise 6.4

1 **Against each set of fractions write whether they are like fractions or unlike fractions.**

(a) $\frac{3}{12}, \frac{1}{12}, \frac{4}{12}, \frac{11}{12}$

(b) $\frac{3}{8}, \frac{2}{3}, \frac{2}{12}, \frac{2}{7}$

(c) $\frac{1}{8}, \frac{4}{8}, \frac{3}{8}, \frac{6}{8}$

(d) $\frac{1}{8}, \frac{1}{10}, \frac{5}{12}, \frac{6}{13}$

2 **Classify the given set of fractions into like fractions and unlike fractions.**

$\frac{1}{4}, \frac{5}{6}, \frac{11}{16}, \frac{1}{16}, \frac{8}{10}, \frac{15}{18}, \frac{10}{16}, \frac{10}{100}, \frac{12}{14}, \frac{13}{111}, \frac{2}{5}, \frac{3}{5}, \frac{25}{111}, \frac{25}{100}, \frac{2}{12}, \frac{1}{8}, \frac{4}{12}, \frac{2}{16}$

Like Fractions	Unlike Fractions

3 **Circle out the unit fractions in each set.**

(a) $\frac{1}{4}, \frac{10}{16}, \frac{2}{5}$

(b) $\frac{11}{12}, \frac{1}{21}, \frac{15}{16}$

(c) $\frac{12}{24}, \frac{14}{36}, \frac{1}{12}$

COMPARISON OF LIKE FRACTIONS

Look at the picture given below.

Which out of $\frac{3}{8}$ and $\frac{5}{8}$ is the bigger fraction?

Look at the figures given below.

$\frac{5}{8}$ is greater than $\frac{3}{8}$.

Therefore, Tinku got more cake.

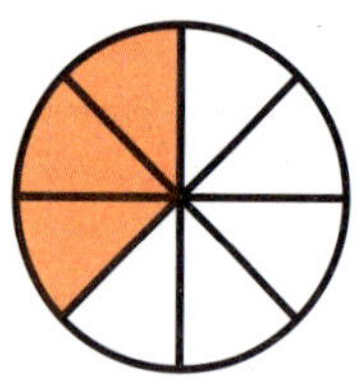

$\frac{3}{8}$

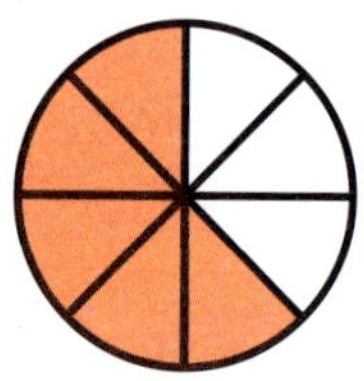

$\frac{5}{8}$

Which fraction has a larger shaded part?

Example 1: Which out of $\frac{3}{6}$ and $\frac{5}{6}$ is bigger?

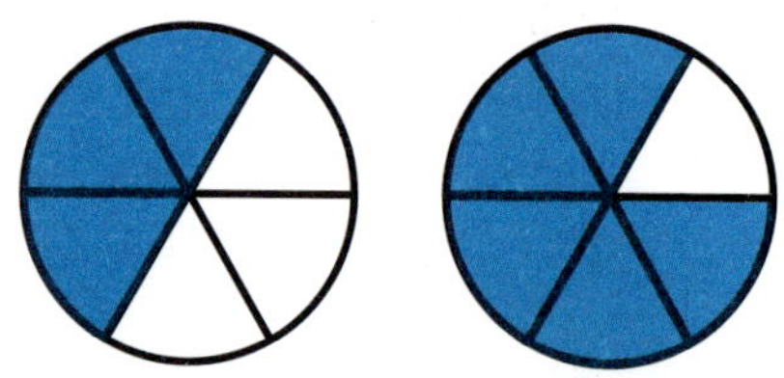

$\frac{3}{6}$ $\frac{5}{6}$

In both the fractions, the whole is divided into 6 equal parts. 3 parts and 5 parts are shaded respectively.

Therefore, out of 6 equal parts, the portion corresponding to 5 parts is greater than the portion corresponding to 3 parts.

Hence, $\frac{5}{6} > \frac{3}{6}$.

Did You Know?

If the denominator of two fractions is the same, then the fraction having a greater value in the numerator is greater than the other fraction.

Exercise 6.5

1 **Compare the fractions given in the following table and use the symbol (=/ >/<) to determine the answer.**

Fraction 1	Symbol (=/ >/<)	Fraction 2
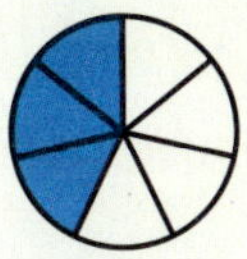 $\frac{3}{7}$		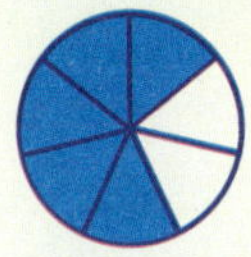 $\frac{5}{7}$
 $\frac{7}{11}$		 $\frac{2}{11}$
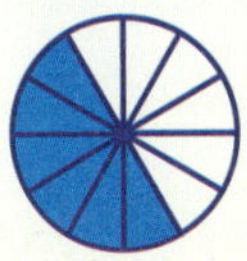 $\frac{6}{12}$		 $\frac{9}{12}$

2 **Compare the fractions and put appropriate sign (=/ >/<) in brackets.**

(a) $\frac{10}{15}$ ( ) $\frac{8}{15}$

(b) $\frac{13}{46}$ ( ) $\frac{32}{46}$

(c) $\frac{3}{9}$ ( ) $\frac{5}{9}$

(d) $\frac{9}{31}$ ( ) $\frac{4}{31}$

(e) $\frac{12}{24}$ ( ) $\frac{11}{24}$

(f) $\frac{10}{19}$ ( ) $\frac{9}{19}$

ADDITION OF LIKE FRACTIONS

Anita got $\frac{2}{5}$ of an apple from her sister and $\frac{1}{5}$ of an apple from her brother.

How much portion of the apple did Anita get?

We need to know how to add two fractions in order to answer such questions.

Consider the fractions $\frac{2}{5}$ and $\frac{1}{5}$.

The fraction $\frac{2}{5}$ is represented as 

The fraction $\frac{1}{5}$ is represented as 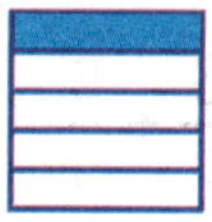

Represent $\frac{2}{5}$ and $\frac{1}{5}$ in the same figure. 

How many boxes are there in all? $\boxed{5}$

What fraction of the whole is shaded in blue? $\boxed{\frac{1}{5}}$

What fraction of the whole is shaded in green? $\boxed{\frac{2}{5}}$

What fraction of the whole is a combination of blue and green? $\boxed{\frac{3}{5}}$

This can also be written as:

$$\boxed{\frac{2}{5}+\frac{1}{5}=\frac{2+1}{5}=\frac{3}{5}}$$

Therefore, Anita got $\frac{3}{5}$ portion of the apple in all.

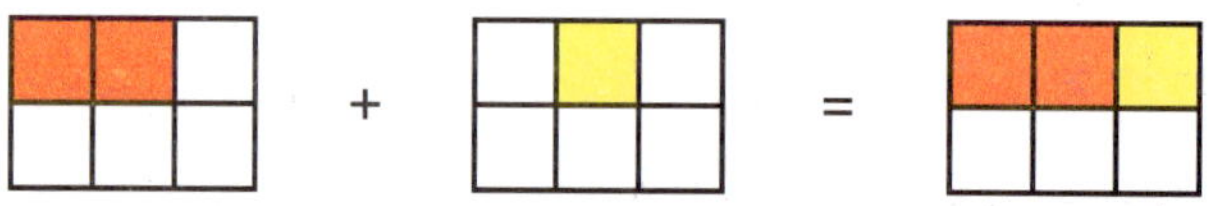

$$\frac{2}{6} \qquad \frac{1}{6} \qquad \frac{2+1}{6}=\frac{\cancel{3}^{1}}{\cancel{6}_{2}}=\frac{1}{2}$$

To add two like fractions, follow the steps given below:

Step 1: Add the numerators.

Step 2: Retain the (common) denominator.

Step 3: Write the fraction as: $\frac{\text{The sum of the numerators}}{\text{Common denominator}}$

Example: *Shubha planted flowers in $\frac{1}{9}$ portion of her garden. Her sister helped her and planted flowers in $\frac{5}{9}$ portion of the garden. In how much portion of the garden did they both planted flowers?*

Shubha and her sister planted:

$$\frac{1}{9}+\frac{5}{9}=\frac{5+1}{9}=\frac{\cancel{6}^{2}}{\cancel{9}_{3}}=\frac{2}{3}.$$

Therefore, they both planted in $\frac{2}{3}$ portion of the garden.

Exercise 6.6

1 **Add the following fractions.**

(a) $\frac{2}{5}+\frac{1}{5}$ (c) $\frac{1}{6}+\frac{3}{6}$ (e) $\frac{1}{3}+\frac{2}{3}$ (g) $\frac{2}{7}+\frac{2}{7}$ (i) $\frac{4}{11}+\frac{6}{11}$

(b) $\frac{2}{8}+\frac{4}{8}$ (d) $\frac{4}{10}+\frac{5}{10}$ (f) $\frac{3}{7}+\frac{1}{7}$ (h) $\frac{3}{15}+\frac{10}{15}$ (j) $\frac{2}{12}+\frac{2}{12}$

2 It was Chhavi's birthday party. Rahul has $\frac{1}{4}$ portion of a cake. He gets $\frac{3}{4}$ portion of a cake from his friend. How much cake does Rahul have now?

3 At the birthday party, the girls ate $\frac{1}{7}$ portion of a pizza and the boys ate $\frac{2}{7}$ portion of the pizza. How much pizza did the boys and girls eat in all?

4 At the party the girls won $\frac{3}{7}$ of the games played and the boys won $\frac{2}{7}$ of the games played. How many games did they win in all?

SUBTRACTION OF LIKE FRACTIONS

Example 1: *Sonal had $\frac{5}{6}$ portion of a cake in her plate. She gave $\frac{3}{6}$ portion out of that to her younger brother. How much portion of the cake is she left with?*

We need to know how to subtract two fractions in order to answer such questions.

Consider the pictorial representation of $\frac{5}{6}$ and $\frac{3}{6}$.

$$\frac{5}{6} - \frac{3}{6} = \frac{5-3}{6} = \frac{\cancel{2}^{1}}{\cancel{6}_{3}} = \frac{1}{3}$$

Therefore, Sonal is left with $\frac{1}{3}$ portion of the cake.

To subtract two like fractions, follow the steps given below:

Step 1: Subtract the smaller numerator from the bigger numerator.

Step 2: Retain the (common) denominator.

Step 3: Write the fraction as: $\frac{\text{The difference of the numerators}}{\text{Common denominator}}$

Exercise 6.7

1 Subtract the following fractions.

(a) $\frac{7}{10}-\frac{4}{10}$ (c) $\frac{6}{6}-\frac{3}{6}$ (e) $\frac{6}{9}-\frac{5}{9}$ (g) $\frac{5}{15}-\frac{2}{15}$ (i) $\frac{11}{12}-\frac{3}{12}$

(b) $\frac{8}{21}-\frac{3}{21}$ (d) $\frac{4}{19}-\frac{2}{19}$ (f) $\frac{12}{23}-\frac{9}{23}$ (h) $\frac{9}{25}-\frac{1}{25}$ (j) $\frac{30}{38}-\frac{1}{38}$

2 Solve the following word problems.

(a) Ramesh bought $\frac{2}{8}$ metre of green ribbon and $\frac{5}{8}$ metre of blue ribbon for tying gifts. How much more blue ribbon did he buy than the green ribbon?

(b) Mohan rode his bicycle for $\frac{3}{5}$ km on Saturday and $\frac{1}{5}$ km on Sunday. How much more distance did Mohan cover on Saturday?

(c) A shopkeeper sold $\frac{7}{9}$ of sugar on Monday and $\frac{2}{9}$ of sugar on Tuesday. How much more sugar did the shopkeeper sell on Monday than on Tuesday?

PROPER AND IMPROPER FRACTIONS

What do you observe from the following set of figures?

$\frac{2}{6}$ $\frac{3}{6}$ $\frac{5}{11}$

In all these fractions, the value of the numerator is lesser than the value of the denominator. These are called proper fractions.

Proper fractions are those fractions in which the numerator is a smaller number than the denominator.

Examples:

$\frac{2}{6}, \frac{4}{11}, \frac{3}{15}, \frac{4}{20}, \frac{12}{16}, \frac{4}{5}, \frac{3}{7}, \frac{1}{6}$ are proper fractions since the numbers in their numerators are smaller than the numbers in their denominators.

Can you think of some examples which are not proper fractions?

Examples:

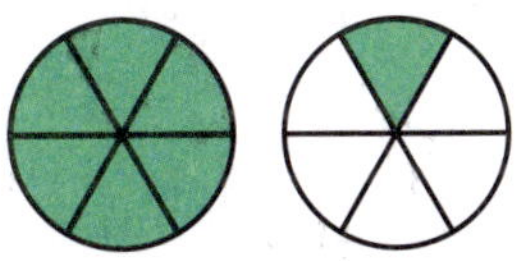 $= \frac{6}{6} + \frac{1}{6} = \frac{6+1}{6} = \frac{7}{6}$

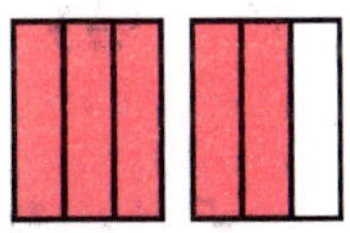 $= \frac{3}{3} + \frac{2}{3} = \frac{3+2}{3} = \frac{5}{3}$

In both the examples above, the value of the numerator is greater than that of the denominator. These are called improper fractions.

Improper fractions are those fractions in which the numerator is a greater number than the denominator.

Examples:

$\frac{21}{6}, \frac{14}{9}, \frac{10}{2}, \frac{16}{5}, \frac{11}{5}, \frac{14}{7}, \frac{5}{2}, \frac{7}{5}$ are improper fractions since the numbers in their numerators are greater than the numbers in their denominators.

Now can you think of some examples which are neither proper fractions nor improper fractions?

Examples:

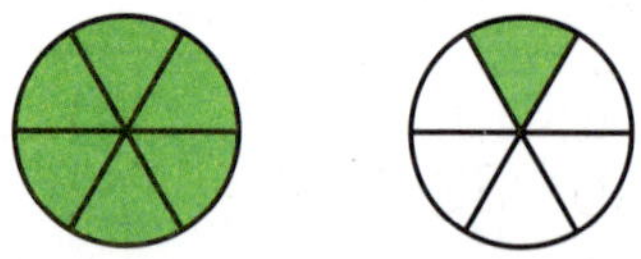

One whole | **Shaded part is $\frac{1}{6}$**

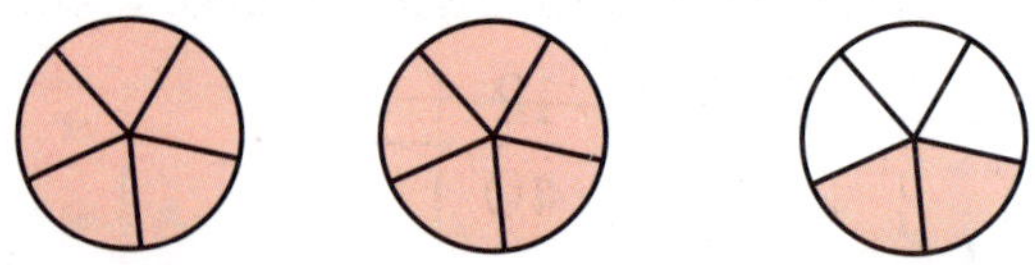

One whole | **One whole** | **The shaded part represents $\frac{2}{5}$**

This figure represents $1 + \frac{1}{6}$.

It can be written as $1\frac{1}{6}$.

This figure represents $2 + \frac{2}{5}$.

It can be written as $2\frac{2}{5}$.

In the above fractions, there is one whole number and one proper fraction. These are called mixed fractions.

A *mixed fraction* is a combination of a whole number and a proper fraction.

Examples:

$1\frac{2}{3}, 3\frac{4}{5}, 9\frac{1}{2}, 11\frac{2}{16}, 4\frac{6}{9}, 3\frac{5}{7}, 7\frac{4}{6}, 12\frac{2}{14}$ are mixed fractions since each of them has one whole number and one proper fraction.

Write a few examples of mixed fractions.

___

Exercise 6.8

1 Classify the following fractions into proper, improper and mixed fractions.

$\frac{1}{3}, \frac{5}{6}, \frac{11}{8}, \frac{12}{13}, 6\frac{1}{3}, \frac{23}{14}, \frac{1}{5}, \frac{5}{7}, 4\frac{1}{3}, \frac{13}{7}, \frac{16}{13}, 8\frac{1}{3}, \frac{11}{6}, \frac{3}{7}, \frac{31}{18}, \frac{5}{8}, 7\frac{5}{6}, \frac{19}{17}, 3\frac{1}{3}, \frac{15}{12}, \frac{11}{17}$

2 Express each of the following mixed fractions as the sum of a whole number and a proper fraction.

(a) $3\frac{1}{4} = 3 + \frac{1}{4}$ (b) $2\frac{5}{7}$ (c) $5\frac{3}{8}$ (d) $1\frac{5}{9}$

Revision Exercise

1 **Write the possible equivalent fractions.**

(a) $\frac{[\ ]}{[\ ]}, \frac{6}{20}, \frac{[\ ]}{[\ ]}, \frac{12}{40}, \frac{[\ ]}{[\ ]}$ (b) $\frac{2}{16}, \frac{4}{32}, \frac{[\ ]}{[\ ]}, \frac{[\ ]}{[\ ]}, \frac{[\ ]}{[\ ]}$

2 **Write the following fractions in their lowest forms.**

(a) $\frac{16}{40}$ (b) $\frac{63}{18}$ (c) $\frac{36}{72}$ (d) $\frac{69}{90}$

3 **Match the following.**

(a) $\frac{4}{9}, \frac{7}{9}, \frac{1}{9}$	Mixed fraction
(b) $\frac{3}{7}, \frac{4}{6}, \frac{5}{13}, \frac{8}{18}$	Improper fraction
(c) $\frac{1}{14}, \frac{1}{16}, \frac{1}{18}, \frac{1}{4}, \frac{1}{6}$	Like fraction
(d) $\frac{4}{7}, \frac{3}{16}, \frac{5}{8}, \frac{9}{21}$	Unlike fraction
(e) $\frac{4}{3}, \frac{9}{6}, \frac{3}{2}, \frac{7}{5}$	Proper fraction
(f) $1\frac{2}{3}, 4\frac{5}{6}, 3\frac{2}{4}, 9\frac{5}{10}$	Unit fraction

4 **Solve the following word problems.**

(a) Radha has a tape of $\frac{2}{4}$ metre in length; Suma gives her a tape of $\frac{2}{4}$ metre in length. How much length of tape does Radha have now?

(b) Rahul bought $\frac{1}{6}$ litres of milk in the morning and $\frac{4}{6}$ litres of milk in the evening. How many litres of milk did he buy that day?

(c) Mrs Gupta bought $\frac{5}{8}$ kg of sugar and used $\frac{2}{8}$ kg of sugar to prepare sweets. How much sugar is Mrs Gupta left with?

(d) Anil had $\frac{5}{7}$ portion of a basket filled with oranges. He took out $\frac{1}{7}$ portion of oranges from the basket. What fraction of oranges was left in the basket?

7 Geometry

Learning Objectives

- To understand the concepts of point, line, line segments, polygons and circles
- To understand the concepts of symmetry, reflections and tessellations

Let's Get Started

Name the points given below using the letters P, Q, R, S and T in two different ways.

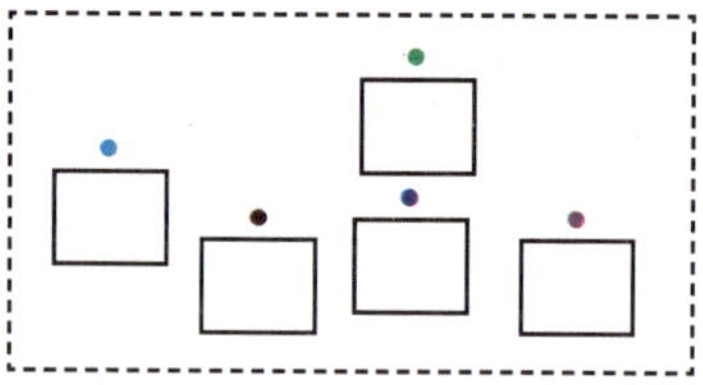

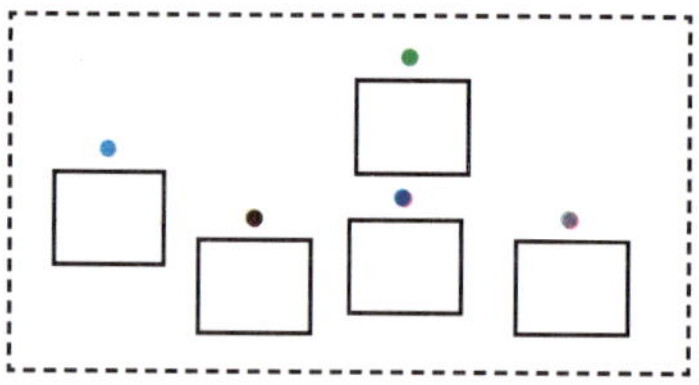

> A dot represents a **point**.
> It determines an **exact location**.
> It is denoted by capital letters.
> Example: **Point M**

Mark two points on a paper and name them as **L** and **M**.

Join these points using a ruler. The figure so obtained is called a **line segment**. It has **two end points**. It is named by the end points, as line segment $\overline{LM}$.

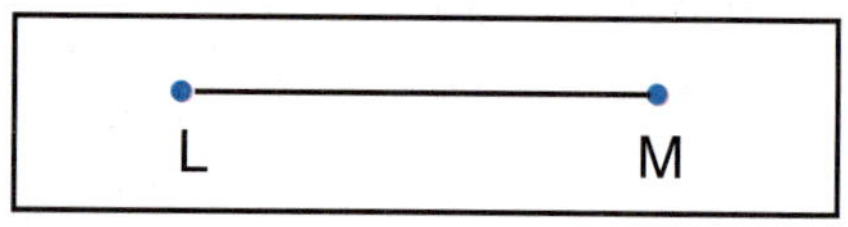

Draw different line segments using the points given in the figure below and write their names.

Line segments:

When you extend a line segment on both the sides without an end, you get a **line**. A line has **no end points**. A line is denoted by taking any two points on a line. For example, consider the line 

To name this line, consider any two points on the line say E and F. It is named as line $\overleftrightarrow{EF}$ 

Draw some lines and name them.

MEASURING THE LINE SEGMENT

Look at the following line segments. Can you say which line is longer without tracing the lines?

You can compare their exact lengths by measuring them.
How to measure the length of a line segment?

Have you seen a scale or a ruler in your geometry box? It looks like one shown below.

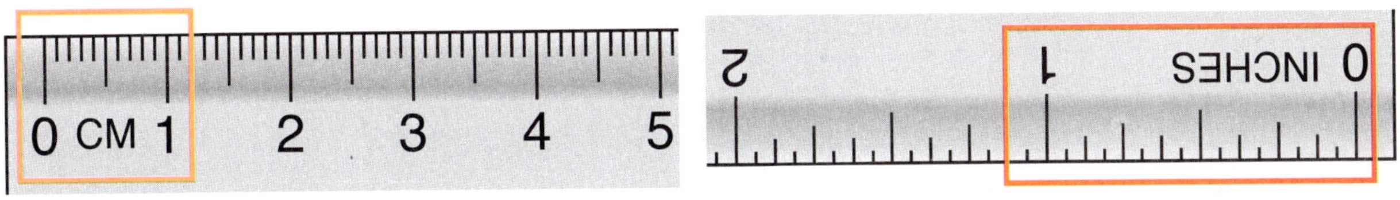

Observe it carefully. It has got one edge marked in **centimetres**. The other edge is marked in **inches**.

One edge is divided into 15 divisions and each division represents a **centimetre**.

Each centimetre is further divided into 10 smaller divisions.

Each smaller division represents $\frac{1}{10}$ of a centimetre and it is known as a **millimetre**.

FACT

10 mm = 1 cm

1 mm = $\frac{1}{10}$ *cm*

Let us measure the length of a line segment, say, DE.

1. Place the ruler along the line segment DE such that the '0' mark coincides with the end point D.

2. Note down the marking on the ruler where the other end point E coincides.

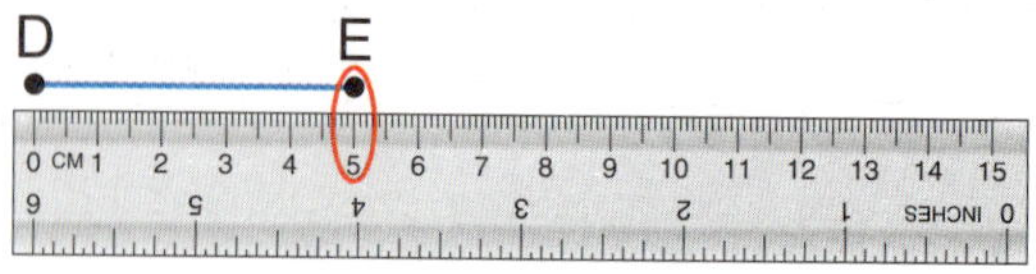

3. The reading gives the length of the line segment DE. Observe that point E is coinciding with 5. Hence, the length of line segment DE is **5 cm**.

Similarly, let us measure the length of PQ and compare it with DE.

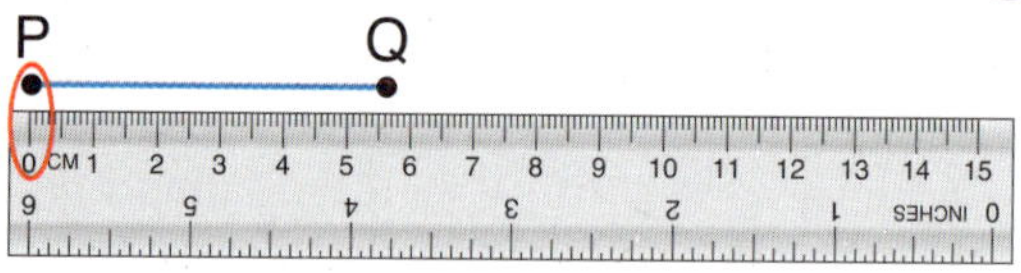

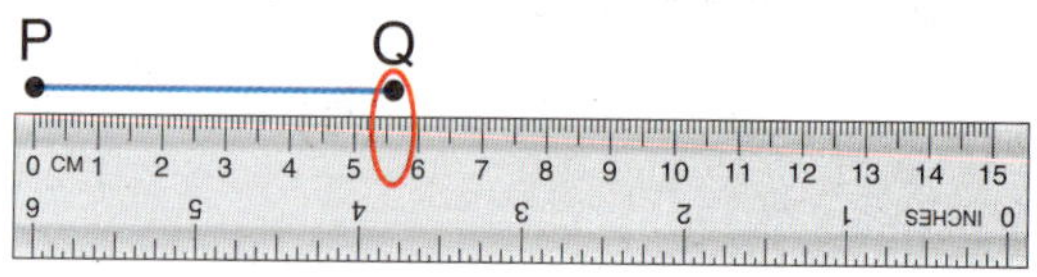

The length of line segment PQ is 5.6 cm. Therefore, PQ > DE.

Common Errors :

Measuring from the end of the ruler instead of zero

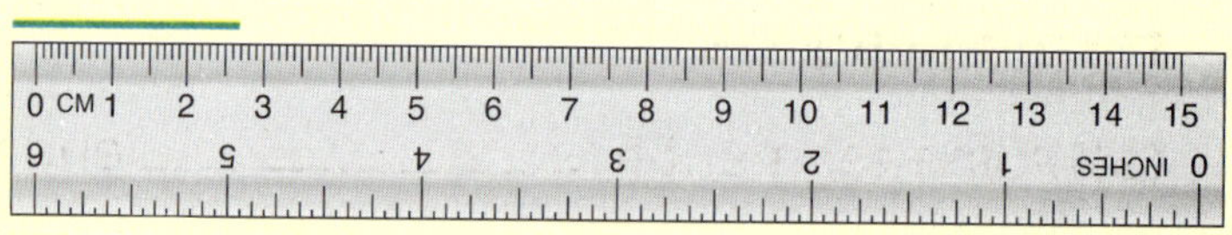

Counting the lines instead of the spaces

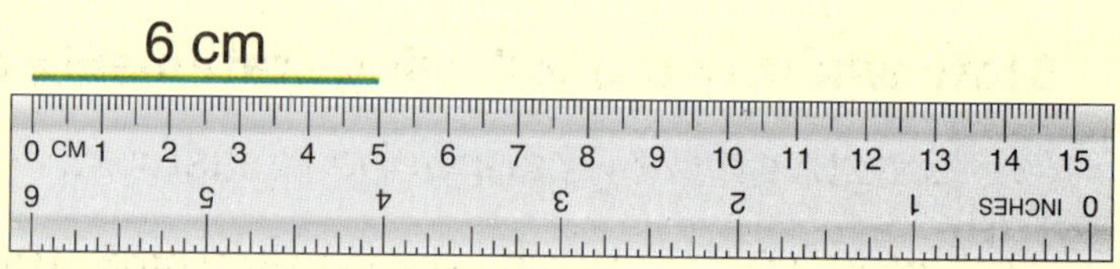

Drawing the Line Segment of a Given Length

To draw a line segment which is **10.5 cm** long:

1. Place the ruler on a sheet of paper and mark a point at '0' and name it A.

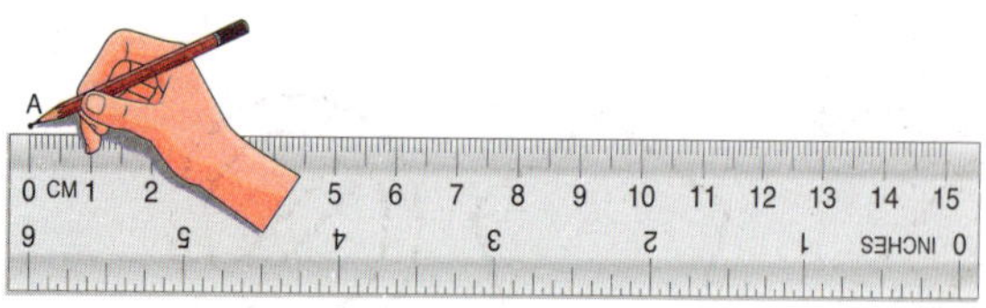

2. Mark another point B against the 10.5 cm mark.

3. Join the points A and B using the ruler. AB is the required line segment of length 10.5 cm.

10.5 cm

Exercise 7.1

1 **Measure the lengths of the line segments given below and write the lengths in the boxes.**

(a) 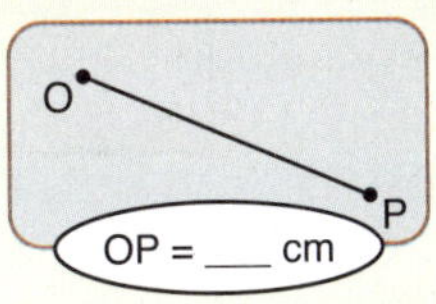

(b) 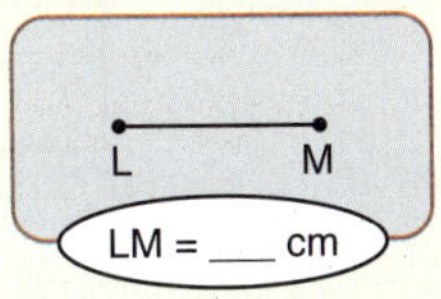

(c) 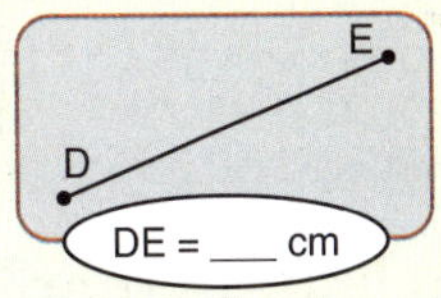

2 **Draw the line segments of the given lengths using a ruler.**

(a) 7 cm (b) 11.5 cm (c) 8.7 cm (d) 14.2 cm

3 **Fill in the blanks.**

(a) A line segment has ____________ end points.

(b) A line has ____________ end points.

4 **State whether the following statements are True or False.**

(a) Length of a line cannot be measured. (True/False)

(b) Length of the book cannot be measured using a ruler. (True/False)

5 **Identify and write the line segments of the following figures in your notebook.**

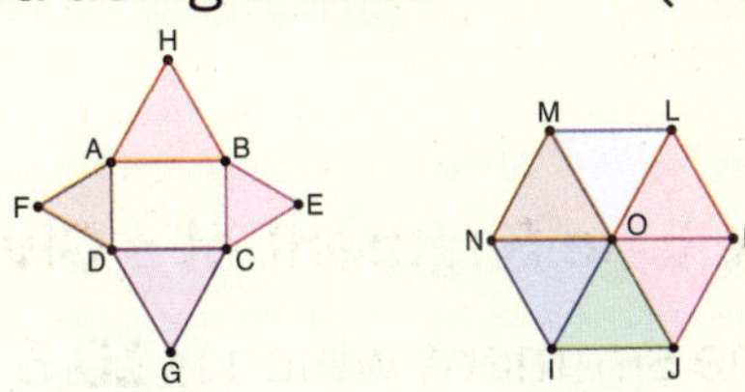

CLOSED AND OPEN CURVES

Open Curves

Closed Curves

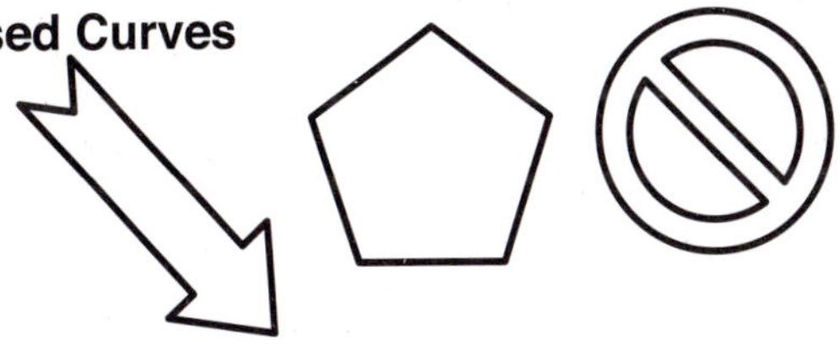

Exercise 7.2

Identify open and closed curves in the following figures and write them in the space provided.

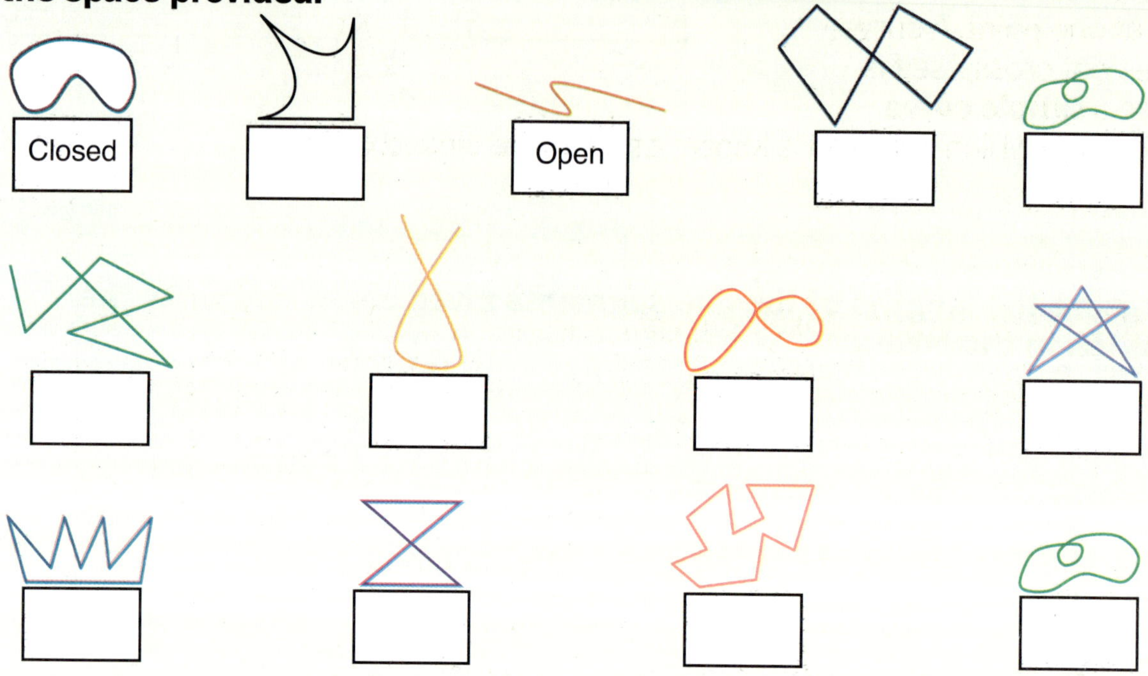

SIMPLE CLOSED CURVES

Closed curves from the above figures are arranged into two groups. Observe both the groups and try to find the difference between the groups.

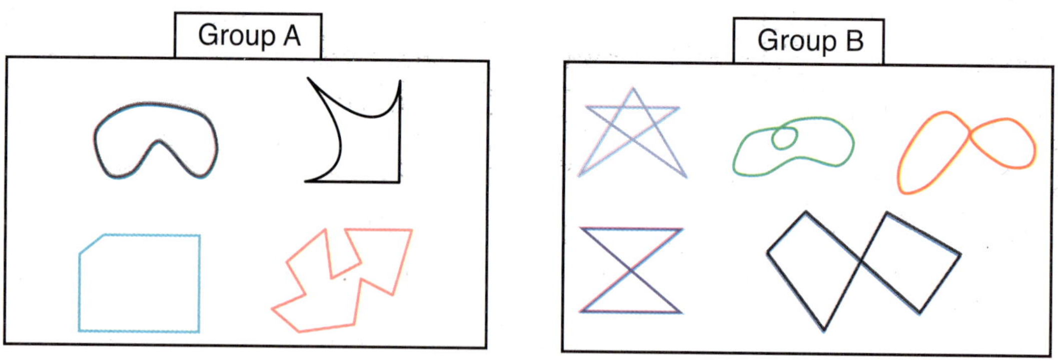

The curves in Group A do not cross themselves at any point whereas the curves in Group B cross themselves at least at one point. A curve that does not cross itself is known as a **simple curve**.

Examples of simple closed curves

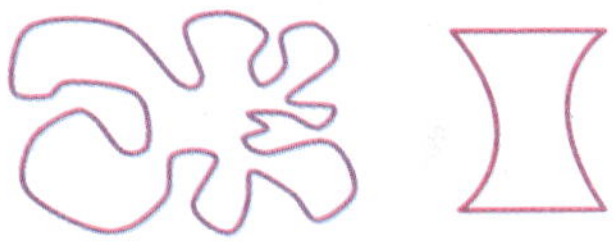

Examples of closed curves which are not simple

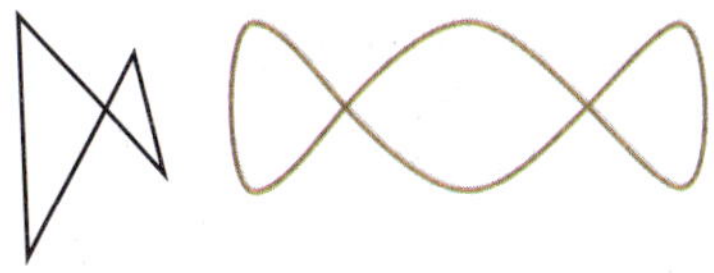

A simple curve which is closed is known as a **simple closed curve**.

Exercise 7.3

1 **Tick (✓) the simple closed curves.**

(a) 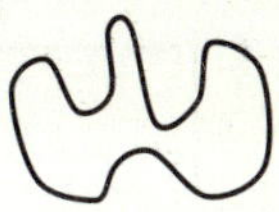

(b) 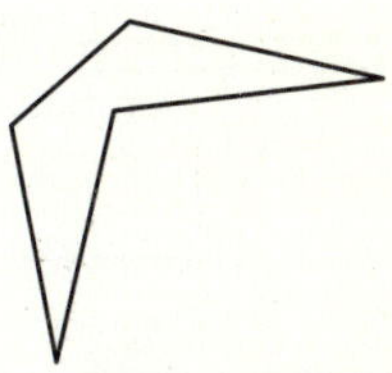

(c) 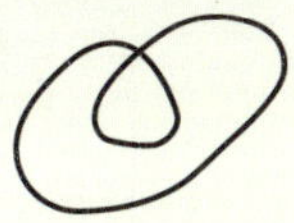

(d) 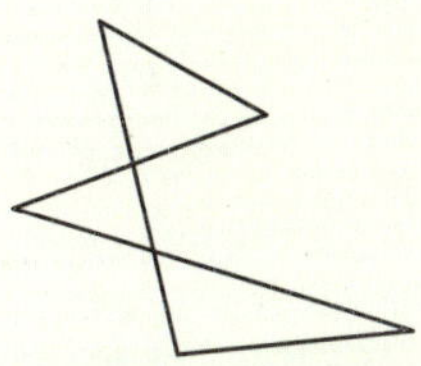

(e) 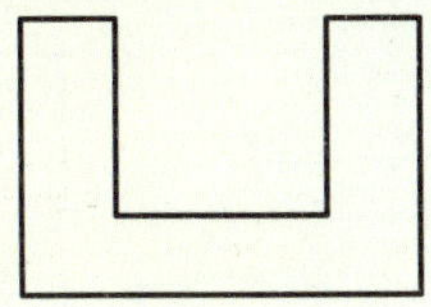

(f) 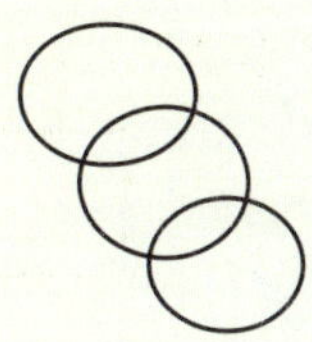

2 **Write the letters of the English alphabet that form simple closed curves when written in capital letters.**

POLYGONS

Look at the following two groups of figures. What is the difference between them?

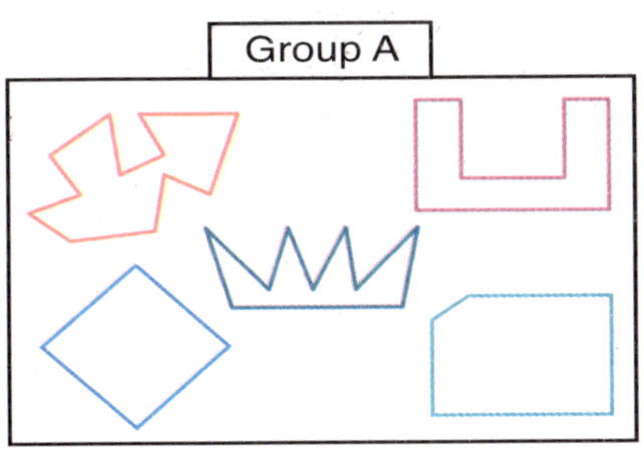

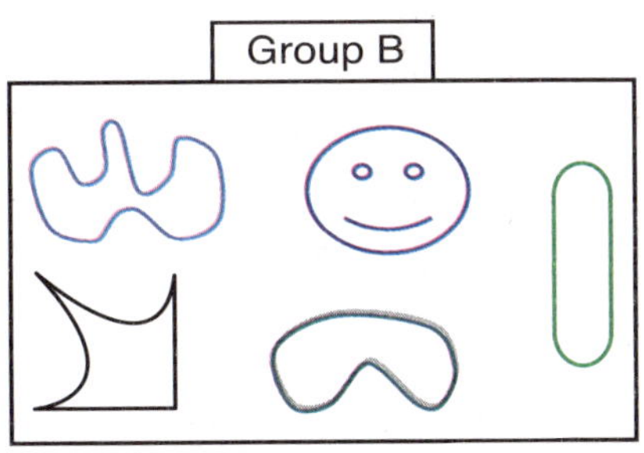

In Group A, all the figures are made up of line segments whereas in Group B, the figures are made up of curves and line segments.

A simple closed figure made up of line segments is known as a **polygon**.

Examples: 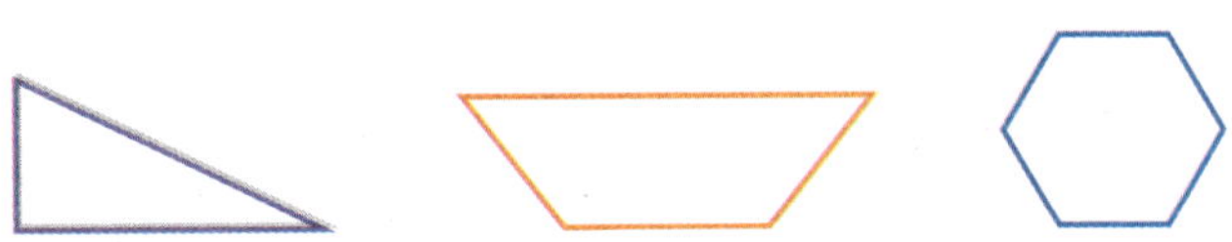

Exercise 7.4

Tick (✓) the polygons in the following figures.

(a) 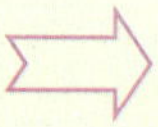 (b)  (c) 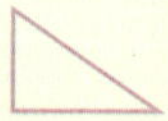 (d) 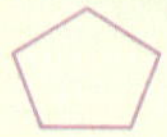 (e)  (f)  (g) 

TYPES OF POLYGONS

A polygon with three line segments is known as a **triangle**.

Example:

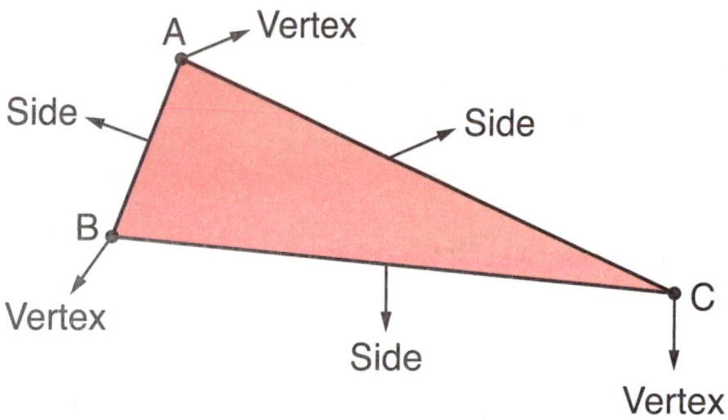

Here the points A, B and C are known as the **vertices** of the triangle ABC.

The line segments AB, BC and CA are known as the **sides** of the triangle ABC.

More examples of triangles:

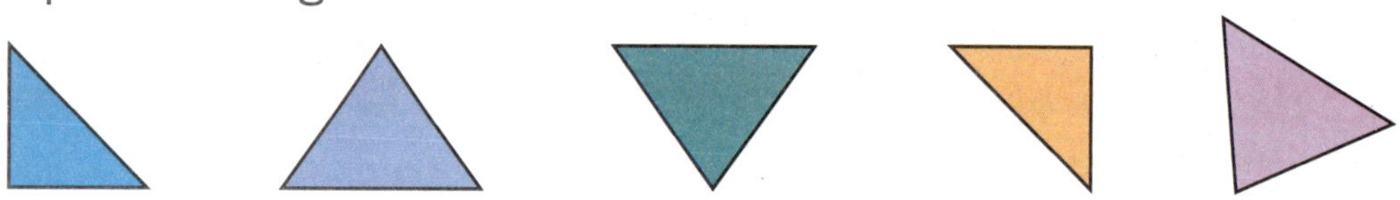

A polygon with four line segments is known as a **quadrilateral**.

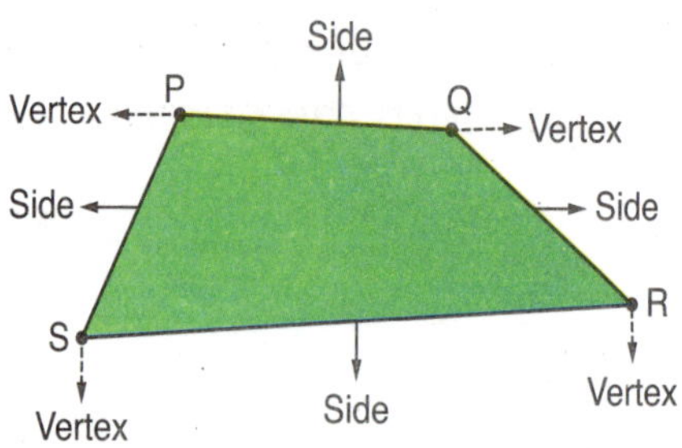

Here the points P, Q, R and S are known as the **vertices** of the quadrilateral PQRS.

The line segments PQ, QR, RS and SP are known as the **sides** of the quadrilateral PQRS.

The sides which have a common vertex are known as **adjacent sides** and the sides which do not have common vertex are known as **opposite sides**.

Here, PQ and SR; PS and QR are the **opposite sides**.

PQ, QR; QR, RS; RS, SP; SP, PQ are the **adjacent sides**.

More examples of quadrilaterals:

Exercise 7.5

1 **Write the vertices and sides of the following figures.**

(a)

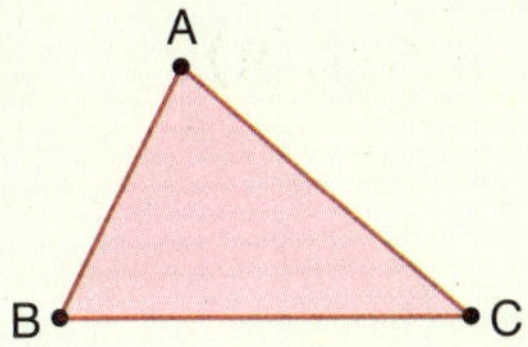

Vertices:

Sides:

(b)

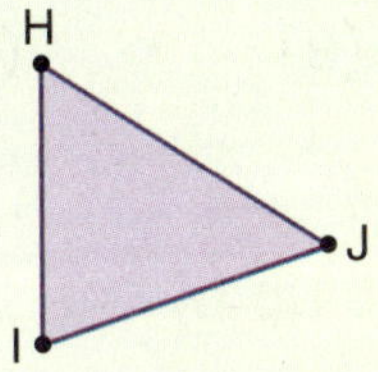

Vertices:

Sides:

(c)

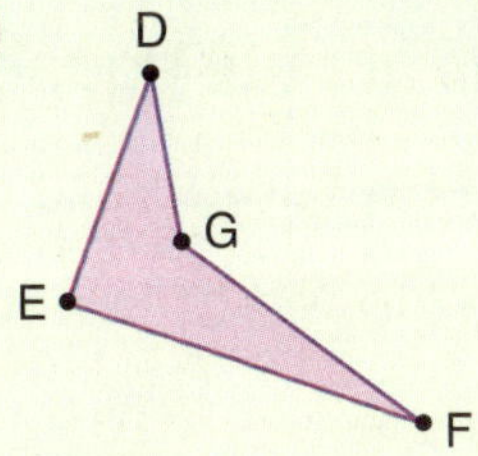

Vertices:

Sides:

(d)

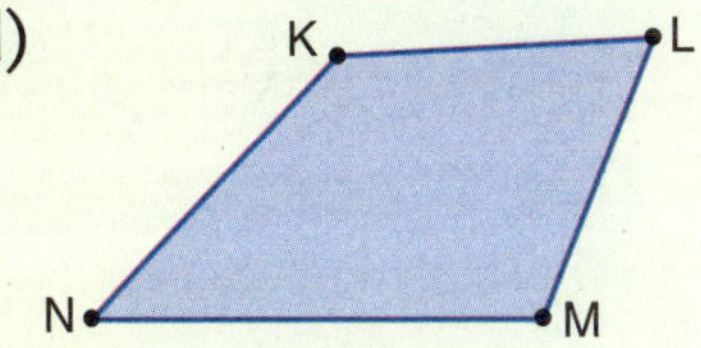

Vertices:

Sides:

2 **Write the opposite sides and adjacent sides of the quadrilateral shown.**

Opposite sides	**Adjacent sides**

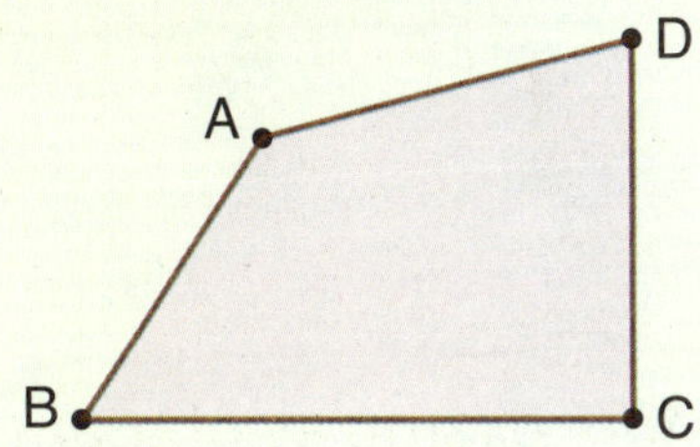

PROPERTIES OF QUADRILATERALS

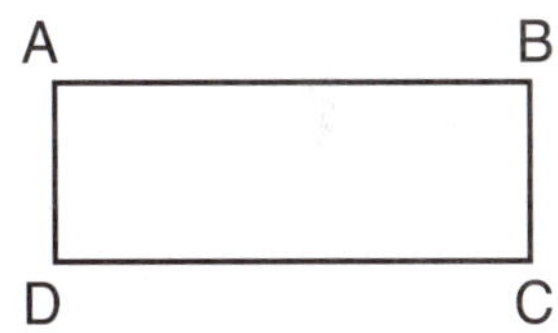

Rectangle is a special type of quadrilateral. Let us understand its speciality.

Try These!

Trace the rectangle given here on a transparent sheet and name its vertices as shown. Take the transparent sheet and coincide different sides with the original rectangle and observe.

You can observe that AB and DC; AD and BC are **equal** in length.
AB and DC; AD and BC are the opposite sides of the rectangle ABCD.

Therefore, in a rectangle opposite sides are equal.

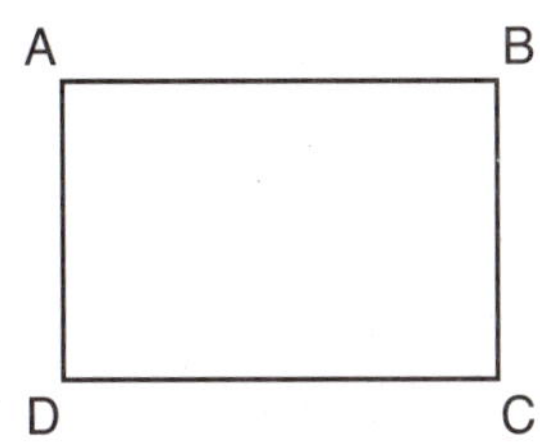

Do a similar activity for square using the square given.

You can observe that all the sides AB, BC, CD and DA are **equal** in length. Therefore, in a square all sides are equal.

Try These!

Collect some rectangular-shaped and square-shaped objects and verify whether these properties are satisfied by them.

Exercise 7.6

1 **State whether the following statements are true (T) or false (F).**

(a) All sides of a square are not equal. ☐

(b) Opposite sides of a rectangle are equal. ☐

(c) Polygon is a simple closed curve made up of line segments. ☐

(d) A square is a rectangle. ☐

2 **Tick (✓) the objects which can be used for tracing a square.**

(a) 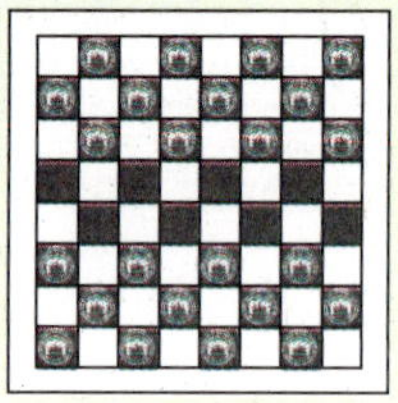

(b) 

(c) 

(d) 

CHALLENGE

Is there any quadrilateral which is not a square or a rectangle? If yes, draw one such quadrilateral.

CIRCLE

Look at the following objects.

Which shape do all these objects remind you of?

Yes, a circle!

Is circle a polygon? Why?

A **circle** is a simple closed curve.

Remember: A circle is not a polygon as it is not made up of straight lines.

Try These!

Collect some pictures of circular objects and prepare a collage and display in your classroom.

How to draw a circle?

Method 1: Take any circular object such as a coin, bottle cap, bangle, etc. and trace its outline.

Method 2: Take a piece of string and tie a pencil to one end of the string. Fix the other end of the string to the paper with a pin. Hold the string tightly and rotate the pencil.

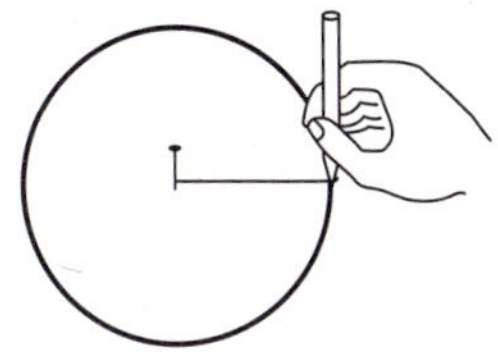

Method 3:

Use a compass

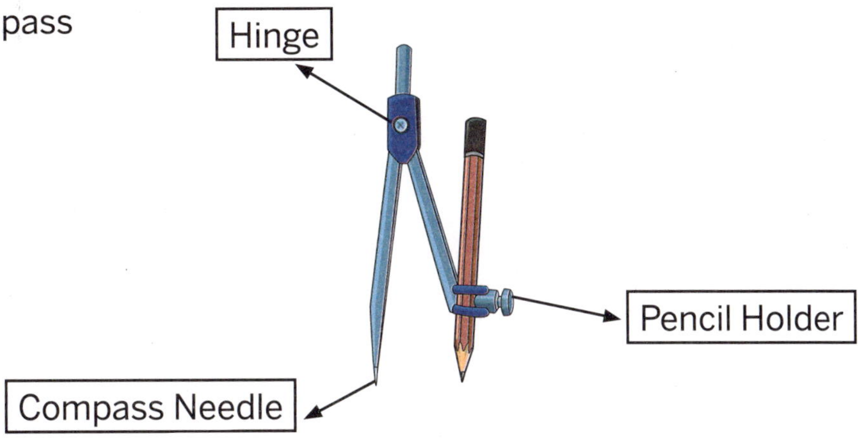

Have you seen the compass in your geometry box? It has a metal-pointed edge at one half and a pencil holder on the other half.

To draw a circle using compass:

Step 1: Fix the pencil to the compass tightly. Adjust the pencil such that the compass needle and the pencil edge are at the same level.

Step 2: Fix the needle of the compass on the paper.

Step 3: Stretch the other arm of the compass which is holding the pencil.

Step 4: Move the pencil around to draw a circle.

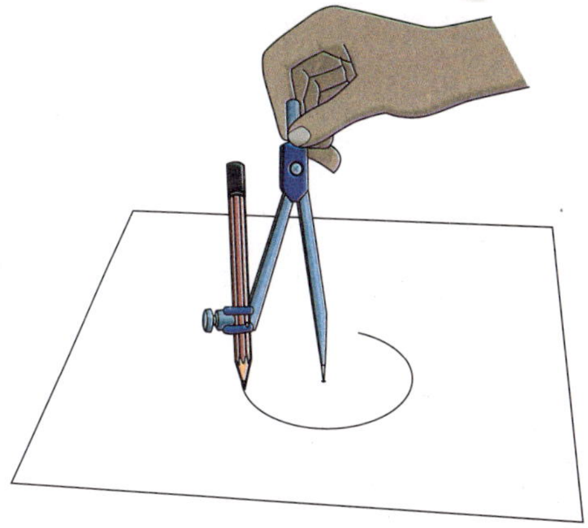

Precautions to be taken: The pencil should be tighlty fixed. The level of the pencil tip and the compass needle should be the same. The compass needle should be held tightly on the paper while drawing a circle.

PARTS OF A CIRCLE

Consider the circle drawn with the string.

The point where you pinned the string gives the **centre** of the circle. The length of the string gives the **radius** of the circle.

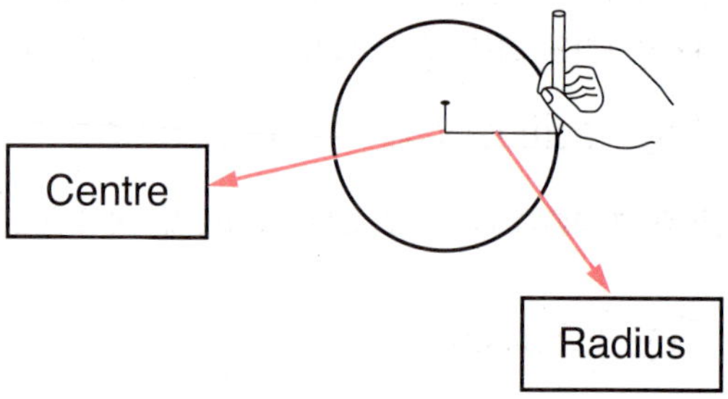

Radii is the plural of radius.

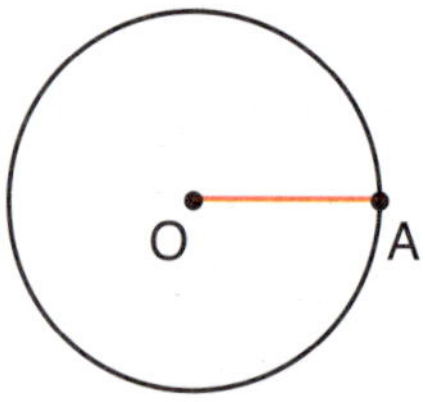

Here, O is the centre and OA is the radius of the circle, where A is any point on the circle.

Try These!

Draw a circle using any of the methods discussed on a transparent sheet. Fold this sheet exactly into half and crease it. Unfold the sheet. Draw a line segment along the folding.

The line segment obtained is known as the **diameter** of a circle. It is a line segment passing through the centre and whose end points lie on the circle.

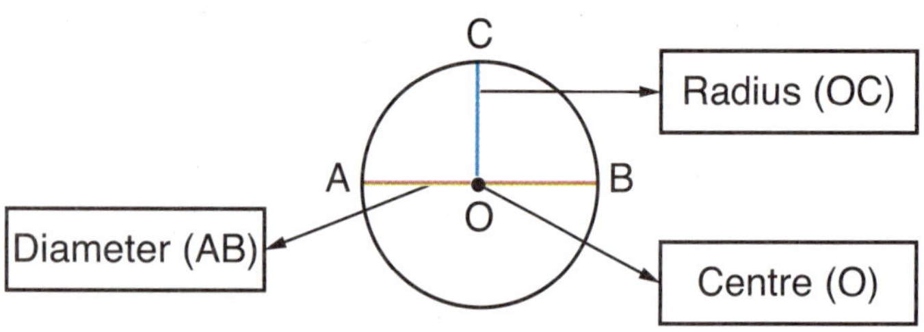

How many radii and diameters can be drawn for a given circle?

Here, O is the centre of circle, AB is the diameter and OC is the radius.

Identify the diameters of the circle and write them.

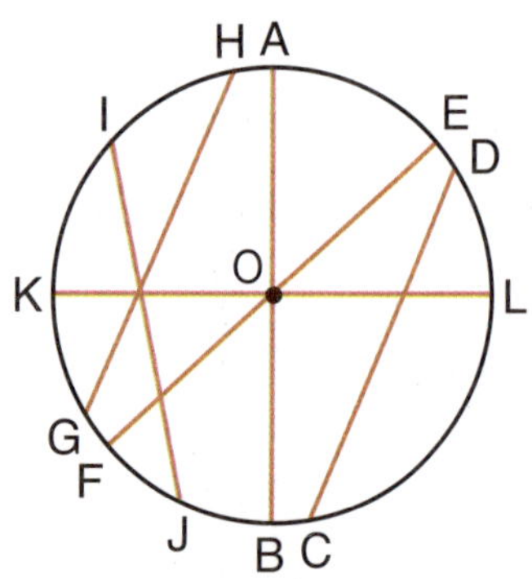

Diameters:

Try These!

Draw different radii of the circle as shown here. Measure their lengths using a ruler. What do you observe?

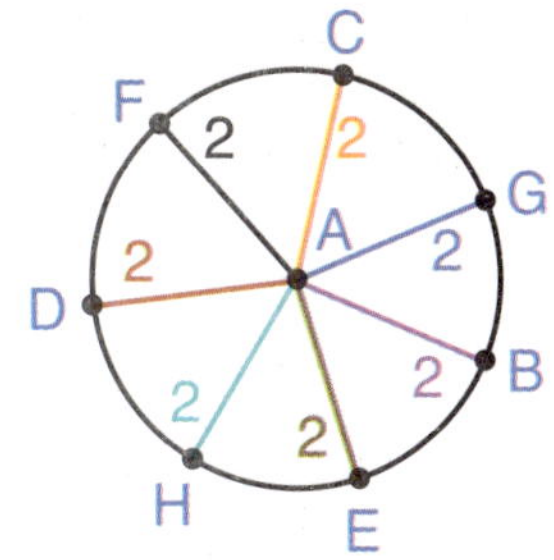

The radii of the circle are same in length.

Relationship between the radius and the diameter of a circle

Try These!

Draw four circles of radii 3 cm, 5 cm, 8 cm and 10 cm. Measure and note down the diameters of all the circles. Can you observe any relationship between the radius and the diameter of each circle?

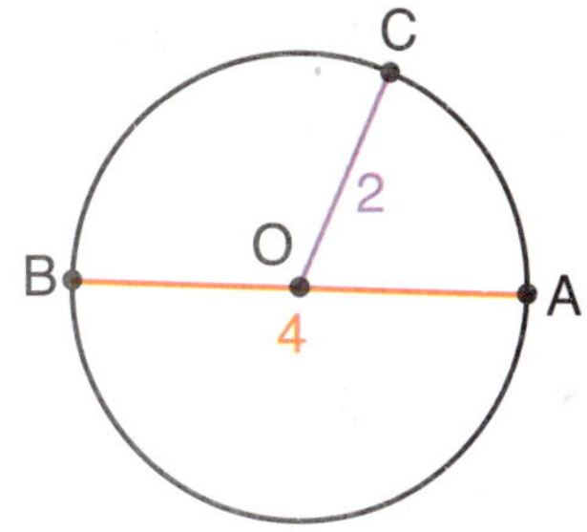

The diameter is twice the length of the radius.
In other words, radius is half the diameter of the circle.

If the radius of a circle is 3 cm, then its diameter is $2 \times 3 = 6$ cm.

If the diameter of a circle is 10 cm, then its radius is $\frac{10}{2} = 5$ cm.

Did You Know?

Circles with same centre are known as concentric circles. You can find many real-life examples of concentric circles such as a dart board.

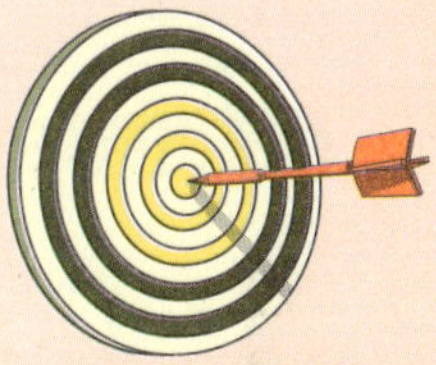

Exercise 7.7

1 **Write the centre and radius of the following circles.**

(a) 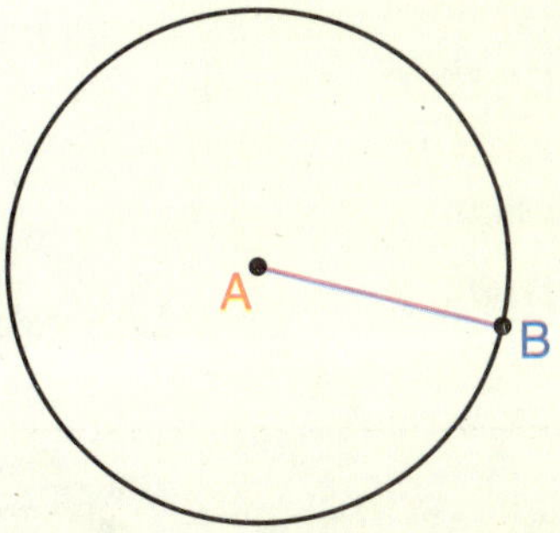

Centre:

Radius:

(b) 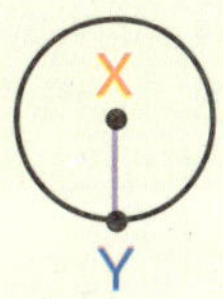

Centre:

Radius:

(c) 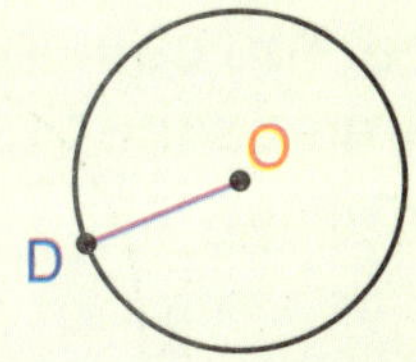

Centre:

Radius:

2 **Draw the radius and diameter for the following circles.**

(a) (b) (c)

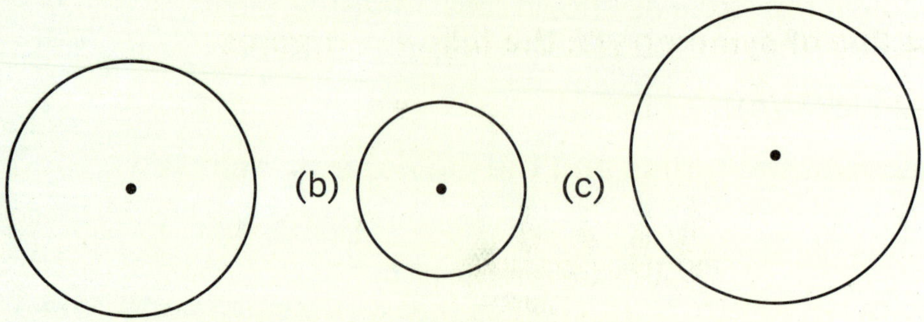

3

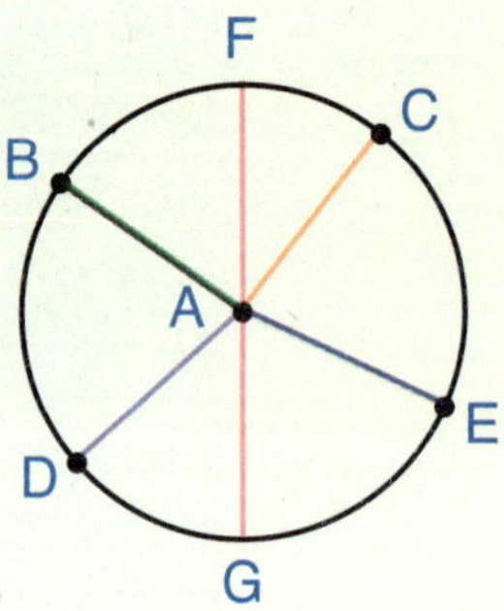

In the diagram shown, AC is 5 cm.

Now write the measurements of the following:

AB = _____cm FG = _____cm

AF = _____cm AE = _____cm

AD = _____cm

4 **Find the radii of the circles whose diameters are given below.**

(a) 14 cm (b) 8 cm (c) 18 cm (d) 30 cm

5 **Find the diameters of the circles whose radii are given below.**

(a) 3 cm (b) 5 cm (c) 11 cm (d) 15 cm

SYMMETRY

A figure is said to be symmetrical if it has **mirror halves**.

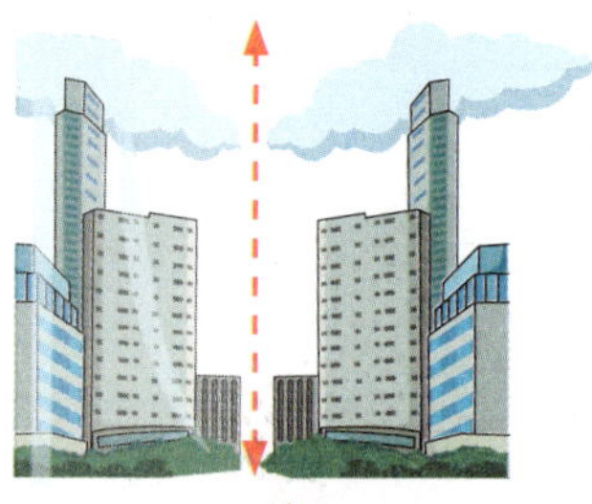

Look at the picture shown here. Place a mirror at the dotted line. You can observe that the image in the mirror is exactly same as the first half. Therefore, this picture is said to be symmetrical. The dotted line is known as **line of symmetry**.

Look at the figure. Place the mirror along all the dotted lines. Identify the line of symmetry and mark it.

Exercise 7.8

1 **Tick (✓) the line of symmetry in the following figures.**

(a)

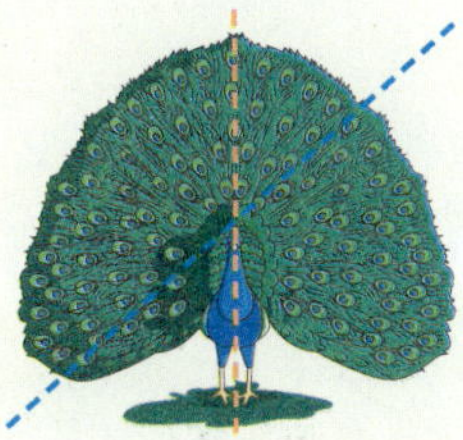

(c)

(e)

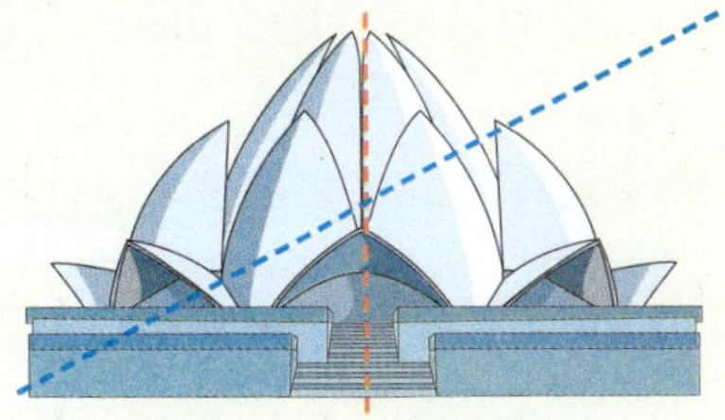

(b)

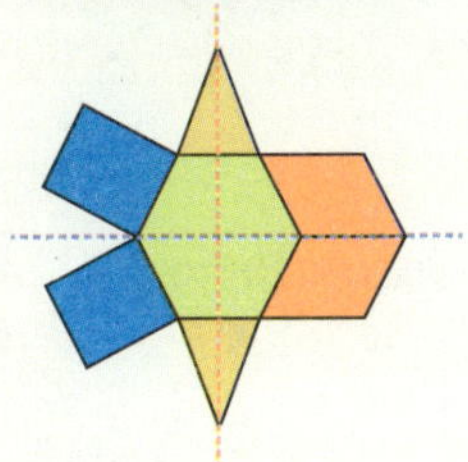

(d)

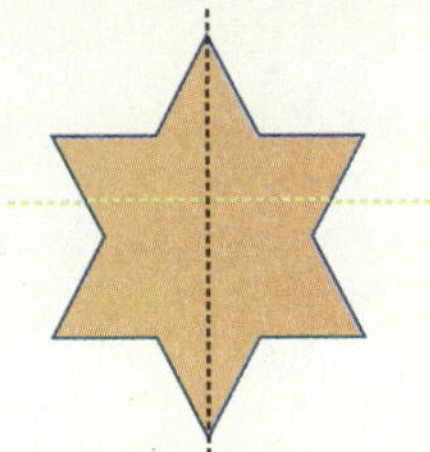

2 **Draw the mirror halves of the following figures to complete them.**

(a)

(b)

(c)

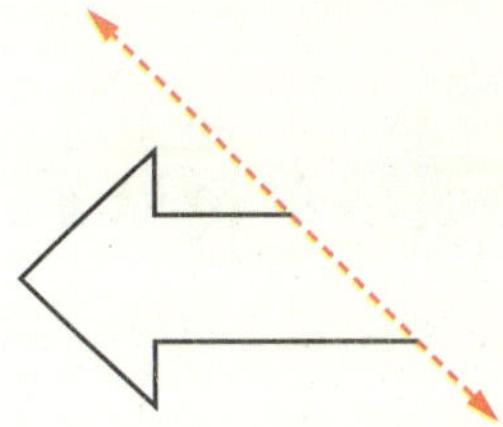

3 **Find out the mirror halves of letters of the English alphabet when written in capital letters..**

Project

Look at the time shown on the digital clock. Is it a symmetric figure? Is the line along the dots the line of symmetry? List the times on a 24-hour digital watch that have a line of symmetry.

Cross-curricular Link: There are many animals which are symmetrical. Some of them are given below. Try to find some more examples.

Beetle

Star Fish

Butterfly

Crab

REFLECTION

Look at the following beautiful sceneries in nature. They have the reflected mirror images along the dotted line.

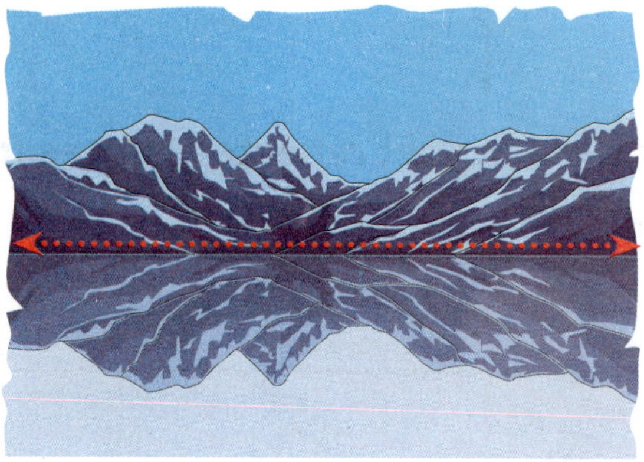

Look at the pictures and their reflected images. They are like mirror images.

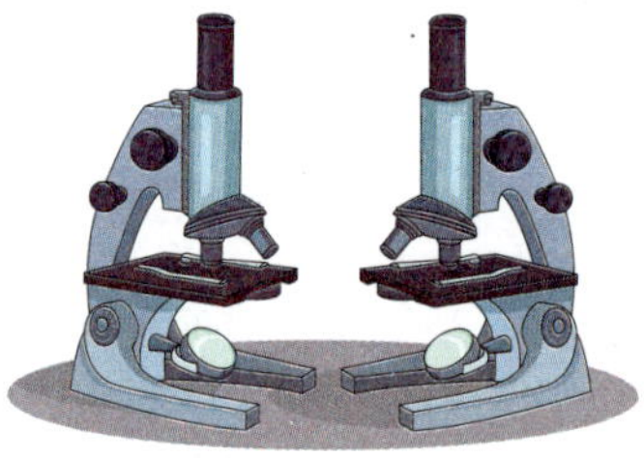

Look at a few more examples of reflected images.

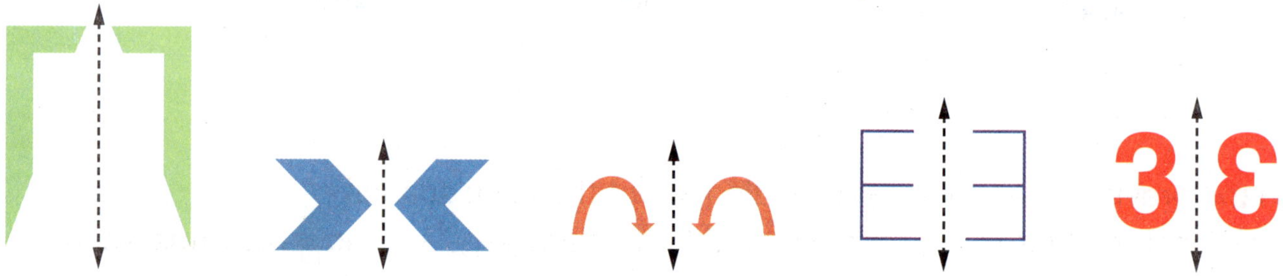

Project

Look at some shapes. Find the reflected images. Observe whether the reflected image is same as the original one. One such example is shown here.

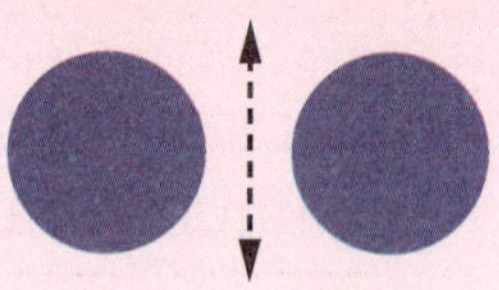

Exercise 7.9

1 **Draw the reflected images of the following shapes.**

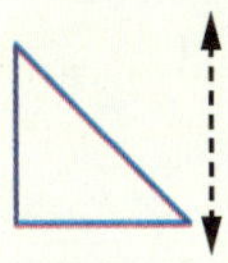 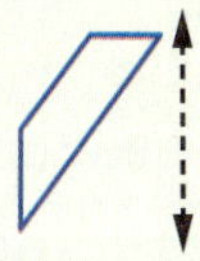 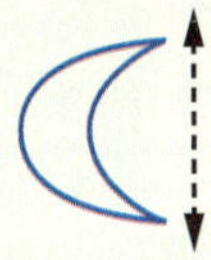 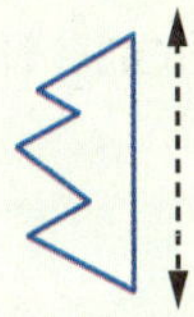

2 **Tick the correct reflected images for the following figures.**

(a) 			
(b) 			
(c) 			
(d) 			
(e) 			

TESSELLATIONS

In the previous class, we have studied about the tiling shapes.

Shapes that fit into each other without leaving any gaps are known as **tiling shapes**.

Shapes that do not fit into each other without leaving gaps are known as **non-tiling shapes**.

Tiling means covering an area with tiles. These tilings are known as **tessellations**.

All shapes do not tessellate. Look at some examples of shapes which tessellate and which do not tessellate.

Shapes that tessellate	Shapes that do not tessellate
	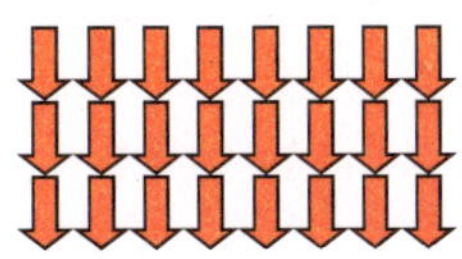 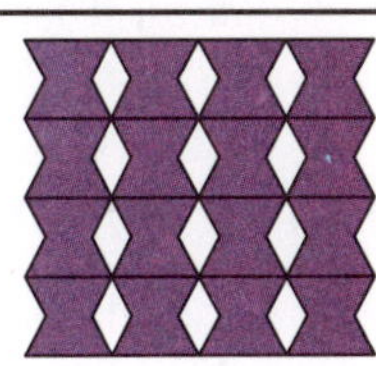

Look at some beautiful tiling patterns that we can find around us.

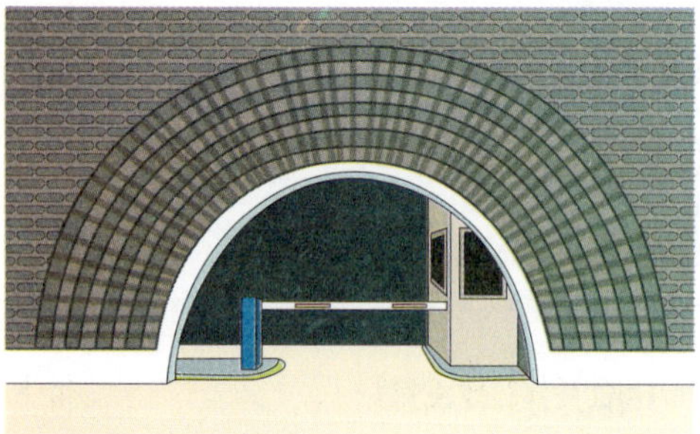

Did You Know?

Beehive constructed by honey bees is also a tiling pattern.

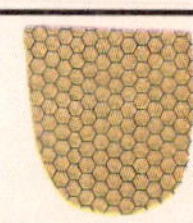

Exercise 7.10

1 Put a tick (✓) mark on the tessellating shapes.

(a) 

(b) 

(c) 

(d) 

(e) 

2 Create different tessellation patterns using the grid paper. Some examples are shown.

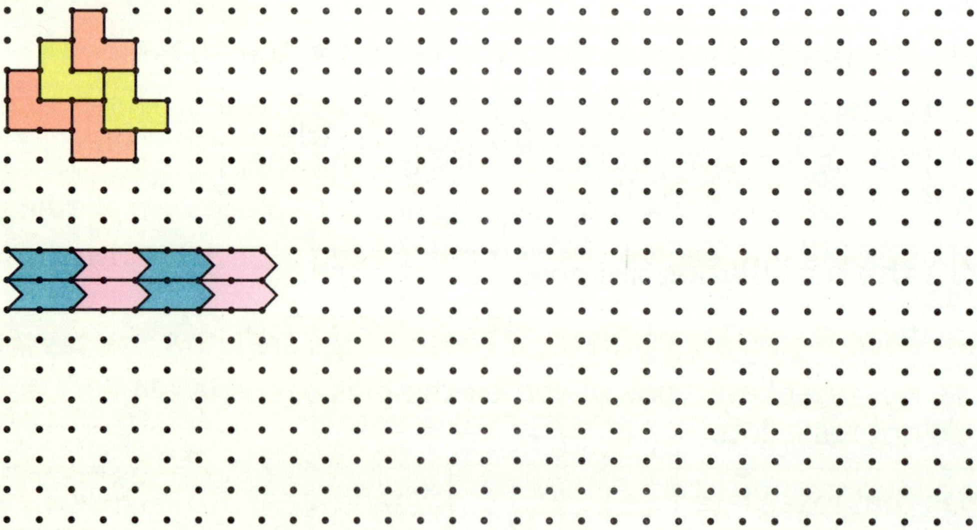

Revision Exercise

1 Measure the lengths of the line segments given below.

(a) 

(b) 

(c) 

2 Draw a the line segments of the given lengths using a ruler.

(a) 5.3 cm (b) 10.2 cm (c) 9 cm (d) 11.9 cm

3 Draw a few simple closed figures which are polygons.

4 Match the following.

(a) A polygon with all four sides equal — (i) Rectangle

(b) A polygon having three sides — (ii) Circle

(c) A polygon having opposite sides equal — (iii) Square

(d) A simple closed curve having no vertices — (iv) Triangle

5 Identify the centre, radius and diameter of the circle.

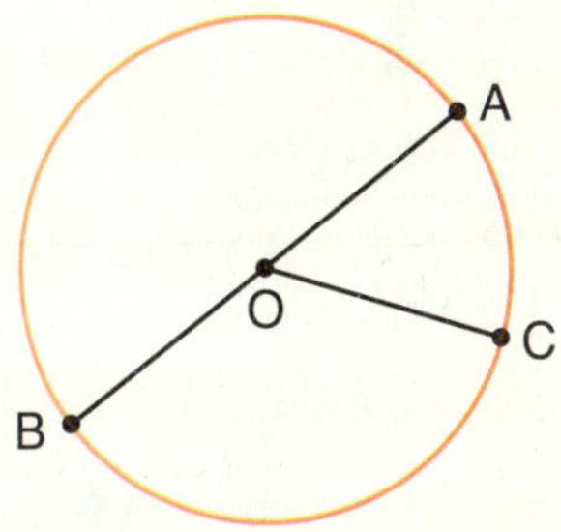

6 Fill in the blanks.

(a) The radius of a wheel with diameter 30 cm is ________ cm.

(b) The diameter of a bangle with radius 3 cm is ________ cm.

7 Identify the pairs of images with correct reflected shapes.

(a) 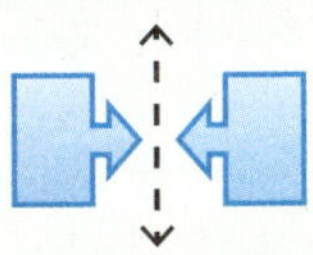 (b) 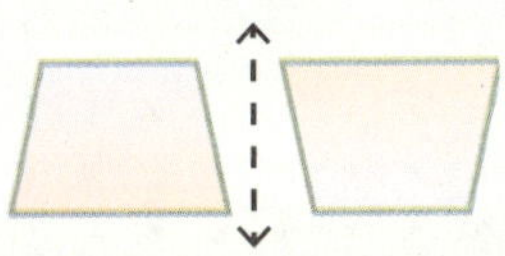 (c) 

(d) 

(e) 

8 Tick (✓) the tessellating shapes.

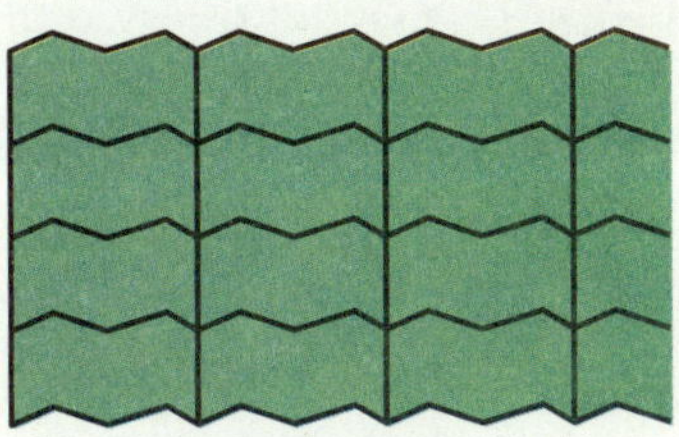  

ASSESSMENT 1

Chapters 1-4

(Maximum Marks = 25)

A Choose the correct option for each of the following. **(10 × 1 = 10)**

1. The digit 3 in the sum of 14789 and 20652 stands for ________.
   (a) 30 (b) 300 (c) 3000 (d) 30000
2. 24 thousands 2 hundreds and 10 ones when written in numeral is ________.
   (a) 24201 (b) 24210 (c) 24300 (d) 24301
3. 35876 ________ 35786.
   (a) > (b) = (c) < (d) None of these
4. 25698 – 19586 = ________.
   (a) 6002 (b) 6112 (c) 6102 (d) 6012
5. 325684 + 132915 = ________.
   (a) 458599 (b) 458959 (c) 192769 (d) 197269
6. ________ × 59 = 2950
   (a) 15 (b) 10 (c) 50 (d) 20
7. A factory can manufacture 132 pairs of boots in a day. In 14 days, how many pairs of boots can it manufacture?
   (a) 1848 (b) 1488 (c) 1884 (d) 1448
8. ________ ÷ 4 = 64
   (a) 16 (b) 24 (c) 256 (d) 246
9. When a number is divided by 9, the quotient is 63 and the remainder is 8. What is the number?
   (a) 504 (b) 513 (c) 567 (d) 575
10. What is the difference between the quotient and the remainder of 4986 ÷ 17?
    (a) 288 (b) 298 (c) 293 (d) 297

B Fill in the blanks. **(5 × 1 = 5)**

1. The difference between the place values of the digit '2' and the digit '7' in 82371 is ________.
2. 10 hundreds more than 69000 is ________.
3. Fill in the blanks with appropriate operational symbols (+/–).
   25689 ________ 458265 ________ 362859 = 121095
4. 150 × ____ = (150 × 3) + (150 × 9)
5. ________ is a number which lies between 50 and 65. It is completely divisible by 3 and 4.

C State whether the following statements are True (T) or False (F). **(4 × 1 = 4)**

1. 99 is expressed in roman numeral as XCVIIII. ☐
2. There were 12063 red buttons and 76355 green buttons. Out of all the buttons, if 23 are damaged then there would be 88385 buttons in good condition. ☐
3. There will be 310 fruits altogether, if we arrange 12 fruits in 25 boxes. ☐
4. If a shopkeeper packs 1080 sweets into 24 boxes, he can pack 45 sweets in each box. ☐

D Match the following: **(2 × 3 = 6)**

1. Add or subtract the numbers and match them.

Column A	Column B
(a) 256852 + 359862	(i) 800000 + 90909
(b) 758625 – 587699	(ii) 714804 – 98090
(c) 989898 – 98989	(iii) 94489 + 76437

2. Mary baked some cookies for selling them. She sold 9 boxes of cookies. There were 12 cookies in each box. She had 3 boxes of 3 cookies in each box left. Match the numbers.

Column A	Column B
(a) Cookies baked	(i) 108
(b) Cookies left	(ii) 99
(c) Cookies sold	(iii) 9

ASSESSMENT 2

Chapters 5-7

(Maximum Marks = 25)

A Choose the correct option for each of the following. **(10 × 1 = 10)**

1. 6, 12, 18, 24, ... These numbers are common multiples of ________________.
   (a) 6 and 8 (b) 2 and 4 (c) 4 and 6 (d) 2 and 3
2. What is the sum of the first five multiples of 8?
   (a) 40 (b) 80 (c) 112 (d) 120
3. Which one of the following is not a factor of 40?
   (a) 5 (b) 10 (c) 15 (d) 20
4. Which of the following fractions is equivalent to $\frac{4}{5}$?
   (a) $\frac{9}{10}$ (b) $\frac{16}{20}$ (c) $\frac{2}{10}$ (d) $\frac{15}{20}$
5. Identify the correct option.
   (a) $\frac{1}{2}<\frac{5}{2}<\frac{3}{2}<\frac{7}{2}$ (b) $\frac{1}{2}<\frac{7}{2}<\frac{5}{2}<\frac{3}{2}$ (c) $\frac{1}{2}<\frac{3}{2}<\frac{5}{2}<\frac{7}{2}$ (d) $\frac{1}{2}<\frac{7}{2}<\frac{3}{2}<\frac{5}{2}$
6. Identify the like fractions from the following set of fractions.
   (a) $\frac{1}{6}, \frac{6}{2}$ (b) $\frac{1}{4}, \frac{1}{2}$ (c) $\frac{9}{11}, \frac{2}{9}$ (d) $\frac{4}{9}, \frac{8}{9}$
7. In the given figure, what is the fraction form of orange-shaded portion?

   (a) $\frac{3}{10}$ (b) $\frac{4}{10}$ (c) $\frac{2}{10}$ (d) $\frac{1}{10}$
8. The two edges of a ruler are marked in
   (a) Centimetres and centimetres
   (b) Inches and inches
   (c) Centimetres and millimetres
   (d) Centimetres and inches

9. Which of the following is not a simple closed curve?

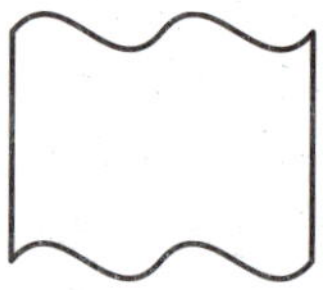
(a)

(b)

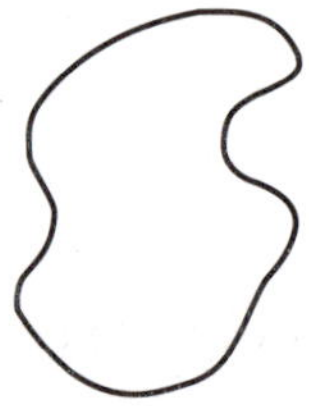
(c)

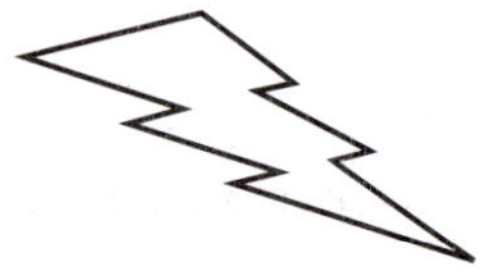
(d)

10. In a rectangle,
    (a) all sides are equal.
    (b) one pair of opposite sides is equal.
    (c) all sides are unequal.
    (d) two pairs of opposite sides are equal.

B Fill in the blanks. **(5 × 1 = 5)**

1. The difference between the 8th multiple of 5 and the 6th multiple of 6 is ________________.
2. "The common factors of 25 and 50 are ____________"
3. $\frac{1}{24} + \frac{11}{24} =$ ________________.
4. A point determines ________________
5. A line is denoted by ________________

C State whether the following statements are True (T) or False (F). **(5 × 1 = 5)**

1. 63 is not a multiple of 9. ☐
2. 7 is a factor of 117. ☐
3. $\frac{2}{10}$ is an example of a unit fraction. ☐
4. The length of the arrow shown below is 7 cm.

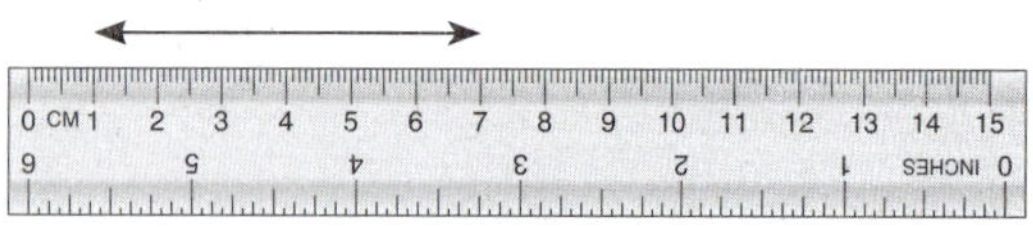

☐

5. The triangle is a polygon with three sides and three vertices. ☐

D Match the following. **(5 × 1 = 5)**

Column A	Column B
(a) Sum of all odd factors of 20	(i) $3\frac{6}{7}, 1\frac{5}{3}, 18\frac{4}{6}, 13\frac{2}{15}$
(b) Sum of all even factors of 20	(ii) $\frac{1}{6}, \frac{3}{10}, \frac{5}{15}, \frac{9}{11}$
(c) Proper fractions	(iii) 36
(d) Improper fractions	(iv) $\frac{12}{8}, \frac{13}{9}, \frac{5}{3}, \frac{7}{2}$
(e) Mixed fractions	(v) 6

COMPREHENSIVE ASSESSMENT

Chapters 1-7

(Maximum Marks = 50)

A Choose the correct option for each of the following. **(10 × 1 = 10)**

1. 67 thousands + 64 hundreds + 23 tens = ____________

   (a) 73630 (b) 67663 (c) 73423 (d) 67870

2. What is the smallest 5-digit even number that can be formed using the digits 3, 9, 2, 0 and 6 (without repeating the digits)?

   (a) 23096 (b) 20369 (c) 20936 (d) 02396

3. Which of the following does not have a remainder when divided by 14?

   (a) 12988 (b) 42920 (c) 51712 (d) 53788

4. The factors of 35 are 1, 5 and ____________.

   (a) 2 (b) 3 (c) 6 (d) 7

5. Find the multiples of 6 which are between 30 and 60.

   (a) 36, 42, 48, 54 (b) 33, 39, 45, 54 (c) 32, 36, 40, 44 (d) 18, 24, 36, 42

6. $$\begin{array}{r} 1\ 5\ 8\ 2\ 3 \\ +7\ 8\ 2\ 0\ 5 \\ \hline 9\ 3\ 0\ 2\ 8 \end{array}$$

   Identify the wrong digit in the answer.

   (a) 9 (b) 3 (c) 2 (d) 8

7. Which of the following options is correct for $\frac{2}{7} = \frac{8}{[\ ]}$?

   (a) $\frac{2}{7} = \frac{8}{16}$ (b) $\frac{2}{7} = \frac{8}{13}$ (c) $\frac{2}{7} = \frac{8}{28}$ (d) $\frac{2}{7} = \frac{8}{35}$

8. The sum of the fractions $\frac{1}{18}$ and $\frac{1}{18}$ is given by

   (a) $\frac{2}{36}$ (b) $\frac{1}{9}$ (c) $\frac{36}{18}$ (d) None of these

9. The number of diameters that can be drawn to a circle is

   (a) one (b) Infinite (c) Depends on the size of the circle (d) Two

10. Which of the following is not a polygon?

    (a) 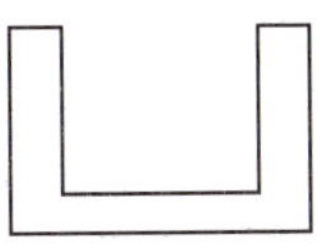 (b) 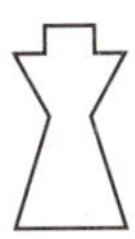 (c) 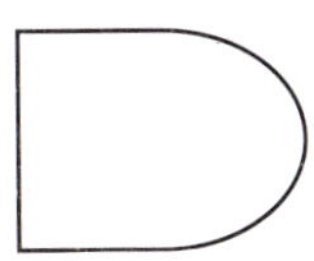 (d) 

B Fill in the blanks. **(5 × 1 = 5)**

1. 3420 ÷ ____________ = 342
2. Find the product of 128 and 6. When it is rounded off to the nearest 100 it would be ____________.
3. 400 books are arranged in 50 shelves equally. The possible combination of books in rows and columns are ____________ and ____________.
4. Difference between the smallest 6-digit number and largest 5-digit number is ____________.
5. The line of symmetry divides the figure into ____________.

C Answer the following questions briefly. **(5 × 2 = 10)**

1. If the number of people watching a performance to the nearest 1000 is 300000, what is the largest possible even number of people watching the performance?
2. Subtract 56725 from the sum of 42238 and 24278.
3. What is the product of 298 and 316?
4. If 12 boxes of wheat weigh 1235 kg, estimate the weight of 1 box.
5. Reduce the fraction $\frac{24}{60}$ to its simplest form.

D Answer the following questions. **(5 × 3 = 15)**

1. Arrange the following in ascending order.

   (a) 67019, 69001, 67109, 68999 (b) C, V, L, X

   ________ , ________ , ________ , ________ ________ , ________ , ________ , ________

2. Lokesh, a fruit seller, has 22150 fruits. 2525 of the fruits are apples. The number of oranges is twice the number of apples. The rest are pears. How many pears does Lokesh have?
3. There are 742 boxes in a storeroom. There are 38 half-sleeve shirts and 12 full-sleeve shirts in each box. Find the total number of half-sleeves shirts, full-sleeve shirts and both the types of shirts.
4. Reena bought 1027 gift articles to distribute to the guests attending the function at home. She wants to pack 3 gifts in each bag. Find to how many guests she can distribute the gifts. Are there any gifts left out? If yes, how many?
5. A sparrow knits $\frac{5}{7}$ part of its nest in 1 day. What part of nest remains to be knit after a day?

E Answer the following. **(2 × 5 = 10)**

1. There are 54 sweets which have to be distributed equally among students. List all the possible number of students and the number of sweets distributed to them in each case.
2. Mr Harish weighs between 60 kg and 80 kg. His actual weight is a multiple of 8 and also a multiple of 9. What is his actual weight?

ANSWERS FOR SELECTED QUESTIONS

Chapter 1

Exercise 1.1

1. **(a)** 91584 – Ninety one thousand five hundred Eighty four
   (b) 23850 – Twenty three thousand eight hundred fifty
   (c) 60008 – Sixty thousand eight

2. **(a)** Forty-three thousand three hundred twenty-one

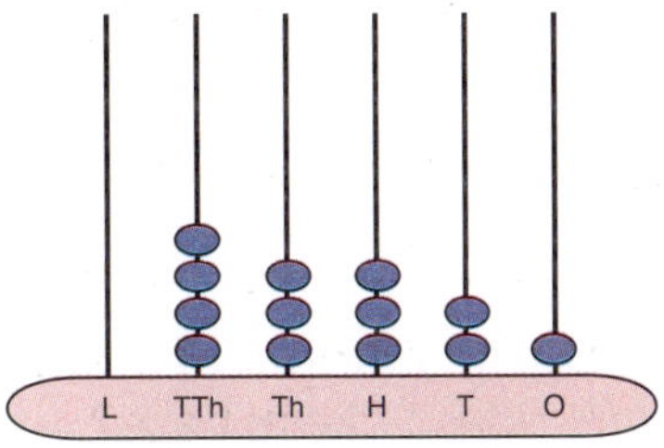

(b) 4,12,014

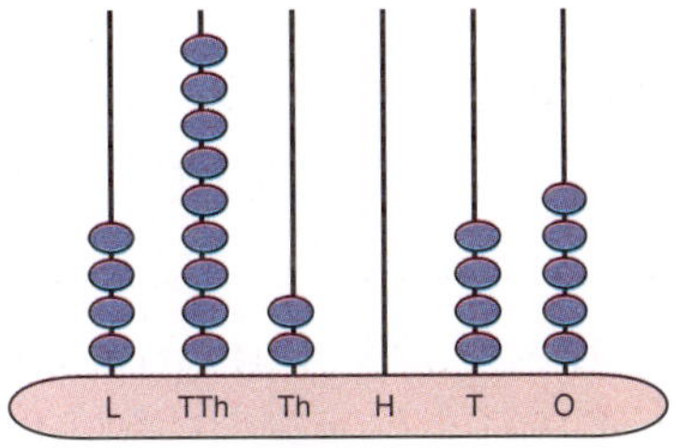

(c) 9,09,890

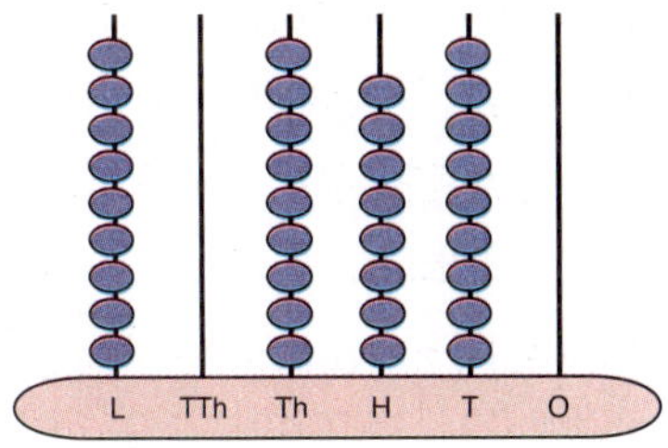

3. **(a)** 45695 **(b)** 102109 **(c)** 206082 **(d)** 86542
4. **(a)** 6 **(b)** 20,000 **(c)** 700000 **(d)** 700 **(e)** 50 **(f)** 9000
5. **(a)** 4000, 84325 **(b)** 800, 4, 511824 **(c)** 800, 40, 74842 **(d)** 600000, 70000, 400, 70, 7, 677477

Exercise 1.2

1. **(a)** 45,251 __<__ 6,81,320 **(d)** 92,475 __>__ 85,784
   (b) 10,024 __<__ 10,204 **(e)** 6,87,999 __>__ 1000
   (c) 8,00,756 __>__ 7,84,245 **(f)** 34,251 __>__ 34,208
2. **(a)** T **(b)** T **(c)** F **(d)** T **(e)** T

Exercise 1.3

1. **(a)** 12054, 20105, 30458, 40306 **(b)** 241475, 413281,430087, 430490 **(c)** 75802, 75871, 750608,750806
2. **(a)** and **(c)**
3. **(a)** 854320 **(b)** 987642 **(c)** 87521 **(d)** 86430
4. **(a)** 59767, 59768, 59769 **(b)** 23874, 23875, 23876
   (c) 65792, 65793, 65794 **(d)** 35986, 35987, 35988

Exercise 1.4

1. **(a)** 78,000 **(b)** 8, 20,000 **(c)** 80,000 **(d)** 30,000
   (e) 1, 50,000 **(f)** 1, 70,000
2. **(b)** and **(d)**
3. **(a)** 51,200 **(b)** 4,60,200 **(c)** 82,500 **(d)** 1,94,900
   (e) 6,71,000 **(f)** 2,47,100
4. **(b)** 4, 20,000 **(c)** 3, 80,000

Revision Exercise

1. **(a)** 43,257 = 40,000 + 3,000 + 200 + 50 + 7 **(b)** 6,74,635 = 6,00,000 + 70,000 + 4,000 + 600 + 30 + 5
   (c) 99,029 = 90,000 + 9,000 + 20 + 9 **(d)** 1,05,061 = 1,00,000 + 5,000 + 60 + 1
   (e) 8,40,499 = 8,00,000 + 40,000 + 400 + 90 + 9 **(f)** 22,009 = 20,000 + 2,000 + 9
2. **(a)** 84,852 = 80,000 + 4,000 + 800 + 50 + 2 Eighty-four thousand eight hundred fifty-two
   (b) 52,901 = 50,000 + 2,000 + 900 + 1 Fifty-two thousand nine hundred one
   (c) 61,509 = 60,000 + 1,000 + 500 + 9 Sixty-one thousand five hundred nine
   (d) 3,17,656 = 3,00,000 + 10,000 + 7,000 + 600 + 50 + 6 Three lakh seventeen thousand six hundred fifty-six
   (e) 7,01,025 = 7,00,000 + 1,000 + 20 + 5 Seven lakh one thousand twenty-five
   (f) 9,93,100 = 9,00,000 + 90,000 + 3,000 + 100 Nine lakh ninety-three thousand hundred
3. **(a)** 6,000 **(b)** 40,000 **(c)** 700 **(d)** 80 **(e)** 10,000 **(f)** 2,00,000
4. **(a)** Smallest number = 13,789 Greatest number = 98,731
   (b) Smallest number = 2,04,568 Greatest number = 8,65,420
   (c) Smallest number = 1,23,456 Greatest number = 6,54,321

5. **(a)** > **(b)** < **(c)** < **(d)** <
   (e) < **(f)** < **(g)** < **(h)** >
6. **(a)** 10,600 **(b)** 7,50,000 **(c)** 22,000 **(d)** 4,17,610
7. **(a)** XVIII **(b)** XII **(c)** 26 **(d)** XXIII **(e)** XXXIX
   (f) 9 **(g)** XXX **(h)** 34 **(i)** 15

HOTS (Higher Order Thinking Skills)

IV = 4 V = 5 XXXVIII = 38 XXXIX = 39
VIII = 8 XVII = 17 XXII = 22

Chapter 2

Exercise 2.1

1. **(a)** 38,074 **(b)** 72,950 **(c)** 99,743 **(d)** 59,091
   (e) 83,993 **(f)** 1, 22,036
2. **(a)** 388074 **(b)** 77,3020 **(c)** 871036 **(d)** 684871
   (e) 789392 **(f)** 801100
3. **(a)** 137575 **(b)** 214196 **(c)** 299998 **(d)** 185740
   (e) 771372 **(f)** 110000
4. **(a)** 139348 **(b)** 833000 **(c)** 257372 **(d)** 54108

Exercise 2.2

1. **(a)** 14239 **(b)** 104150 **(c)** 96002 **(d)** 17912
   (e) 273928 **(f)** 27709
2. **(a)** Candidate A has 23655 votes **(b)** Other number is 76430 **(c)** Unsold cars are 86082

Revision Exercise

1. **(a)** i, ii **(b)** ii, iv **(c)** ii **(d)** i
2. **(a)** – **(b)** + **(c)** + **(d)** + **(e)** + **(f)** +
3. **(a)** ₹1,70,030 **(b)** ₹1,16,19 **(c)** 77,887 litres **(d)** 4,03,749 votes
   (e) 7,62,103 kg **(f)** 12,868 km

Chapter 3

Exercise 3.1

1. **(a)** 241 × 124 (i) 1,75,032
   (b) 468 × 374 (ii) 88,072
   (c) 101 × 872 (iii) 29,884
   (d) 456 × 470 (iv) 3,06,030
   (e) 100 × 943 (v) 2,14,320
   (f) 606 × 505 (vi) 94,300
2. **(a)** 74400 **(b)** 237384 **(c)** 184 * 612 = 1, 12,608 **(d)** 131850

Revision Exercise

1. **(a)** 37,935 **(b)** 1,50,944 **(c)** 1,34,830 **(d)** 81,500 **(e)** 2,53,368
   (f) 98,044 **(g)** 70,528 **(h)** 21,780 **(i)** 1,16,844 **(j)** 2,21,008
2. **(a)** 192172 **(b)** 18724 **(c)** 86815 **(d)** 157798 **(e)** 37944
   (f) 122256 **(g)** 30098 **(h)** 37800
3. **(a)** ₹72,500 **(b)** ₹3,855 ₹7,710 ₹11,565
4. **(a)** 4,500 **(b)** 6,000 **(c)** 1,80,000 **(d)** 20,000

Chapter 4

Exercise 4.1

(a) Remainder = 11 Quotient = 4 **(b)** Remainder = 0 Quotient = 6
(c) Remainder = 0 Quotient = 3 **(d)** Remainder =9 Quotient = 2
(e) Remainder = 3 Quotient = 6 **(f)** Remainder = 16 Quotient = 2

ANSWERS

Exercise 4.2

(a) Remainder = 11 Quotient = 36
(b) Remainder = 39 Quotient = 13
(c) Remainder = 0 Quotient = 25
(d) Remainder = 0 Quotient = 13
(e) Remainder = 4 Quotient = 17
(f) Remainder = 11 Quotient = 46

Exercise 4.3

(a) Remainder = 9 Quotient = 59
(b) Remainder = 10 Quotient = 122
(c) Remainder = 16 Quotient = 233
(d) Remainder = 0 Quotient = 425
(e) Remainder =0 Quotient = 214
(f) Remainder = 64 Quotient = 130

Exercise 4.4

1. **(a)** Remainder = 0 Quotient = 45
(b) Remainder = 0 Quotient = 27
(c) Remainder = 14 Quotient = 30
(d) Remainder = 13 Quotient = 24
(e) Remainder = 0 Quotient = 124
(f) Remainder = 35 Quotient = 119
(g) Remainder = 0 Quotient = 208
(h) Remainder = 0 Quotient = 70
2. **(a)** 78 **(b)** 80 **(c)** 345 **(d)** 152 **(e)** 101
(f) 63 **(g)** 37 **(h)** 82 **(i)** 119
3. Message 1 HYDERABAD Message 2 BOMBAY

Revision Exercise

1. **(a)** remainder = 0, quotient = 26 **(b)** remainder = 0, quotient = 87
(c) remainder = 5, quotient = 345 **(d)** remainder = 5, quotient = 87
(e) remainder = 22, quotient = 78
2. **(a)** 18 **(b)** 85 **(c)** 24 **(d)** 101
(e) 405 **(f)** 69
3. **(a)**, **(d)**, **(e)**
4. **(a)** 350 (7000 ÷ 20) **(b)** 400 (8000 ÷ 20) **(c)** 50 (4000 ÷ 80) **(d)** 100 (9000 ÷ 90) **(e)** 40 (400 ÷ 10)
5. **(a)** ₹630 **(b)** 975 km **(c)** ₹250 **(d)** 4
(e) 53 years **(f)** ₹6,250

Chapter 5

Exercise 5.1

1.

Number	Divisible by 2	Divisible by 5	Divisible by 10	Divisible by 3	Divisible by 9
24	yes	no	no	yes	no
1,025	no	yes	no	no	no
876	yes	no	no	yes	no
9,122	yes	no	no	no	no
1,000	yes	yes	yes	no	no

2. Not Divisible by 5 – 24, 876 Not Divisible by 2 – 1025, 2005 Not Divisible by 10 –1025, 9122
Not Divisible by 3 – 1000, 2005 Not Divisible by 9 – 24, 40, 2005

Exercise 5.2

1.

Number	Factors
27	1, 3, 9, 27
4	1, 2, 4
45	1, 3, 5, 9, 45
19	1, 19

Number	Factors
14	1, 2, 7, 14
9	1, 3, 9
30	1, 3, 2,5, 6, 10, 30
15	1, 3, 5, 10, 15

2.

Number	First Five Multiples
7	7, 14, 21, 28, 35
8	8, 16, 24, 32, 40
1	1,2, 3, 4, 5
3	3, 6, 9, 12, 15
9	9, 18, 36, 27, 45

Number	First Five Multiples
10	10, 20, 30, 40, 50
2	2, 6, 4, 8, 10
12	12, 24, 36, 48, 60
6	6, 12, 18, 21, 24, 30
5	5, 10, 15, 20, 25

ANSWERS

3. **(a)** 7 **(b)** 2 and 8 **(c)** 5 and 11 **(d)** 8 and 6 **(e)** 19
(f) 1 and 13 **(g)** 5 **(h)** 1 and 11 **(i)** 9 and 3

4. **(a)** 56 and 77 **(b)** 11 and 88 **(c)** 80 and 32 **(d)** 81 and 18 **(e)** 5, 100, 150 and 200
(f) 72, 63, 21 and 27 **(g)** 60 and 55 **(h)** 22, 33 and 66 **(i)** 45, 30 and 60

Revision Exercise

1. **(a)** Factors of 10 are 1, 2, 5 and 10. Factors of 15 are 1, 3, 5 and 15. Common factor is 5.
(b) Factors of 12 are 1, 2, 3, 4, 6 and 12. Factors of 16 are 1, 2, 4, 8 and 16. Common factors are 2, 4.
(c) Factors of 18 are 1, 2, 3, 6, 9 and 18. Factors of 24 are 1, 2, 3, 4, 6, 8, 12 and 24. Common factors are 2, 3 and 6.
(d) Factors of 16 are 1, 2, 4, 8 and 16. Factors of 18 are 1, 2, 3, 6, 9 and 18. Common factor is 2.
(e) Factors of 14 are 1, 2, 7 and 14. Factors of 35 are 1, 5, 7 and 35. Common factor is 7.

2. **(a)** First ten multiples of 3 are 3, 6, 9, 12, 15, 18, 21, 24, 27 and 30.
First ten multiples of 7 are 7, 14, 21, 28, 35, 42, 49, 56, 63 and 70.
Common multiple = 21

(b) First ten multiples of 2 are 2, 4, 6, 8, 10, 12, 14, 16, 18 and 20.
First ten multiples of 6 are 6, 12, 18, 24, 30, 36, 42, 48, 54 and 60.
Common multiples = 6, 12 and 18

(c) First ten multiples of 8 are 8, 16, 24, 32, 40, 48, 56, 64, 72 and 80.
First ten multiples of 3 are 3, 6, 9, 12, 15, 18, 21, 24, 27 and 30.
Common multiple = 24

(d) First ten multiples of 2 are 2, 4, 6, 8, 10, 12, 14, 16, 18 and 20.
First ten multiples of 5 are 5, 10, 15, 20, 25, 30, 35, 40, 45 and 50.
Common multiples = 10 and 20

(e) First ten multiples of 4 are 4, 8, 12, 16, 20, 24, 28, 32, 36 and 40.
First ten multiples of 3 are 3, 6, 9, 12, 15, 18, 21, 24, 27 and 30.
Common multiples = 12 and 24

3. **(a)** ii **(b)** v **(c)** i **(d)** vi **(e)** iv

4. **(a)** 2 **(b)** 3, 9 **(c)** 5, 3 **(d)** 2 **(e)** 1, 11 **(f)** 2, 4

5. **(a)** 14, 56 **(b)** 6, 12, 18 **(c)** 16 **(d)** 12, 36
(e) 50, 100 **(f)** 30, 60, 90

6.

Number	Divisible by 2	Divisible by 5	Divisible by 10
120	yes	yes	yes
35	no	yes	no
5,872	yes	no	no

HOTS (Higher Order Thinking Skills)

1. No, for example, 2 is a factor of 4 but it is not a multiple of 4.
2. **(a)**, **(d)**

Chapter 6

Exercise 6.1

1.

Pairs of equivalent fractions: $\frac{2}{5} = \frac{4}{10}$

2. **(a)** $\frac{2}{3} = \frac{4}{6} = \frac{6}{9} = \frac{8}{12} = \frac{10}{15}$ **(b)** $\frac{1}{7} = \frac{2}{14} = \frac{3}{21} = \frac{4}{21} = \frac{5}{35}$
(c) $\frac{3}{5} = \frac{6}{10} = \frac{9}{15} = \frac{12}{20} = \frac{15}{25}$ **(d)** $\frac{1}{4} = \frac{3}{12} = \frac{4}{16} = \frac{6}{24} = \frac{7}{28}$

Exercise 6.2

(a) $\frac{8}{9}$ **(b)** $\frac{1}{3}$ **(c)** $\frac{1}{2}$ **(d)** $\frac{1}{5}$
(e) $\frac{1}{2}$ **(f)** $\frac{1}{5}$ **(g)** $\frac{1}{7}$ **(h)** $\frac{8}{17}$

Exercise 6.3

1 **(a)** Equivalent **(b)** Equivalent **(c)** Equivalent **(d)** Not equivalent **(e)** Equivalent
(f) Not equivalent **(g)** Not equivalent **(h)** Not equivalent

Exercise 6.4

1. (a) $\frac{3}{12}, \frac{1}{12}, \frac{4}{12}, \frac{11}{12}$ — Like Fractions
   (b) $\frac{3}{8}, \frac{2}{3}, \frac{2}{12}, \frac{2}{7}$ — Unlike Fractions
   (c) $\frac{1}{8}, \frac{4}{8}, \frac{3}{8}, \frac{6}{8}$ — Like Fractions
   (d) $\frac{1}{8}, \frac{1}{10}, \frac{5}{12}, \frac{6}{13}$ — Unlike Fractions

2. Like Fractions – $\frac{11}{16}, \frac{1}{16}, \frac{10}{16}, \frac{10}{100}, \frac{11}{111}, \frac{2}{5}, \frac{3}{5}, \frac{25}{111}, \frac{25}{100}, \frac{2}{16}$
   Unlike Fractions – $\frac{1}{4}, \frac{5}{6}, \frac{8}{10}, \frac{15}{18}, \frac{12}{14}, \frac{2}{12}, \frac{1}{8}, \frac{4}{12}$,

3. (a) $\frac{1}{4}$ (b) $\frac{1}{21}$ (c) $\frac{1}{12}$

Exercise 6.5

1.

Fraction 1	Symbol (=/ >/<)	Fraction 2
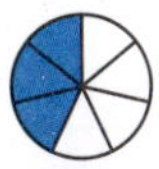 $\frac{3}{7}$	<	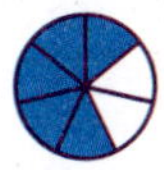 $\frac{5}{7}$
 $\frac{7}{11}$	>	 $\frac{2}{11}$
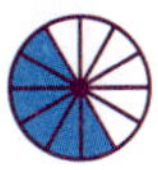 $\frac{6}{12}$	>	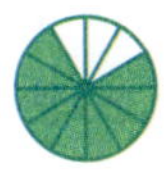 $\frac{9}{12}$

2. (a) $\frac{10}{15}$ (>) $\frac{8}{15}$ (c) $\frac{3}{9}$ (<) $\frac{5}{9}$ (e) $\frac{12}{24}$ (>) $\frac{11}{24}$
   (b) $\frac{13}{46}$ (<) $\frac{32}{46}$ (d) $\frac{9}{31}$ (>) $\frac{4}{31}$ (f) $\frac{10}{19}$ (>) $\frac{9}{19}$

Exercise 6.6

1. (a) $\frac{3}{5}$ (b) $\frac{3}{4}$ (c) $\frac{2}{3}$ (d) $\frac{9}{10}$ (e) $\frac{3}{3}$
   (f) $\frac{4}{7}$ (g) $\frac{4}{7}$ (h) $\frac{13}{15}$ (i) $\frac{10}{11}$ (j) $\frac{2}{3}$
2. 1 3. $\frac{3}{7}$ 4. $\frac{5}{7}$

Exercise 6.7

1 (a) $\frac{3}{10}$ (b) $\frac{5}{21}$ (c) $\frac{1}{2}$ (d) $\frac{2}{19}$ (e) $\frac{1}{9}$
  (f) $\frac{3}{23}$ (g) $\frac{1}{5}$ (h) $\frac{8}{25}$ (i) $\frac{2}{3}$ (j) $\frac{29}{38}$
2. (a) $\frac{3}{8}$ (b) $\frac{2}{5}$ (c) $\frac{5}{9}$

Exercise 6.8

1. Proper Fraction– $\frac{1}{3}, \frac{5}{6}, \frac{12}{13}, \frac{1}{5}, \frac{5}{7}, \frac{3}{7}, \frac{5}{8}, \frac{11}{17}$
   Improper Fraction – $\frac{11}{8}, \frac{23}{14}, \frac{13}{7}, \frac{11}{6}, \frac{16}{13}, \frac{31}{18}, \frac{19}{17}$
   Mixed Fraction – $6\frac{1}{3}, 4\frac{1}{3}, 8\frac{1}{3}, 7\frac{5}{6}, 3\frac{1}{3}$
2. (a) Ramesh bought $\frac{3}{8}$ more blue ribbon
   (b) $\frac{2}{5}$ more distance covered by mohan on Saturday
   (c) $\frac{5}{9}$ more sugar sold on Monday

Revision Exercise

1. (a) $\frac{3}{10}, \frac{6}{20}, \frac{9}{30}, \frac{12}{40}, \frac{15}{50}$ (b) $\frac{2}{16}, \frac{4}{32}, \frac{6}{48}, \frac{8}{64}, \frac{10}{80}$
2. (a) $\frac{2}{5}$ (b) $\frac{7}{2}$ (c) $\frac{1}{2}$ (d) $\frac{23}{30}$
3. **Match the following.**

(a) $\frac{4}{9}, \frac{7}{9}, \frac{1}{9}$ Mixed fraction
(b) $\frac{3}{7}, \frac{4}{6}, \frac{5}{13}, \frac{8}{18}$ Improper fraction
(c) $\frac{1}{14}, \frac{1}{16}, \frac{1}{18}, \frac{1}{4}, \frac{1}{6}$ Like fraction
(d) $\frac{4}{7}, \frac{3}{16}, \frac{5}{8}, \frac{9}{21}$ Unlike fraction
(e) $\frac{4}{3}, \frac{9}{6}, \frac{3}{2}, \frac{7}{5}$ Proper fraction
(f) $1\frac{2}{3}, 4\frac{5}{6}, 3\frac{2}{4}, 9\frac{5}{10}$ Unit fraction

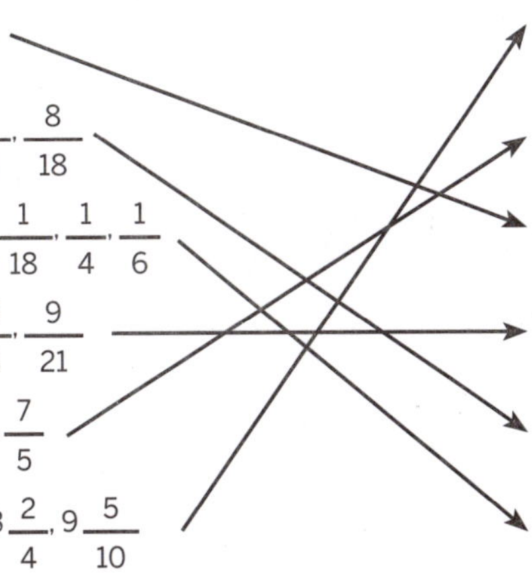

4. **(a)** 1 metre **(b)** $\frac{5}{6}$ litre **(c)** $\frac{3}{8}$ kg **(d)** $\frac{4}{7}$

HOTS (Higher Order Thinking Skills)

We can form 42 numbers of improper fractions.

Explanation: Numbers: 1, 2, 3, 4, 5, 6, 7, 8, 9, 10

Fractions with denominator	Improper fractions	Total
1	$\frac{2}{1}, \frac{3}{1}, \frac{4}{1}, \frac{5}{1}, \frac{6}{1}, \frac{7}{1}, \frac{8}{1}, \frac{9}{1}, \frac{10}{1}$	9
2	$\frac{3}{2}, \frac{4}{2}, \frac{5}{2}, \frac{6}{2}, \frac{7}{2}, \frac{8}{2}, \frac{9}{2}, \frac{10}{2}$	8
3	$\frac{4}{3}, \frac{5}{3}, \frac{6}{3}, \frac{7}{3}, \frac{8}{3}, \frac{9}{3}, \frac{10}{3}$	7
4	$\frac{5}{4}, \frac{6}{4}, \frac{7}{4}, \frac{8}{4}, \frac{9}{4}, \frac{10}{4}$	6
5	$\frac{6}{5}, \frac{7}{5}, \frac{8}{5}, \frac{9}{5}, \frac{10}{5}$	5
6	$\frac{7}{6}, \frac{8}{6}, \frac{9}{6}, \frac{10}{6}$	4
7	$\frac{8}{7}, \frac{9}{7}, \frac{10}{7}$	3
8	$\frac{9}{8}, \frac{10}{8}$	2
9	$\frac{10}{9}$	1
Total number of improper fractions		**45**

Chapter 7

Exercise 7.1

1. **(a)**

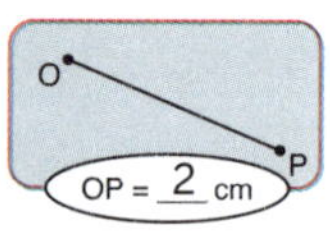

(b)

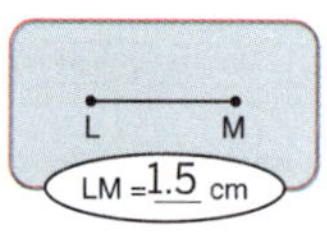

(c)

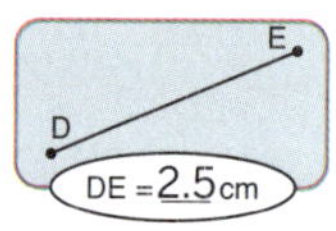

2. Follow instruction given in question

3. **(a)** A line segment has 2 end points **(b)** A line has no end point

4. **(a)** True **(b)** False

5. Follow instruction given in question

Exercise 7.2

Closed

Closed

Open

Closed

Closed

Open

Open

Closed

Closed

Closed

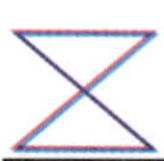

Closed

Closed

Closed

Exercise 7.3

1. (a) 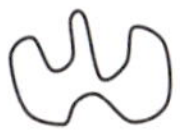 (c) 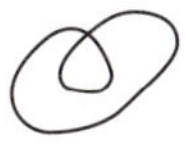 (e) 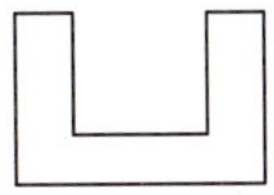 (b) 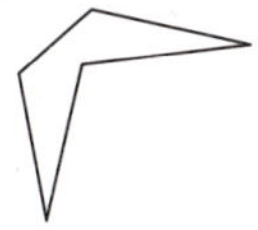 (d) 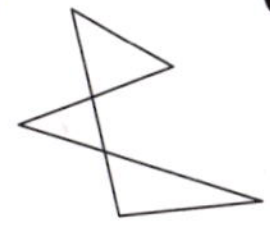 (f) 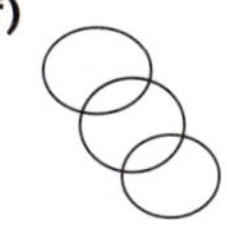

2. **D, O, B, Q**

Exercise 7.4

(a)  **(b)**  **(c)** ✓ 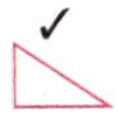 **(d)** ✓ 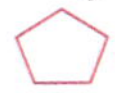 **(e)**  **(f)**  **(g)** 

Exercise 7.5

1. **(a)**

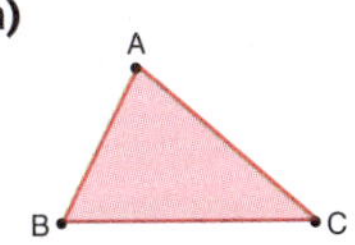

Vertices: A, B, C Sides: AB, BC, CA

(b)

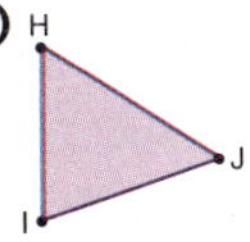

Vertices: H, I, J Sides: IJ, HI, HJ

(c)

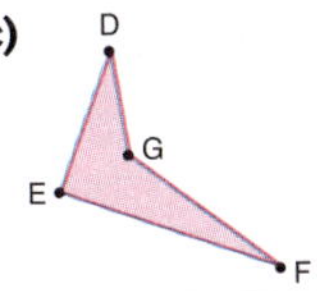

Vertices: D, G, F, E Sides: DG, GF, EF, ED

(d)

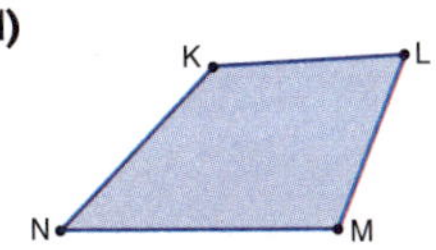

Vertices: k, L, M, N Sides: KL, MK, NM, NK

2.

Opposite sides
AD and BC; AB and DC

Adjacent sides
AD, DC, CB, BA

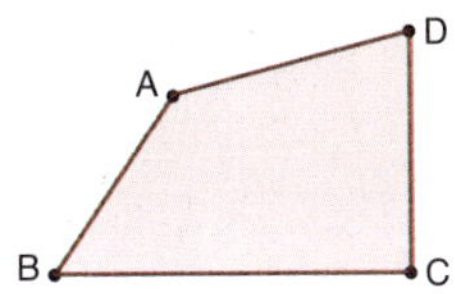

Exercise 7.6

1. **(a)** F **(b)** T **(c)** T **(d)** F

2. **(a)** 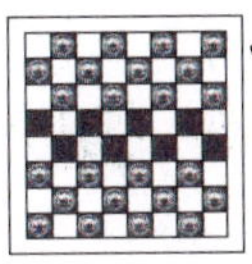 ✓ **(b)**  ✓ **(c)**  **(d)** 

Exercise 7.7

1. **(a)** Centre: A Radius: AB **(b)** Centre: X Radius: XY **(c)** Centre: O Radius: OD

2. **(a)**

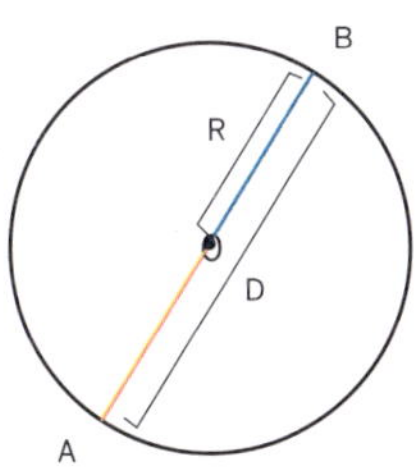

(b)

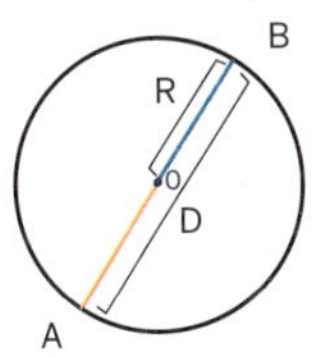

(c)

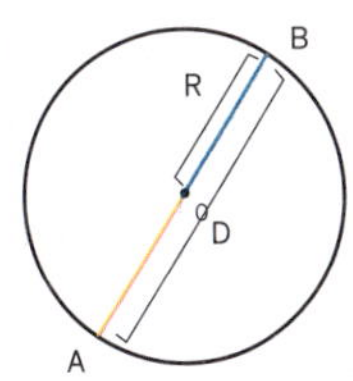

3. AB = 5 cm AF = 5 cm AD = 5 cm FG = 10 cm AE = 5 cm

4. **(a)** 7 cm **(b)** 4 cm **(c)** 9 cm **(d)** 15 cm

5. **(a)** 6 cm **(b)** 10 cm **(c)** 22 cm **(d)** 30 cm

Exercise 7.8

1. **(a)** 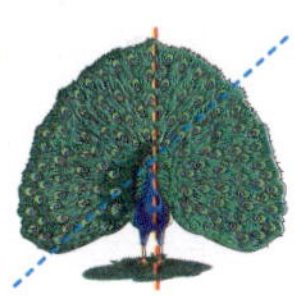 **(b)** ✓ 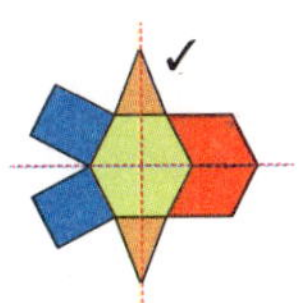 **(c)** ✓  **(d)** 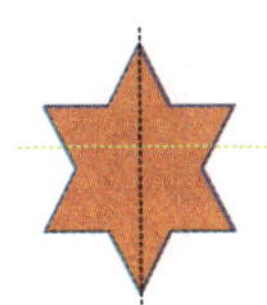 **(e)** 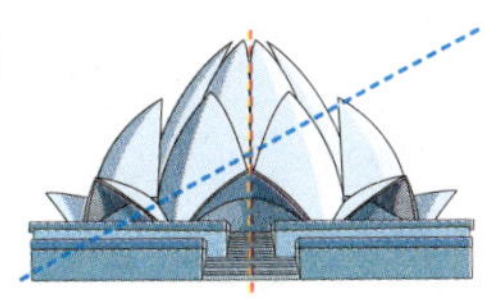

Exercise 7.9

1. Follow instructions given in question
2.

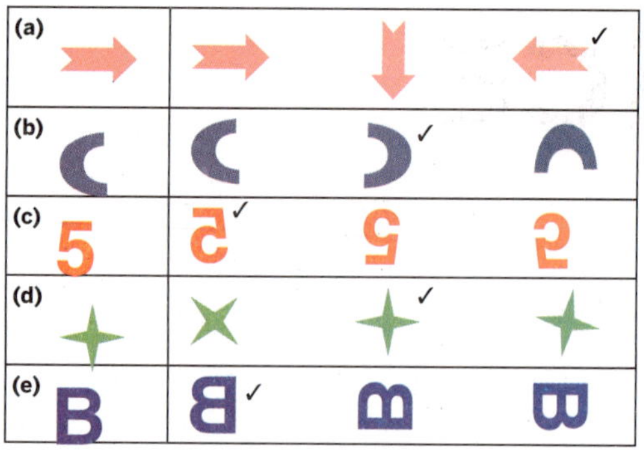

Exercise 7.10

1.

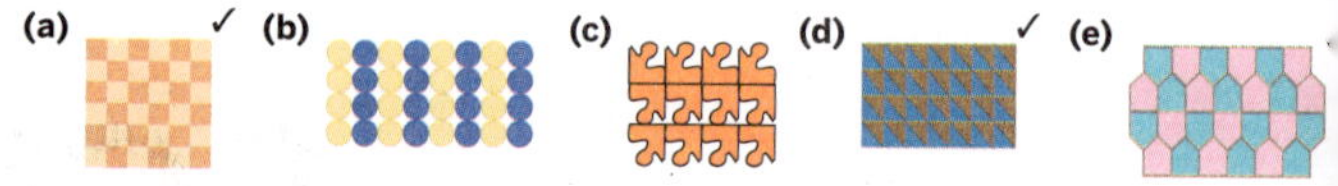

Revision Exercise

3.

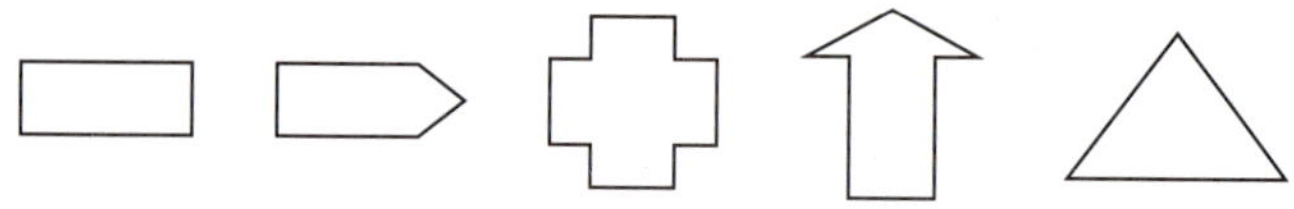

4. **(a)** iii **(b)** iv **(c)** i
   (d) ii
5. Centre – O, Radius – OC or OA or OB, Diameter – AB
6. **(a)** 15cm **(b)** 6 cm
7. a, c and d
8. a and b

SCIENCE

1 The Green Plants

Learning Checklist

- Leaf
- How do plants make their food?
- Interdependence of plants and animals

Leaves of different plants differ in shape, size and colour. Let us learn more about leaves and their functions in this chapter.

LEAF

A leaf is a flat structure growing from the stem or branch of a plant. Most plants have green leaves. The green colour is due to a green pigment[1] called **chlorophyll** present in the leaves.

The flat part of the leaf is called **leaf blade** or the **lamina**. The part that attaches the leaf to the stem or supports the leaf is called the **petiole**. Leaf has a main vein called **midrib** and many small veins branching off from it. These veins help in transporting water, minerals and nutrients to and from the leaves of a plant.

The underside of every leaf has tiny openings called **stomata** (singular: stoma). Stomata are like nostrils of a plant which help them to breathe. Bean-shaped structures called **guard cells** surround the stomata. Guard cells control the opening and closing of stomata.

Word Web

[1]**Pigment**: coloured substance

Parts of a leaf

Leaf cells

HOW DO PLANTS MAKE THEIR FOOD?

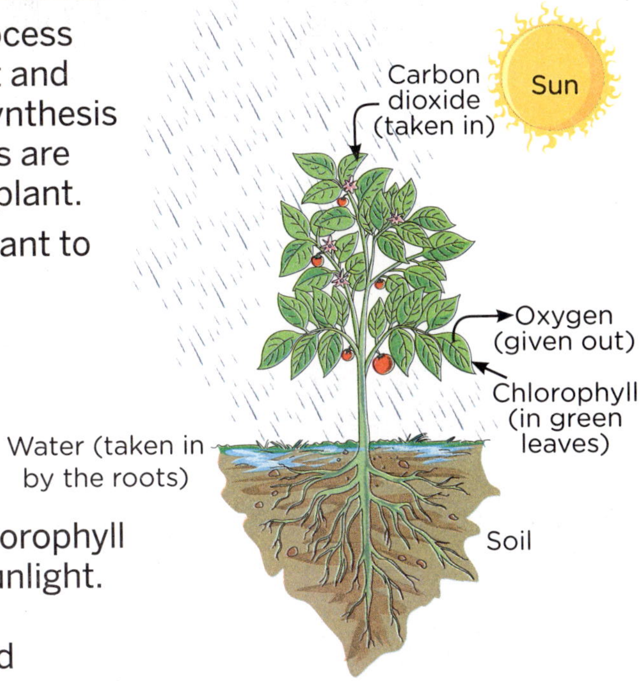

Green plants make their own food by a process called **photosynthesis** (*photo* means light and *synthesis* means to put together). Photosynthesis takes place in the leaves, that is why leaves are called the food factory or the kitchen of a plant.

The following things are necessary for a plant to carry out photosynthesis:

(a) Carbon dioxide

(b) Light

(c) Water

(d) Chlorophyll

Light is mostly obtained from the sun. Chlorophyll present in the green leaves absorbs the sunlight. Carbon dioxide enters the leaves through stomata. Water is taken in by the roots and carried to the leaves by the stem. The products of photosynthesis are sugar and oxygen.

$$\text{Carbon dioxide + Water} \xrightarrow[\text{Chlorophyll}]{\text{Light}} \text{Sugar + Oxygen}$$

Plants use the prepared food for growth and other routine functions. Extra food is stored in the form of starch in different parts of a plant.

Activity

Aim: To show that leaves prepare food which is stored in the form of starch.

Materials required: A potted plant, black paper, beaker, burner, water, forceps, Petri-plate, dropper, alcohol and iodine solution

Procedure:

1. Keep the potted plant in a dark room for two or three days.
2. Clip some black paper to a green leaf of the plant. Keep the plant exposed to sunlight for one day.
3. Remove the black paper from the leaf.
4. Take some water in a small beaker and heat it on a burner.

6. Dip the leaf into the boiling water with the help of forceps. Keep it for about two minutes.
7. Remove the leaf from the boiling water and dip it completely in warm alcohol.
8. Heat the set-up using a burner till the leaves turn white.
9. Take out the leaf carefully using forceps and wash it with cold water.
10. Place it on the Petri-plate and pour a few drops of iodine solution over it with the help of a dropper.

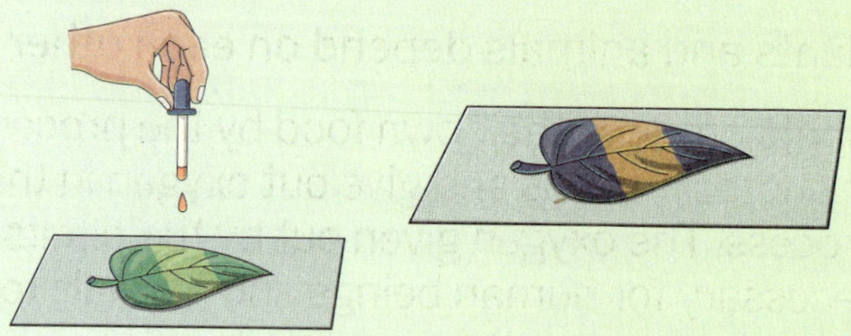

Observation: The portion of the leaf that was exposed to sunlight shows a blue-black colour, while the portion covered with the black paper does not show blue-black colour.

Conclusion: The blue-black colour indicates the presence of starch and is a positive result for starch test. The portion of the leaf which was exposed to sunlight was able to prepare its food and store starch. The one covered with black paper could not prepare its food because it did not receive any sunlight. Thus, no starch formation takes place in this part of the leaf.

FA

Revise and recall

1. Look at the picture of a leaf shown below and fill in the names of its parts.

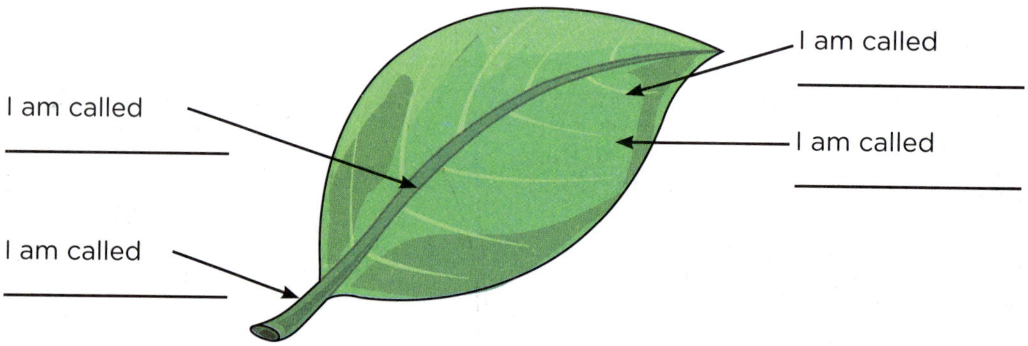

2. Select the words from the help box and fill in the blanks.

Oxygen, Sunlight, Chlorophyll, Sugar, Carbon dioxide, Water

Photosynthesis is:

________ + ________ ————→ ________ + ________

INTERDEPENDENCE OF PLANTS AND ANIMALS

Plants and animals depend on each other for their survival.

Plants produce their own food by the process of photosynthesis and give out oxygen in this process. The oxygen given out by the plants is necessary for human beings and animals to live. Animals also depend on plants for food.

> **Science in Context**
>
> Plants not only provide us with food to eat and oxygen to breathe, but also provide us with medicines. Most of the medicines that we use are made from plants.

Herbivorous animals eat plants for their food. Carnivores depend on the herbivores for their food. Plants eaten by herbivores and the herbivores eaten by carnivores form a chain. A chain that shows how one organism is dependent on another organism for food is called the **food chain**.

A food chain

Animals help the plants by carrying their seeds to far off places where they can germinate. Animals breathe out carbon dioxide which is used by the plants for photosynthesis.

The interdependence[1] of plants and animals creates a balance in nature. If the number of either plants or animals increases or decreases suddenly, this balance will be disturbed.

Humans beings and animals obtain food and oxygen from plants

> **Word Web**
>
> [1]**Interdependence**: dependence on each other

Keywords

Chlorophyll: The green pigment in the leaves of plants that gives green colour to the leaves
Stomata: Tiny openings on the underside of leaves that help the plant to breathe
Petiole: The part of a leaf that holds it to the stem of the plant
Photosynthesis: The process by which the green leaves of plants make their own food.
Food chain: The chain that shows how one organism is dependent on another food.

Summary

1. The parts of a leaf are leaf blade, petiole, midrib and veins.
2. The green colour of plants is due to the presence of a pigment called chlorophyll.
3. Plants make their own food by a process called photosynthesis, using sunlight, carbon dioxide, water and chlorophyll.
4. The underside of leaves have small openings called stomata. Exchange of gases like oxygen and carbon dioxide takes place through the stomata.
5. Plants and animals depend on each other for their survival.

EXERCISE

A Choose the correct option for each of the following.

1. Leaves are green in colour due to the presence of
   (a) Stomata (b) Chlorophyll (c) Carbon dioxide (d) Oxygen
2. The part of a leaf that attaches it to the stem is
   (a) Midrib (b) Blade (c) Petiole (d) Vein
3. Plants make their own food using
   (a) Carbon dioxide (b) Sunlight (c) Water (d) All of them
4. During photosynthesis, plants produce
   (a) Sunlight (b) Sugar (c) Carbon dioxide (d) All of them

B Fill in the blanks with the correct words.

1. The flat part of a leaf is called ____________________. (vein/leaf blade)
2. Tiny openings on the underside of leaves of plants are called ____________________. (stomata/vein)

3. Chlorophyll gives ____________________ colour to the plant. (white/green)
4. Plants give us ____________________ to breathe. (oxygen/carbon dioxide)

C Match the following.

Column A	Column B
(a) Photosynthesis	(i) Transport substances
(b) Chlorophyll	(ii) Tiny openings on the underside of leaves
(c) Veins	(iii) Preparation of food by the plants
(d) Stomata	(iv) Green pigment

D State whether the following statements are true (T) or false (F).

1. The midrib branches into smaller structures called veins. ☐
2. Sunlight gives the leaf energy to make food. ☐
3. Leaves give out oxygen through the veins. ☐
4. In a food chain, one organism is the food for another organism. ☐

E Give one word for each of the following.

1. The flat, broad part of the leaf ____________________
2. The pigment that helps in absorbing sunlight ____________________
3. The form in which extra food is stored in plant parts ____________________
4. A gas which is the product of photosynthesis ____________________

F Answer the following questions briefly.

1. What is the function of veins in a leaf?
2. How do stomata help a leaf?
3. What is photosynthesis?
4. What is a food chain? Give your own example of a food chain.

G Answer the following questions.

1. Explain the parts of a leaf with the help of a labelled diagram.
2. Name the four things that the plants use to make food and the sources from which they get them.
3. Why is the interdependence of plants and animals important?

H HOTS (Higher Order Thinking Skills)

What would happen if you take a potted plant and lock it up inside a dark room for one week?
(Hint: Plants use light to prepare food)

I Complete the photosynthesis chart.

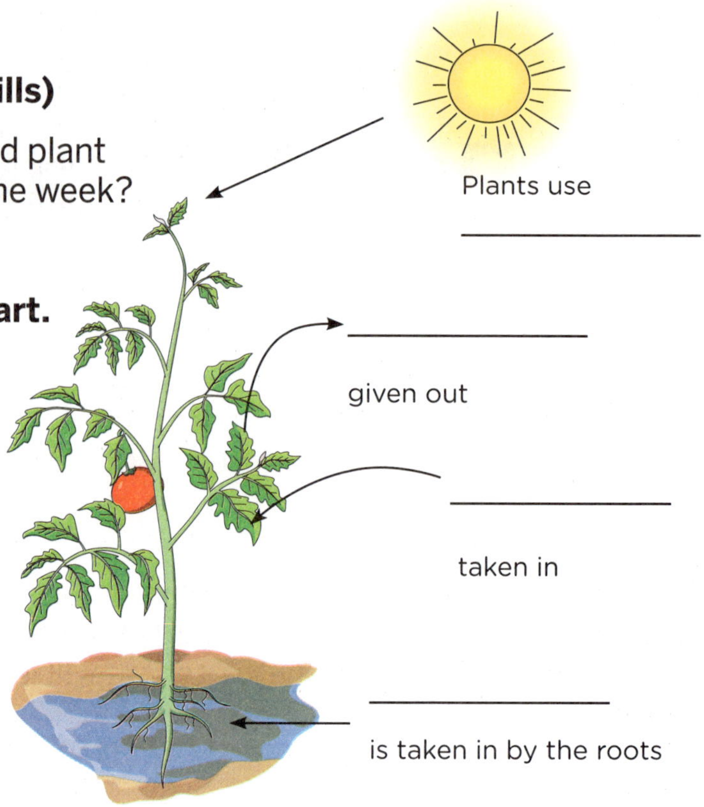

J Life Skills

Read the story of the tree and the woodcutter.

Based on the above story, give any five uses of tress.

K Project

Visit a green house or nursery in your city or town. Interact with the gardener and find out the names of any five plants grown there and their uses. Prepare a report on your findings; if possible, include pictures of those plants.

2 Plant Adaptations

Learning Checklist

- Plant adaptations—terrestrial, aquatic, insectivorous, non-green, parasitic

The place where an organism naturally lives is called its **habitat**. The changes undergone or the features acquired by an organism to adjust itself in a habitat are called **adaptations**. In this chapter, we will learn more about different adaptations shown by plants.

PLANT ADAPTATIONS

We know that different kinds of plants grow in different places. These plants adapt certain features to survive in their habitat.

According to the habitat they grow in, plants can be grouped into two broad categories: aquatic plants and terrestrial plants.

Aquatic Plants

Plants that grow and live in water are called aquatic plants. The following figure shows the different types of aquatic plants.

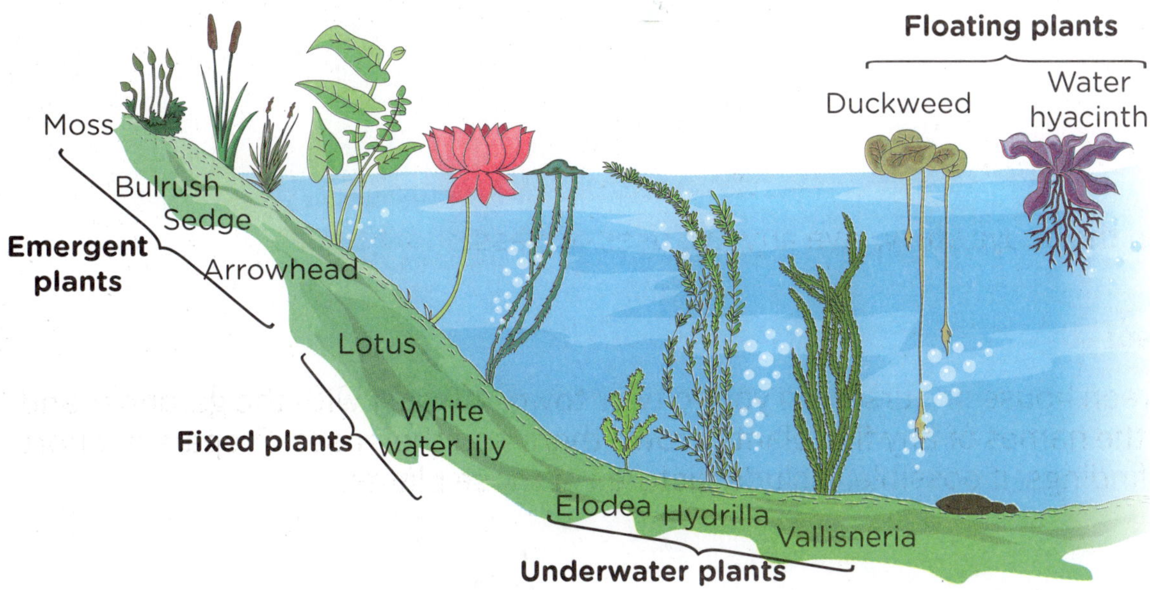

Floating Plants

Plants that float in water are called floating plants. Examples are duckweed, water lettuce and water hyacinth. These plants float in water because either they have air filled inside their stems, for example water hyacinth, or they are very small and light weight, for example duckweed. The roots absorb the nutrients directly from the water.

Duckweed

Fixed Plants

These plants are fixed to the waterbed with the help of strong roots. Hence, they are called fixed plants. Examples are the lotus and water lily. They have thin, long stalks[1] that are hollow inside and light in weight. This keeps the flowers and leaves floating on the surface of the water. The leaves of these plants have a waxy coating that prevents the water from getting into the plant. The leaves have stomata on the upper side instead of the lower side. These plants absorb nutrients from the soil in the waterbeds through their roots.

Lotus

Underwater Plants

These plants grow and remain completely submerged[2] into the water. They are also called submerged plants. Examples are *Hydrilla*, *Vallisneria* and pondweed. They have thin, narrow, ribbon-like leaves to prevent them from getting torn by the force of water currents.

Their leaves do not have stomata but take in carbon dioxide from the water through their body surface. These plants do not bear flowers. They get nutrients through the roots from the soil in the waterbeds. Underwater plants support animal life to a great extent because they give out oxygen during photosynthesis which keeps the animals alive.

Vallisneria

Emergent Plants

Some water plants are called emergent plants because even when their roots are fixed into the soil of the shallow waterbed, their leaves and stem extend out on to the surface of the water body they are growing in. Examples of emergent plants are the bulrush, cattail, arrowhead and sedges.

Bulrush

Sedges

Word Web

[1]**Stalk**: a thin stem that supports the leaves and flowers of a plant
[2]**Submerged**: growing beneath the surface of water

Revise and recall

FA

State whether the following statements are true (T) or false (F).

1. Water lettuce floats on water. ☐
2. Sedges are fixed in water and hence called fixed plants. ☐
3. Fixed plants have stomata on the upper surface of leaves, which helps the plants in breathing. ☐
4. Duckweed is an example of emergent plant. ☐

Terrestrial Plants

Plants that grow on land are called terrestrial plants. Terrestrial plants grow in deserts[1], mountains[2] and plains[3]. Let us study the different types of terrestrial plants and their adaptations:

Word Web

[1]**Deserts**: dry lands that get very little rainfall

[2]**Mountains**: lands that are raised higher than hills

[3]**Plains**: large areas of flat land

[4]**Spines**: sharp-pointed structures on a plant

Plants in Deserts

Desert plants are also called **xerophytes**. They are adapted to grow in very hot and dry conditions. Examples of plants that grow in deserts are cactus and date palms. The following adaptations of desert plants help them to survive in such conditions:

(a) The stem of a cactus is thick and fleshy. This helps the plant to collect and store water, which is required to carry out photosynthesis.

(b) The leaves of these plants are reduced to spines[4]. Spines protect the plants and reduce water loss.

(c) These plants also have long roots that grow deep into the ground. They help in absorbing groundwater.

A cactus growing in a desert

Plants on Mountains and Hills

Plants on mountains and hills are adapted to grow in very cold temperatures. Examples of plants that grow on mountains and hills are pine trees and alpine plants. The following adaptations are seen in these plants:

(a) The trees are straight, tall and cone-shaped so that snow can easily slide off their branches.

(b) Their leaves have a waxy coating and are needle-shaped which helps to wade off the snow and prevent rotting of the plant.

(c) These plants have cones with seeds instead of flowers.

Pine tree

Plants in Plains

These plants are adapted to survive in varying climates of both hot and cold weather. Examples of plants that grow in plains are mango, banyan and teak. The following adaptations are seen in plants that grow on plains:

Mango tree

(a) They have many branches with plenty of leaves and flowers.
(b) They shed their leaves in autumn which grow back again during spring.

Plants in Marshy Areas

Marshy areas are places that have clayey and sticky soil with water covering their surface. The plants growing in such areas develop roots that emerge out from the surface of the marsh. These roots are called breathing roots and help the plants to breathe. Most of the plants that grow in marshy areas are called **mangroves**. Some examples are *Avicennia* and *Rhizophora*.

Mangroves

Plants in Forests

Forests usually have warm climates and get a lot of rain throughout the year. The plants that grow in forests grow tall with broad and abundant leaves which can capture the sunlight for photosynthesis and produce abundant food for themselves and for the animals to feed on. The leaves have waxy surface and pointed tips which help the rain to drain off from the leaves onto the ground. Examples of plants that grow in forest are pineapple, banana and coconut.

Forest

Insectivorous Plants

Some plants live in a habitat where the soil is poor in nutrients, or in thick forests where enough sunlight is not available to carry out photosynthesis. These plants feed on small insects for nutrition. Such plants are called insectivorous plants. Some examples are pitcher plant and Venus flytrap.

Venus flytrap

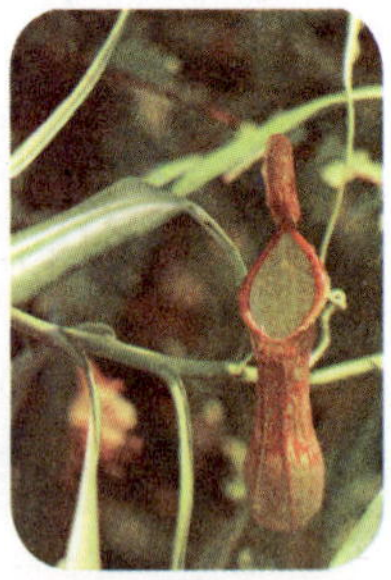

Pitcher plant

Insectivorous plants show unique features that help them to catch their prey. The venus flytrap has two lobes with hair-like spikes on their edges. These lobes snap shut when an insect sits on it. The pitcher plant is shaped like a pitcher. Its edges secrete a slippery substance due to which the insects sitting on it slip and fall inside the pitcher, thus getting trapped.

Non-green Plants

Some plants do not contain the green pigment called chlorophyll, and hence cannot carry out photosynthesis. These plants are called non-green plants. These plants are adapted to absorb their food from dead plants and animals. Examples are coralroot and Indian pipe.

Indian pipe

Know the Fact!

There are about 600 types of carnivorous plants found all over the world except in Antarctica.

Parasitic Plants

There are certain plants which grow on other plants and absorb nutrients from them. These plants are unable to obtain nutrients from the soil. Such plants are called parasitic plants. They often harm the plant on which they grow. Examples are *Cuscuta* and mistletoe.

Cuscuta

Revise and recall

FA

Write an example for each of the following.

1. Desert plant __________
2. Mountain plant __________
3. Plant in plains __________
4. Marshy plant __________
5. Insectivorous plant __________

Keywords

Adaptation: An organism developing special features to adjust to the surroundings in which it lives and grows

Aquatic plants: Plants that grow in water

Terrestrial plants: Plants that grow on land
Breathing roots: The roots, developed by the plants growing in marshy land, which emerge from the soil
Xerophytes: Plants that grow in the deserts
Insectivorous plants: Plants that trap insects for obtaining nutrients
Parasitic plants: Plant which grow on other plants and absorb nutrients from the parent plant

Summary

1. Plants adapt themselves to their habitat in order to grow and keep themselves alive.
2. Aquatic plants adapt themselves by developing special features to either float or stay completely under the water.
3. Terrestrial plants are found in plains, mountains, deserts, marshy areas and forests.
4. Insectivorous plants and non-green plants are also terrestrial plants and they are adapted to the surroundings in which they live.
5. Plants that grow on other plants and absorb nutrients from them are called parasitic plants.

EXERCISE

A Choose the correct option for each of the following.

1. Plant that floats in water is
   (a) Duckweed (b) Pondweed (c) Water lily (d) Hydrilla
2. Which of the following is a xerophyte?
   (a) Cactus (b) Teak (c) Palm (d) All of them
3. Plants that are adapted to grow in deserts have
   (a) Spines (b) Thin stem (c) Short roots (d) All of them
4. An example of a non-green plant is
   (a) Pineapple (b) Cuscuta (c) Venus flytrap (d) Neem

B Fill in the blanks with the correct words.

1. Arrowhead is an example of ________________ plant. (floating/emergent)
2. Coralroot is a ________________ plant. (parasitic/non-green)
3. Mangroves grow in ________________ . (deserts/marshy areas)
4. Non-green plants do not have ________________ . (chlorophyll/stems)

C Match the following.

Column A	Column B
(a) Cactus	(i) Mountain plant
(b) Pines	(ii) Insectivorous plant
(c) Indian pipe	(iii) Desert plant
(d) Pitcher plant	(iv) Non-green plant

D State whether the following statements ar true (T) or false (F).

1. Water lily is a floating plant. ☐
2. Terrestrial plants can grow both on land and in water. ☐
3. Desert plants are called xerophytes. ☐
4. The leaves of forest plants have waxy surfaces and pointed tips. ☐
5. All non-green plants need not be carnivorous. ☐

E Name the following.

1. Plants having cones with seeds instead of flowers ____________
2. Plants that obtain nutrients from insects ____________
3. Plants that remain completely submerged in water ____________
4. Plants that absorb food from dead plants and animals ____________

F Answer the following questions briefly.

1. What is adaptation?
2. Give two adaptations of underwater plants.
3. Give two examples of emerging plants and parasitic plants.
4. Why do desert plants have thick stems?
5. Non-green plants cannot carry out photosynthesis. Why?

G Answer the following questions.

1. What are the types of aquatic plants? Give one example for each.
2. List any four types of terrestrial plants and give one adaptation of each type.
3. Explain the adaptations shown by mountain plants.
4. List three features that would make a plant live in a forest.
5. What are insectivorous plants? Explain with examples.

H HOTS (Higher Order Thinking Skills)

A plant with broad leaves will not survive in a desert. Do you think this statement is correct? Explain. (Hint: Role of spines)

I Match the adaptation to the plant type. One has been done for you.

These plants are adapted to live in very cold places.

These plants trap insects to get nutrients.

These plants are adapted to grow their roots above the ground to help in breathing.

These plants are fixed to the soil but their leaves float on the surface of water.

These plants can live in very dry places as they have long roots to absorb water from deep under the Earth.

These plants grow in shallow waters but their leaves and stems are found growing out into the air.

FA

J Life Skills

Plants give us oxygen to breathe. We cannot live without oxygen. We can take care of plants and save them from dying by taking small steps mentioned below:

1. We know that paper is made from plants. So do not waste paper and reuse it whenever possible. Always use both sides of the paper.
2. Whenever you go out to play in a park, do not pluck leaves or pull them out. Stop others also if they are doing so. The leaves of many plants are home to insects, birds and small animals.

FA

K Project

Find out the different types of forests and the places where they are found. Refer to the books in your school library or use the Internet to get the information. Write the special features of a few plants that are adapted to grow there.

FA

L Fun Activity (Cross-curricular)

Write a letter to the forest authority telling them the benefits of plants and trees, so that they do not allow cutting down of trees in the future.

3 Animals and Their Young Ones

Learning Checklist

- Animals that lay eggs
- Animals that give birth to babies

One of the characteristics of living things is that they produce young ones of their own kind. This process is called reproduction. Some animals lay eggs from which their young ones hatch, whereas other animals give birth to their young ones directly without laying eggs. Let us learn more about how animals reproduce.

ANIMALS THAT LAY EGGS

The animals that reproduce by laying eggs are called **egg-laying animals**. Examples are birds, frog, fish, snake, lizard and insects like cockroach and butterfly.

The eggs are kept in a warm place or the parent animals sit on their eggs to keep them warm. This is known as **incubation**.

Birds

Birds lay eggs in their nests and incubate the eggs by sitting on them until the eggs hatch into young ones. The eggs then hatch and chicks come out. They cannot fly as they are featherless and cannot see. Their parents help them in feeding and take care of them until they develop feathers and learn to fly.

Structure of an egg

Eggs produced by all the birds have the same kind of internal structure. The thin, hard outer layer of the egg that protects the contents of the egg is called the **egg shell**. The jelly-like white coloured substance that is present inside the egg shell is called the **albumen**. The yellow-coloured substance present within the albumen is called the **yolk**.

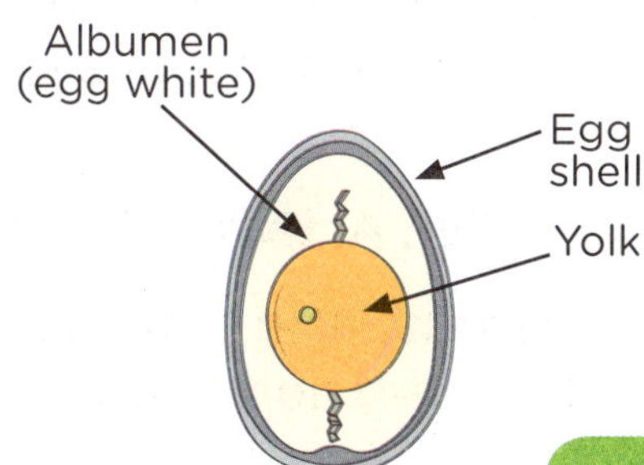

The yolk consists of the essential nutrients required for the development of a growing baby called an **embryo**. The embryo ultimately develops into a young one.

The different stages of the development of an embryo into an adult are called the **life cycle** of an animal.

Life cycle of a hen

Science in Context

Yolk is rich in nutrients like fats, minerals and vitamins, whereas albumen is rich in proteins.

Fish

Fish lay plenty of eggs in the water at a time. Out of these eggs, only a few develop into baby fish as some of the eggs get eaten by larger fish and other animals. Generally, these eggs obtain warmth for incubation from the sunrays.

Frogs

Life cycle of a frog

Like fish, frogs also lay a large number of eggs in the water. These eggs appear as large clusters of jelly-like substance known as **spawn**. The young ones that hatch from these eggs are called **tadpoles**. Tadpoles look very different from the adult frog. The process of the transformation of a young one into an adult which looks completely different is called **metamorphosis**. After undergoing metamorphosis, the tadpole becomes an adult frog.

Butterfly

Butterflies lay their eggs on leaves. A small worm-like larva called **caterpillar** hatches from the eggs. The larva grows in size by eating the leaves of the plants and develops a protective covering around itself. This form is known as **pupa**. The pupa sheds its old skin many times. This process of shedding old skin is called **moulting**. Finally, the adult butterfly comes out from the pupa.

Life cycle of a butterfly

Grasshoppers and Cockroaches

The life cycle of cockroaches and grasshoppers involves three main stages. The tiny larvae that hatch from the eggs are called **nymph**. The nymphs closely resemble their parent. The nymph undergoes moulting several times and eventually develops into an adult.

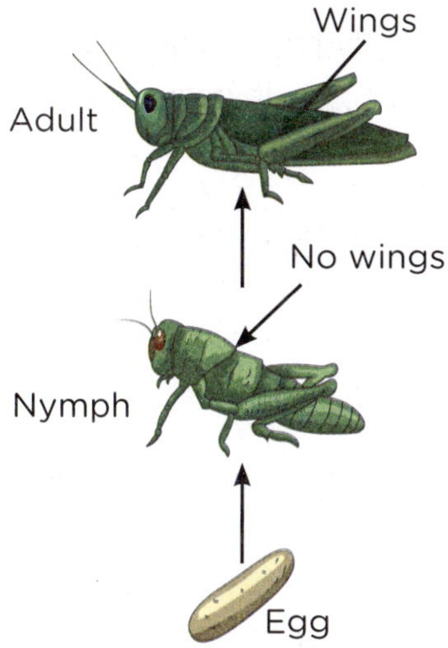

Life cycle of a grasshopper

Reptiles

Reptiles such as snakes and lizards lay their eggs on the ground. Out of these eggs, only a few develop into adults with the help of the sun's rays that provide warmth to these eggs. Some of the eggs are eaten by other animals.

Revise and recall

FA

State whether the following statements are true (T) or false (F).

1. Lizards reproduce by laying eggs. ☐
2. The eggs produced by all the birds have the same kind of internal structure. ☐
3. Fish lay only one egg in water at a time. ☐
4. The young ones produced from the eggs of frogs are referred to as pupa. ☐

ANIMALS THAT GIVE BIRTH TO BABIES

Animals that give birth to their young ones and suckle[1] them with milk are called **mammals**. Dogs, cats, cows, monkeys, rabbits, elephants, kangaroos, giraffes, lions and human beings are examples of mammals.

The complete development of the young ones takes place inside the mother's body. The mother feeds the young ones with her milk after they are born.

Mammals have a well-developed brain. They have hair on their body and most of them live on land. They breathe through their lungs.

Word Web

[1]**Suckle**: feed young ones with one's own milk

Cow with its calf

Some mammals such as dolphins and whales live in water. They are called **aquatic mammals**. They do not have hair on their body. They breathe through lungs and often come up to the water surface to breathe in air.

Know the Fact!

Blue Whale is the largest mammal.

Dolphin: An aquatic mammal

MAMMALS CARE FOR THEIR YOUNG ONES

Mammals take care of their young ones for a long time. They keep their babies clean and warm. They feed their babies and protect them from enemies. Most fish, reptiles and insects do not take care of their young ones. They lay their eggs in a safe place and leave the young ones to live on their own.

Mammals care for their young ones

Wonder!

The *Tilapia* fish carries its eggs in its mouth until they hatch. The small fish hide in the parent's mouth when faced with danger.

Revise and recall

State whether the following statements are true (T) or false (F).

1. In mammals, the complete development of the young ones takes place inside the mother's body. ☐
2. Mammals do not have well-developed brains. ☐
3. All mammals have hair on their body. ☐
4. Human beings do not take care of their young ones. ☐

FA

Keywords

Incubation: The period of time when animals sit on their eggs to keep them warm
Metamorphosis: The transformation of a young one into an adult which looks completely different
Spawn: A cluster of eggs laid by a frog
Nymph: Larva of grasshoppers and cockroaches
Caterpillar: The larval stage of a butterfly
Moulting: The process of shedding of old skin by animals
Mammals: Animals that give birth to their young ones and suckle them with milk

Summary

1. Living organisms produce young ones by the process of reproduction.
2. Some animals lay eggs. Young ones come out when the eggs hatch.
3. Eggs of all the birds contain the egg shell, albumen and yolk.
4. The transformation of a young one into an adult which looks completely different is called metamorphosis.
5. The shedding of old skin by some insects to develop into an adult is called moulting.
6. Animals that give birth to young ones and suckle them with milk are called mammals.

EXERCISE

A Choose the correct option for each of the following.

1. Identify the animal that does not reproduce by laying eggs.
   (a) Housefly (b) Deer (c) Butterfly (d) Fish
2. The jelly-like white-coloured substance that is present inside the egg is
   (a) Albumen (b) Yolk (c) Egg shell (d) Embryo
3. The process of shedding of old skin by the animals is called
   (a) Incubation (b) Metamorphosis (c) Moulting (d) Life cycle
4. Identify the egg-laying animal from the following.
   (a) Hippopotamus (b) Zebra (c) Frog (d) Cat

B Fill in the blanks with the correct words.

1. Birds reproduce by ____________ . (laying eggs/giving birth to their young ones)
2. The large cluster of frog's eggs is called ______________ . (spawn/nymph)
3. Lizards lay their eggs ______________ . (in water/on the ground)
4. ____________ (Mammals/Insects) suckle their young ones with milk.

C Match the following.

Column A	Column B
(a) Butterfly	(i) Tadpole
(b) Hen	(ii) Caterpillar
(c) Frog	(iii) Chick
(d) Grasshopper	(iv) Nymph

D State whether the following statements are true (T) or false (F).

1. Reproduction helps the organisms to maintain their own kind on Earth. ☐
2. Yolk is the yellow-coloured substance that is present inside the egg. ☐
3. Mammals like dolphins come out from the surface of water to breathe in air. ☐
4. The larval form of frogs is called the spawn. ☐

E Give two examples for each of the following:

1. Egg-laying animals
2. Animals that give birth to their young ones
3. Aquatic mammals
4. Animals that lay eggs in water

F Answer the following questions briefly.

1. Define reproduction.
2. What is incubation?
3. What is metamorphosis?
4. How do animals take care of their young ones?

G Answer the following questions.

1. Describe the structure of an egg with the help of a diagram.
2. Describe the process of metamorphosis in a frog.
3. Define aquatic mammals and mention their specific features.

H Look at the pictures given below. Name each stage that belongs to the life cycle of a frog.

____

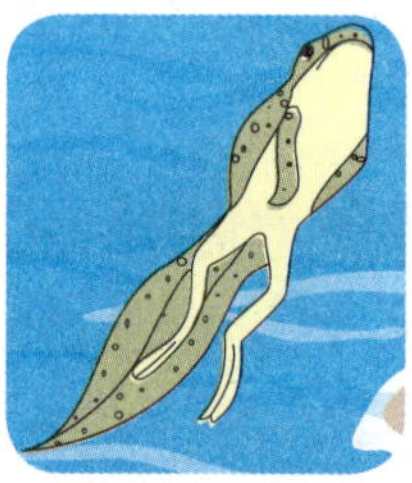
____

____

I HOTS (Higher Order Thinking Skills)

A dolphin lives in water but does not have gills like other fish. Why? (Hint: Dolphin is an aquatic mammal.)

J Project

FA

Collect pictures of various animals from old newspapers and magazines. Group them as egg-laying animals and the animals that give birth to their young ones. Paste these pictures in a scrapbook. Display your scrapbook in the classroom.

4 Animal Adaptations

Learning Checklist

- Adaptations to environment
- Adaptations for food
- Adaptations for protection
- Extinct and endangered animals

Like plants, animals also undergo changes over a period of time to adapt to their surroundings. Let us learn about the adaptations of different animals in detail in this chapter.

ADAPTATIONS TO ENVIRONMENT

Based on the environment in which they live, animals are grouped as terrestrial, aquatic, aerial and arboreal.

Terrestrial Animals

Polar bear

Animals that live on land are called **terrestrial animals**. The climatic conditions on land vary from place to place. Polar regions are extremely cold.

To protect themselves from cold animals like polar bears, Arctic foxes, penguins, seals and walruses live there and have a thick layer of fat under the skin called **blubber**.

Yak

Due to the scarcity of food during cold periods, animals like bear, frog and snake prefer to sleep throughout the winter and remain inactive. This long winter sleep is called **hibernation**.

Mountains are also very cold. Animals that live on mountains such as the mountain sheep, mountain goats and yaks have thick fur on their body which keeps them warm during cold weather. These animals have strong hooves[1] that help them to walk on the slopes of mountains.

Word Web

[1]**Hooves**: the hard covering present in the foot of some animals

Deserts are usually very hot. Animals that live in deserts such as camels have less hair on their body and have thick skin. This helps to prevent water loss from their body.

Camel

Some animals like snails, lizards and earthworms sleep for a long time during summer months to escape the heat. This long summer sleep is called **aestivation**.

Aquatic Animals

Animals that live in water are called aquatic animals. Fish, whale, turtle and octopus are a few examples of aquatic animals. Fishes have fins, whales and turtles have paddle-like flippers that help them in swimming. Most aquatic animals respire through gills.

Whale

Turtle

Amphibians

Animals such as frog and salamander that can live both in water and on land are called amphibians. Most amphibians have lungs that help them to breathe on land and moist skin that helps them to breathe underwater. Frogs have well-developed, strong hind limbs which help them to hop on land and webbed feet to help them swim in water.

Frog

Aerial Animals

Animals that can fly are called aerial animals. Birds are examples of aerial animals. The hollow bones, boat-shaped body, wings and feathers help the birds to fly in the air easily. Bats are the only mammals that can fly. Insects such as butterflies and dragonflies have thin papery wings which help them to fly.

Bird

Arboreal Animals

Animals that spend a majority of their time on trees are called arboreal animals. Monkeys, squirrels, tree lizards and koala bears are examples of arboreal animals. These animals have strong limbs and sharp claws that help them in climbing the trees. The tail of monkeys helps them to hang on the branches of trees.

Koala bear

ADAPTATIONS FOR FOOD

Based on the type of food that they eat, animals are grouped into the following categories:

Herbivores

Deer

Animals that eat only plants are called herbivores. These animals have strong and broad teeth in the front to bite off the leaves and grass, and strong chewing teeth with space in between them (for grinding) at the back. They are able to travel long distances with the help of their long and strong legs in search of food.

Carnivores

Tiger eating flesh

Animals that eat the flesh of other animals are called carnivores. These animals have pointed, sharp, long and curved canines to tear the flesh of their prey. Carnivores chew the flesh and bones with the help of broad and flat grinding teeth present at the back of their mouth.

Omnivores

Crow

Animals such as bears, crows and human beings eat both plants and the flesh of other animals. They are called omnivores.

Scavengers

Hyena

Vultures, jackals, wild dogs and hyenas feed on the remains of dead animals. These animals are called scavengers.

Parasites

Organisms that live on or inside the body of other living organisms and depend on them for food are called **parasites**. The animal on which the parasite depends for nutrition is called the **host**. Roundworms, hookworms and tapeworms live inside the body of the host.

Roundworm

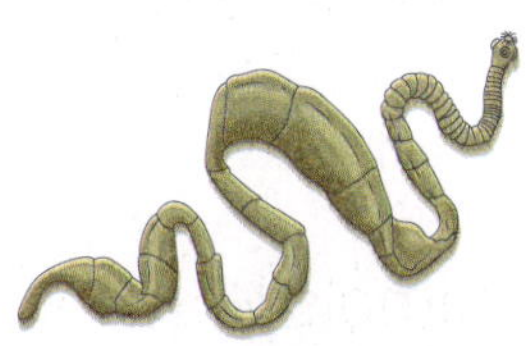

Tapeworm

Lice (singular: louse), ticks and fleas live on the surface of the host's body. The mouth of these organisms is adapted to suck blood from the host's body.

Louse

Flea

ADAPTATIONS FOR PROTECTION

Animals show different types of adaptations to protect themselves from danger.

(a) Rabbits, deer, fishes and mice can move very fast to protect themselves from their enemies and danger.

(b) The thick skin of elephants and hippopotamus helps in protecting them from the hot climate.

(c) Insects like cockroaches have a hard outer body covering for protection.

(d) The hard shell of crabs and turtles protects their soft bodies from getting damaged and from danger.

(e) The sharp spines of porcupines protect them from their enemies.

The characteristics of animals (colour and shape) that help them to mix or merge with their surroundings are called **camouflage**. Most animals escape from their enemies or catch their prey by camouflaging themselves.

(a) Polar bears have white fur which merges with snow. Thus, it gets difficult to detect a polar bear and hence keeps them safe.

(b) Tigers have black stripes over an orange-coloured body which helps them to blend with the forest or the grassland.

(c) Some insects have the structure of the leaves (leaf insect) or a twig (stick insect) so that they can hide from their enemies.

(d) Chameleons can change colours to match themselves according to their surroundings.

Porcupine

Leaf Insect

Stick Insect

Chameleon

EXTINCT AND ENDANGERED ANIMALS

Animals such as dodos, passenger pigeons, Caribbean monk seals, and Tecopa pupfish are some of the species that are no longer found on Earth. These animals are called **extinct animals**.

Animals which are unable to adapt to their surroundings die and eventually become extinct. Millions of years ago, huge animals called dinosaurs lived on Earth. When it became very cold on Earth, they were not able to adjust to the cold climate and became extinct. That is why we do not see dinosaurs today.

Dodo

Indian rhinoceros

Many animals are in threat due to the destruction of forests by humans for their needs. The numbers of some animals such as tigers, cheetahs, giant pandas and Indian rhinoceros are fast declining and they may soon disappear. These animals that are in danger of disappearing from the Earth are called **endangered animals**.

Revise and recall

FA

State whether the following statements are true (T) or false (F).

1. Walrus is a terrestrial animal that lives in polar regions. ☐
2. Rabbit undergoes aestivation. ☐
3. Koala bear is an arboreal animal. ☐
4. Wolf is an omnivore. ☐
5. Roundworms live inside the body of the host. ☐

Keywords

Hibernation: The long sleep of animals during winter months
Aestivation: The long sleep of animals during summer months
Aerial animals: Animals that can fly and spend a majority of their time in the air
Arboreal animals: Animals that spend a majority of their time on the trees
Parasites: Animals that live on or inside other living organisms and depend on them for food
Camouflaging: The characteristics of animals (colour and shape) that help them to match with their surroundings in order to escape from their enemies or to catch their prey
Extinct animals: Animals that are no longer found on Earth
Endangered animals: Animals that are in danger of becoming extinct and may disappear soon

Summary

1. The features and habits that enable living organisms to live in their surroundings are called adaptations.
2. Based on their habitat, animals are grouped as terrestrial animals, aquatic animals,amphibians aerial animals and arboreal animals.
3. Based on the type of food that they eat, animals are grouped into herbivores, carnivores, omnivores, scavengers and parasites.
4. Animals protect themselves from enemies by adopting special features like fast movement, thick skin and camouflaging.
5. Many animals are in threat due to the destruction of forests.

EXERCISE

A Choose the correct option for each of the following.

1. Identify the animal that sleeps throughout the summer months.
   (a) Bear (b) Snail (c) Rabbit (d) Frog
2. The aquatic animals respire mostly through the
   (a) Skin (b) Lungs (c) Gills (d) Lungs and skin
3. Identify the parasite that lives on the host's body.
   (a) Roundworm (b) Hookworm (c) Lice (d) Tapeworm
4. Identify the animal that cannot protect itself by camouflaging.
   (a) Chameleon (b) Tiger (c) Hippopotamus (d) Polar bear

B Fill in the blanks with the correct words.

1. A polar bear has ______________ to keep it warm. (blubber/flesh)
2. Winter sleep is also called ______________. (hibernation/aestivation)
3. Eagle is an example of ______________. (aerial animal/arboreal animal)
4. Koala bear is ______________ animal. (an arboreal/a terrestrial)

C Match the following.

Column A	Column B
(a) Deer	(i) Aquatic animal
(b) Seal	(ii) Terrestrial animal
(c) Salamander	(iii) Amphibian
(d) Sparrow	(iv) Arboreal
(e) Flying squirrel	(v) Aerial

D State whether the following statements are true (T) or false (F).

1. All terrestrial animals undergo aestivation. ☐
2. The thick fur of the yak helps in protecting it from the cold weather. ☐
3. Insects such as butterflies have thin papery wings, which help them to fly. ☐
4. Amphibians breathe through lungs as well as moist skin. ☐
5. Bear is an example of herbivore. ☐

E Give two examples for each of the following.

1. Arboreal animals ______
2. Animals that undergo hibernation ______
3. Animals that eat the flesh of other animals ______
4. Scavengers ______

F Answer the following questions briefly.

1. Why do some animals undergo hibernation?
2. Mention the adaptations shown by arboreal animals.
3. Distinguish between parasites and scavengers.
4. How are extinct animals different from endangered animals?

G Answer the following questions.

1. Define adaptation and explain how it is helpful for the animals.
2. Describe in brief about the various adaptations of terrestrial animals.
3. Explain the grouping of animals according to their adaptations to their habitats.
4. Describe in brief about the grouping of animals according to their feeding habits.
5. Describe various adaptations by the animals for their protection.

H HOTS (Higher Order Thinking Skills)

How is a camel different from yak even though both are terrestrial animals?
(Hint: Recall about various adaptations of terrestrial animals)

I Look at the pictures shown below and circle the odd one out. Give a reason for your selection.

______

J Project

FA

Collect pictures of various animals from old newspapers and magazines. Group them according to their habitat as terrestrial, aquatic, amphibians, aerial and arboreal animals and paste these pictures in a scrapbook. Write a few lines about the adaptations shown by the animals in each habitat. Display your scrapbook in the classroom.

5 Food: Our Basic Need

Learning Checklist

- Food groups and balanced diet
- Preservation of food
- Rest, posture and exercise

WHY DO WE NEED FOOD?

In our day-to-day lives we do many activities such as going to school, studying, playing, going for a walk, dancing, swimming, etc. To do all these activities, we need a lot of energy.

Food gives us the energy to do our everyday activities. We should eat healthy food in order to stay fit.

FOOD GROUPS

Substances present in food which help the body to grow, stay healthy and become strong are called **nutrients**. The main nutrients found in food are carbohydrates, proteins, fats, vitamins and minerals. Food also contains roughage and water. Based on what nutrients the food contains, they are grouped into three food groups. The three food groups are energy-giving food, body-building food and protective food.

Carbohydrates

Carbohydrates are known as **energy-giving food**. There are two types of carbohydrates present in food—sugar and starch. Wheat, rice, potato and sweet potato contain starch. Food items such as pastries and bananas contain sugar.

Carbohydrates

People who do more physical work need more energy. Therefore, an athlete needs more carbohydrates in his diet than a person who sits and works in office all day.

Proteins

Proteins

Proteins help in the growth of body and repair of worn-out tissues and cells. They build our muscles too. They are known as **body-building food**. Growing children need more proteins than adults. Food items such as milk, cheese, egg, fish, meat and pulses are rich in proteins.

Fats

Fat is present in food items such as oil, butter, ghee, cream, cheese, paneer and nuts. Fats are also energy-giving food. The provide more energy than carbohydrates. Our body needs very little fat. Consumption of fat in excess is not good for health as they get stored in the body and increase the body weight.

Butter

Cream

Oil

Vitamins and Minerals

Fruits and vegetables

Our body requires vitamins and minerals in very small quantities. These are very important for us to stay healthy as they protect us from diseases. Hence, they are known as **protective food**.

Fresh fruits, leafy vegetables, cereals, milk are some important sources of vitamins.

Minerals such as iron and calcium are also required to keep our body healthy and strong. Calcium makes bones and teeth strong. Milk, curd, nuts are some of the calcium-rich foods. Lack of iron in our body makes us feel tired and weak. Green leafy vegetables, oranges, apples are some of the iron-rich foods. To get minerals, we should have vegetables, fruits, egg, fish, milk, salt and cereals.

Roughage and Water

Roughage is the fibre present in some green vegetables, fruits, cereals, etc. It cannot be digested and does not provide any nutrient to our body, but it helps in the movement of food through the intestines and in removal of wastes from the body.

Water is very important for our body. It helps in digestion and maintains the body temperature. Our body loses water through sweat, breath and urine. In order to compensate for this loss, we should drink plenty of water every day.

BALANCED DIET

A balanced diet is a meal that contains carbohydrates, proteins, fats, vitamins, minerals, water and fibre in the right proportion[1]. To stay healthy, we should always have a balanced diet[2].

Word Web

[1]**Proportion**: amount
[2]**Diet**: the kind of food that we eat

FA

Revise and recall

State whether the following statements are true (T) or false (F).

1. Carbohydrates are known as energy-giving food. ☐
2. Consumption of fat in excess is very good for health. ☐
3. Vitamins are known as body-building food. ☐
4. Roughage is the fibre present in the food. ☐
5. To stay healthy, we should not drink water. ☐

PRESERVATION OF FOOD

The process of treating food to prevent it from getting spoilt is called **preservation**. Following are some ways of preserving foods:

(a) **Refrigerating**: Keeping fruits, vegetables and cooked food in the fridge prevents them from getting spoilt.

(b) **Drying**: In this method, water is completely removed from the food item. One simple way is to keep the food item out in the open under the sun. For example, dates and raisins are preserved as dry fruits.

(c) **Canning**: The moisture in the air can spoil the food. Hence, food can be kept in airtight containers to prevent them from getting affected by moisture. For example, *rasgullas* and *jamuns*.

(d) **Pickling (using salt)**: Salt and oil forms a concentrated solution in which germs cannot live. It is a good method of preserving pickles (e.g., mango or chilly pickle).

(e) **Jellying (using sugar)**: Keeping fruits/vegetables in sugar syrups is one of the ways of preserving food (e.g., mixed fruit jam).

Refrigerating

Drying

Canning

Pickling

Jellying

REST, POSTURE AND EXERCISE

In addition to a balanced diet, sufficient amount of rest, a good posture and regular exercise are essential to stay healthy.

Rest

Rest is very important for the body. We need at least 6 to 8 hours of sleep in a day. Lack of sleep makes us feel tired and it can also make us fall sick.

Posture

Posture is the position in which we keep our body while standing, sitting or walking. Having the correct posture helps us in many ways:

(a) Our bones and joints are in line so that our muscles can be used properly.
(b) We do not get tired quickly and do not suffer from back and muscle pain.
(c) We look good.

Standing

Exercise

Regular exercise like running, walking, cycling and playing different sports helps us to keep fit and stay healthy. Nowadays, Yoga has also become a popular form of exercise. If we exercise regularly, then

(a) our bones and muscles get stronger.
(b) we sleep well and do not feel tired
(c) we have more energy to work.

Exercise

Keywords

Nutrients: Substances present in food which help the body to grow and stay healthy

Roughage: The fibre present in green vegetables, fruits and cereals

Balanced diet: A meal that contains carbohydrates, proteins, fats, vitamins, minerals, water and fibre in the right proportion

Preservation: The process of treating food to prevent it from getting spoilt

Summary

1. The main nutrients found in food items are carbohydrates, proteins, fats, vitamins, minerals, roughage and water.
2. Carbohydrates and fats provide us energy.
3. Proteins help in the growth and repair of our body parts.
4. Vitamins and minerals protect our body from diseases.
5. A balanced diet contains all the nutrients in the right proportion.

6. Treating food to prevent it from getting spoilt is called preservation.
7. Proper rest, good posture and exercise keeps us fit and healthy.

EXERCISE

A Choose the correct option for each of the following.

1. Which of these is essential for people who do more physical work?
   (a) Proteins (b) Carbohydrates (c) Fats (d) None of these
2. Proteins are also known as
   (a) Iron-rich food (b) Body-building food (c) Fibre-rich food (d) None of these
3. Drying is a method of preserving food by
   (a) Adding salt (b) Adding sugar (c) Removing water (d) Freezing
4. Posture refers to the body's
   (a) Position (b) Shape (c) Muscles (d) None of these

B Fill in the blanks with the correct words.

1. Food items which contain ________________ help us to grow and stay healthy. (nutrients/preservatives)
2. Food items that are rich in ________________ are called energy-giving foods. (carbohydrates/vitamins)
3. Roughage is the ________________ present in some green vegetables, fruits and cereals. (fibre/nutrient)
4. The process of treating food to prevent it from getting spoilt is called ________________. (balanced diet/preservation)

C Match the following.

Column A	Column B
(a) Carbohydrates	(i) Prevent diseases
(b) Fat	(ii) Makes food last longer
(c) Vitamins	(iii) Helps in formation of bones and teeth
(d) Preservation	(iv) Butter
(e) Calcium	(v) Potato and sweet potato

D Name the following.

1. The diet that contains all the nutrients in the right proportion ____________
2. Position of the body while standing or sitting ____________
3. The fibre present in some green vegetables, fruits and cereals ____________
4. Substances present in food which help the body to grow, stay healthy and become strong ____________

E Answer the following questions briefly.

1. What are carbohydrates?
2. Why do athletes need more carbohydrates than a person sitting in office?
3. What is the role of roughage?
4. Why is water essential in our diet?
5. What is a balanced diet?

F Answer the following questions.

1. Name the different food groups. Explain proteins and vitamins with examples.
2. Name the different ways of preserving food and give examples for each.
3. How does the correct posture help us?

G HOTS (Higher Order Thinking Skills)

1. Food does not get spoiled quickly in winter as compared to summer. Why? (Hint: High and low temperature)
2. Renu falls sick very often. Which food items would you suggest she eats to prevent her from falling sick? (Hint: What is the role of protective food?)

H Write B for body-building foods, E for energy-giving foods and P for protective foods.

 ☐  ☐  ☐  ☐

 ☐  ☐  ☐  ☐

6 Digestion of Food

Learning Checklist

- Care of teeth
- Digestive system
- Microbes

Teeth help us to bite and chew the food we eat. They also help us to speak. In this chapter, we will learn about the types of teeth, and how teeth and other organs in our body help in the breakdown of food.

TEETH

A new-born baby does not have any teeth, it starts developing teeth when it is six months old. This first set of teeth that are formed is called the **milk teeth**. Milk teeth are about 20 in number.

> **Science in Context**
>
> Some people have only 28 teeth in the permanent set of teeth. The remaining 4 teeth appear later during the age of 17–21 and are called **wisdom teeth**. Some people do not have wisdom teeth at all!

Between the age of 6 and 12, the milk teeth begin to fall off one by one. Hence, milk teeth are also called temporary teeth. New teeth start growing in their places. This second set of teeth is called **permanent teeth**. There are 32 permanent teeth in total, 16 in the upper jaw and 16 in the lower jaw. This set of teeth continues to last until old age.

Structure of Teeth

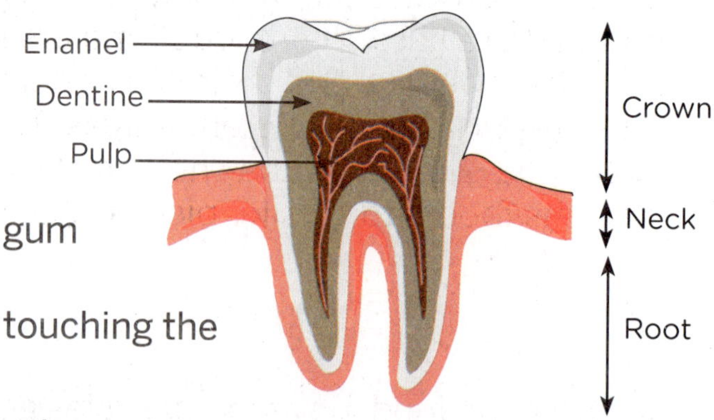

A tooth has three parts:

Crown: The visible part of the tooth above the gum is called the crown.

Neck: The part of the tooth below the crown touching the gums is the called the neck.

Root: The part of the tooth inside the gums is the root.

Enamel is the hard outer covering of the tooth which is white in colour. Enamel covers each tooth and is known to be the hardest part of our body.

There is another layer below the enamel called the **dentine**. Below the dentine lies the pulp. **Pulp** is the soft part of the tooth. It has blood vessels and nerves inside it which are connected to the gums through a hole in the root.

Types of Teeth

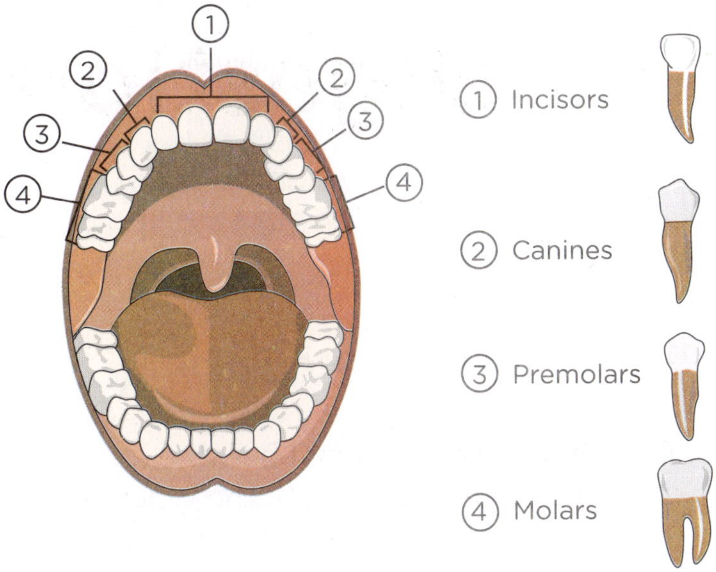

Teeth are mainly classified into four types based on their functions incisors, canines, premolars and molars.

Let us learn more about each type.

Incisors

These teeth help in cutting and biting off pieces of food. There are four incisors in the upper jaw and four in the lower jaw. They are placed in the front in both the jaws.

Canines

These teeth are seen on either side of the incisors in both the upper and lower jaws. They help in holding and tearing the food. There are a total of four canines, two in the upper and two in the lower jaw. Carnivores have canines which are longer and sharper as they are modified to tear raw flesh faster and with ease.

Premolars

These teeth help in crushing and grinding soft foods. There are four premolars each in the upper and lower jaws which are found next to the canines. These teeth are usually broader than other types of teeth.

Molars

These are the last teeth towards the end of the mouth which are used for chewing and grinding food that are hard. There are 12 molars in total, six in the lower jaw and six in the upper jaw. These teeth grow at different stages. They are bigger and broader as they help to chew and grind the food into smaller pieces easily.

Science in Context

Herbivores use incisors to bite off the leaves from plants and molars to grind the bitten off leaves.

CARE OF TEETH

When we eat food, tiny food particles get stuck to the teeth and also between them while chewing. If these food particles are not removed regularly, germs start growing in these areas. These germs first attack the enamel, then dentine and finally move into the pulp. There, the germs start attacking the nerves resulting in toothache as they spread to other nerves through the roots.

Here are a few ways by which you can keep your teeth clean and healthy:

1. Brush your teeth properly in the morning and at night before going to bed. Moving your toothbrush upwards and downwards in a circular motion is the proper way to brush your teeth.
2. Gargle[1] and rinse your mouth after every meal.
3. Use a mouthwash and dental floss[2], if possible.
4. Avoid eating too many candies and chocolates.
5. Eat lots of salads and fruits.
6. Drink milk and eat food items that are rich in calcium such as cheese, eggs, etc.
7. Visit a dentist[3] regularly to know how healthy your teeth are and get them treated, if required.

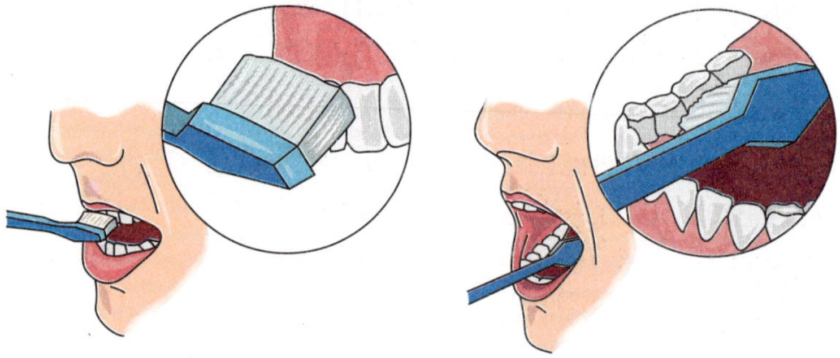

Teeth should be brushed properly to keep them healthy

Word Web

[1]**Gargle**: clean the mouth with water or a mouth freshener by moving it around inside the mouth

[2]**Dental floss**: a soft thread used for cleaning the spaces between the teeth

[3]**Dentist**: a person qualified to treat people suffering with tooth problems

FA

Revise and recall

Put a tick (✓) against the correct statements and cross (✗) against the wrong ones.

I can take care of my teeth by:

1. Brushing them only once a day. ☐
2. Eating only chocolates. ☐
3. Gargling my mouth after I eat every meal. ☐
4. Visiting the dentist only when I have toothache. ☐

DIGESTIVE SYSTEM

Our body gets energy from the food we eat. To get energy from the food, it has to be broken down into smaller substances which are easily absorbed by the body.

The process of breaking down of food into smaller particles which can be easily absorbed by the body is called **digestion**.

The organs that help in the process of digestion make up the digestive system. The figure given alongside shows the human digestive system.

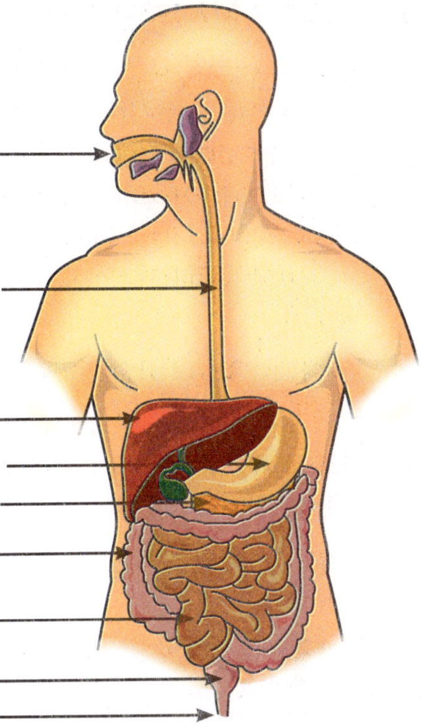

Human digestive system

Process of Digestion

Digestion of the food we eat starts in the **mouth**. The teeth bite and chew the food into smaller pieces.

Saliva is a digestive juice secreted in the mouth which mixes with the food and makes it soft and moist to make it easy to swallow. This is called the **bolus**. Food that contains starch, such as rice, is broken down into sugar by the saliva and hence tastes sweet.

The bolus then enters the **food pipe**. The food pipe moves by contracting and relaxing alternatively. This movement helps in pushing the food down into the **stomach**. The food stays in the stomach for many hours where some part of digestion takes place. Stomach produces acid and digestive juices that help to digest the food.

From the stomach, the remaining undigested food is pushed into a long coiled tube called the **small intestine**. Here the digestive juices produced by the small intestine, the **liver** and the **pancreas** mix with the food and digest it.

All the useful nutrients from the digested food get absorbed by the walls of the intestine. These nutrients are then absorbed by the blood vessels which carry them to different parts of the body.

The undigested food then enters the **large intestine** where the extra water and minerals are absorbed.

The remaining solid waste is stored in the **rectum** until it passes out from the body through the **anus**.

Science in Context

The rumbling sound in your stomach occurs when there is no food in the stomach and the stomach and intestines contract.

FA **Revise and recall**

Fill in the blanks using the names of the organs of the digestive system.

From the mouth, the food enters the ________________ and then passes into the ________________. From the stomach, the digested food then moves into a long coiled tube called the ________________. The food is completely digested as the juices of the ________________, ________________ and ________________ also mix with the food. The undigested food passes into the ________________ where the extra water and minerals are absorbed. The remaining solid waste is stored in the ________________ until it passes out of the body through the ________________.

MICROBES

Microbes are very tiny living things which cannot be seen with the naked eye. They can only be seen under a microscope[1]. They grow everywhere: on food, soil, standing water, inside and outside our body and even in animals.

Word Web

[1]**Microscope**: an instrument that makes very small objects appear big

Bacteria, viruses, fungi and protozoa are the main categories of microbes.

Bacteria

Bacteria (singular: bacterium) are made up of only one cell. They can be of different shapes such as rod shape, round or spiral.

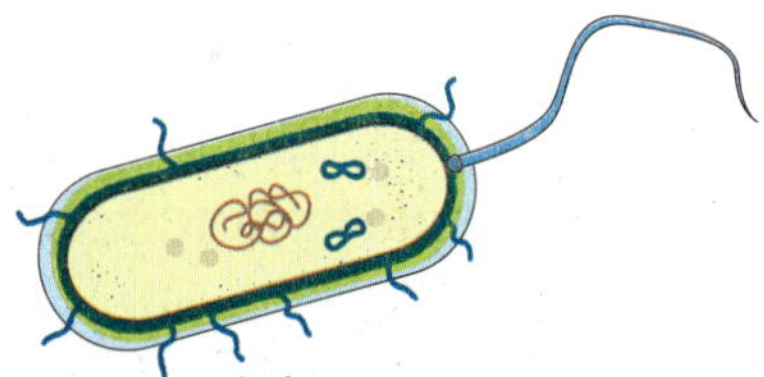

A bacterium

Viruses

Viruses are the smallest living things that can only be seen under a very powerful microscope.

A virus

Fungi

Fungi (singular: fungus) are the microbes that grow mainly on dead and decaying matter.

Protozoa

Protozoa (singular: protozoan) are single-celled microbes.

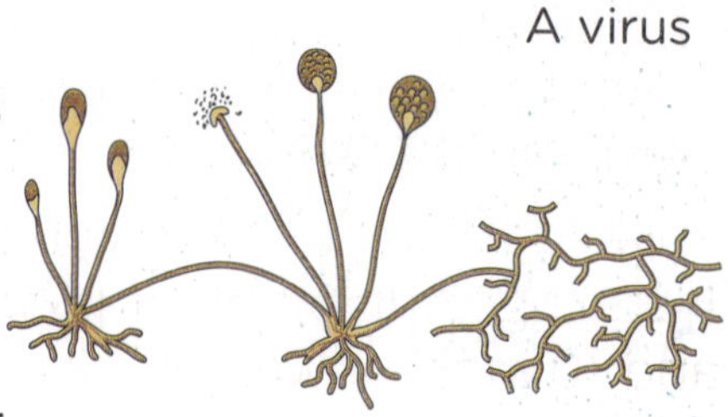

Fungi

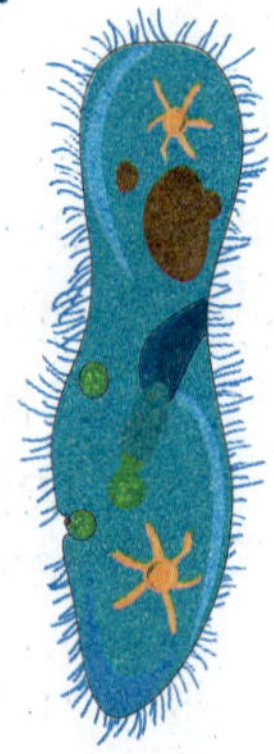

A protozoan

Some microbes are useful to us. Useful microbes help us in the following ways:

(a) Bacteria help in changing milk into curd.

(b) Bacteria and fungi help in breaking down the dead matter.

(c) Protozoa are used as soil fertilizers.

(d) Fungi like yeast help in making bread.

(e) Some bacteria help in digesting the food we eat.

(f) We obtain medicines from some bacteria and viruses.

Some microbes are harmful to us and cause diseases. These microbes are called **germs** or **pathogens**.

(a) Bacteria cause diseases such as typhoid, tetanus and cholera.

(b) Viruses cause diseases such as flu, chicken pox, dengue, mumps and even common cold.

(c) Fungi mainly cause skin diseases such as ringworm, candidiasis and athlete's foot.

(d) Protozoa cause diseases such as dysentery and malaria.

Keywords

Crown: The upper part of the tooth above the gum which is visible to us

Enamel: The white outer hardest substance of the teeth

Dentine: The part of the teeth found below the enamel

Pulp: The part of the teeth that has blood vessels and nerves

Digestion: The process of breaking down food into simpler substances so that it can be absorbed by the body

Digestive system: The organ system that helps to digest and absorb the food in our body

Microbes: Very small living things which are found everywhere and which can be seen only under a microscope

Summary

1. There are two sets of teeth in humans. They are the milk teeth and the permanent teeth.
2. The milk teeth fall off between the age of 6 and 12 and permanent teeth start growing in their place and forms 32 teeth; 16 in the upper jaw and 16 in the lower jaw.

3. Brushing, gargling, avoiding too many sweets and chocolates, eating healthy foods like salads, fruits and milk, and visiting a dentist regularly are some of the ways to take care of our teeth.
4. The organs of the digestive system are the mouth, food pipe, stomach, liver, pancreas, small intestine, large intestine, rectum and anus.
5. Microbes are very small living things that can only be seen under a microscope. The different types of microbes are bacteria, virus, fungi and protozoa.
6. Microbes can be harmful or useful. Harmful microbes cause diseases like cholera, typhoid, dengue, athlete's foot and many more. Useful microbes help in preparing different kind of food items, medicine, manure and many more things.

EXERCISE

A Choose the correct option for each of the following.

1. Toothache can be avoided by
   (a) Eating very little sweets (c) Eating lot of salads and drinking lots of milk
   (b) Brushing teeth regularly (d) All of these
2. The organ(s) of the digestive system
   (a) Pancreas (b) Large intestine (c) Liver (d) All of these
3. The tube that connects your mouth to your stomach
   (a) Liver (b) Food pipe (c) Intestine (d) Pancreas
4. The types of microbes are
   (a) Bacteria (b) Protozoa (c) Virus (d) All of these

B Fill in the blanks with the correct words.

1. There are ____________ teeth in the permanent set of teeth. (16/32)
2. The part of the tooth inside the gum is called the ____________. (crown/root)
3. From the stomach, the remaining undigested food is pushed into a long coiled tube called the ____________. (small intestine/large intestine)
4. ____________ grow mainly on dead and decaying matter. (Fungi/Bacteria)

C Match the following.

Column A	Column B
(a) Bacteria	(i) Common cold
(b) Useful microbe	(ii) Malaria
(c) Virus	(iii) Manure
(d) Protozoa	(iv) Typhoid

D State whether the following statements are true (T) or false (F).

1. Milk teeth are formed after the permanent teeth fall off. ☐
2. Digestion is breaking down of food into simpler substances. ☐
3. Saliva helps to digest our food. ☐
4. Microbes that cause diseases in living beings are called germs. ☐

E Answer the following in one word.

1. The first set of teeth that is formed ____________
2. The outer hard white covering of the tooth ____________
3. The process of breaking down food into simpler substances ____________
4. Small living things that can be seen only under a microscope ____________

F Answer the following questions briefly.

1. Name the parts of a tooth.
2. List the organs of the digestive system.
3. What is the function of the stomach in the digestive system?
4. What are the different types of microbes?

G Answer the following questions.

1. Describe the structure of a tooth with the help of a diagram.
2. List four ways by which you can take care of your teeth.
3. How are microbes useful to us?
4. Name one disease each caused by the four types of microbes.

H HOTS (Higher Order Thinking Skills)

Richa, who is 12 years old, has 14 teeth in her upper jaw. Her father, who is 40 years old, has 16 teeth in his upper jaw. Can you explain why? (Hint: What are wisdom teeth?)

ASSESSMENT 1

Chapters 1-3

(Maximum Marks = 25)

A Choose the correct option for each of the following. **(7 × 1 = 7)**

1. Which of the following is not required by the plants to prepare their food?
   (a) Sunlight (b) Water (c) Carbon dioxide (d) Oxygen
2. The part of a plant that holds or supports the leaf is:
   (a) Vein (b) Midrib (c) Petiole (d) Calyx
3. Which of the following animals reproduces by laying eggs?
   (a) Deer (b) Frog (c) Hippopotamus (d) Rabbit
4. The large cluster of eggs of a frog is referred as
   (a) Tadpole (b) Maggot (c) Nymph (d) Spawn
5. Duckweed, water lettuce and water hyacinth are examples of:
   (a) Desert plants (b) Plants grown on plains
   (c) Terrestrial plants (d) Floating plants
6. The area where mangrove plants grow is:
   (a) Marshy area (b) Clayey area (c) Sandy area (d) Desert area
7. Which among the following are called xerophytes?
   (a) Plants on mountains and hills (b) Plants in plains
   (c) Plants in deserts (d) Plants in forests

B State whether the following statements are true (T) or false (F) **(6 × 1 = 6)**

1. The major products of photosynthesis are carbon dioxide and oxygen. ☐
2. Interdependence of one organism on another for its food is called the food chain. ☐
3. Floating plants are able to float, as they do not have stem to fix themselves to the soil bed. ☐
4. Cattail is an emergent plant. ☐
5. Fish lay only one egg in water at a time. ☐
6. Non-green plants absorb their food from dead plants and animals. ☐

C Replace the underlined word in each of the following statements with the correct word. **(6 × 1 = 6)**

1. The midrib branches into smaller structures called <u>arteries</u>.
2. Animals that eat only plants are called <u>omnivores</u>.
3. Mango trees are an example of plants in <u>forests</u>.
4. The yellow-coloured substance that is present within the egg is <u>albumen</u>.
5. Egg-laying animals are also called <u>viviparous</u> animals.
6. <u>Dolphin</u> is the largest mammal.

D Answer each of the following questions in one word. **(6 × 1 = 6)**

1. Name the process of shedding of skin in some animals.
2. Name the process by which living organisms produce young ones of their own kind.
3. By which name do we know the tiny openings in the leaf through which carbon dioxide enters into a plant?

4. Which pigment in the green leaves helps in absorbing sunlight?
5. Which gas is released by the plants during the process of photosynthesis?
6. What is the process of keeping the eggs warm by the parent birds called?

ASSESSMENT 2

Chapters 4-6

(Maximum Marks = 25)

A Pick the odd one out from each of the following groups of words. (7 × 1 = 7)

1. Ticks, Tapeworm, Lice, Fleas
2. Crown, Neck, Root, Stem
3. Small intestine, Stomach, Blood, Saliva
4. Yogurt, Cheese, Tomato soup, Milk
5. Sapling, Canning, Jellying, Drying
6. Mouth, Food pipe, Stomach, Bolus
7. Wheat, Rice, Potato, Pulses

B Circle YES if the statement is correct and NO if the statement is wrong (6 × 1 = 6)

1. Penguin is a terrestrial animal that lives in Polar Regions. YES NO
2. Saliva makes the food soft and easy to swallow. YES NO
3. Liver and pancreas are not the part of digestive system. YES NO
4. Different foods contain different nutrients. YES NO
5. Resting for 5 hours a day is sufficient for a healthy life. YES NO
6. The diet that contains all the nutrients in the right proportion is called a balanced diet. YES NO

C Fill in the blanks with the correct words. (6 × 1 = 6)

1. The animals on which the parasite depends for nutrition is called the __________. (carnivore/host)
2. Animals that live in water are referred as __________ animals. (arboreal/aquatic)
3. The undigested food passes into the __________ where the extra water and minerals are absorbed. (large intestine/small intestine)
4. __________ are the microbes that grow on dead and decayed substances. (Fungi/ Virus)
5. The process of keeping the food safe without getting it spoilt is called __________. (balanced diet/preservation)
6. Our body loses water by __________. (eating/sweating)

D Answer each of the following questions in one word. (6 × 1 = 6)

1. What is the other name for winter sleep?
2. What is the term used for the animals that may disappear soon from the earth?
3. What is the other name for summer sleep?
4. Through which organ does the undigested food passes before it is passed out of the body?
5. Name the method of preserving food in sugar syrup.
6. What is the name of the very long coiled tube connected to the stomach, where digestion is completed?

COMPREHENSIVE ASSESSMENT

(Maximum Marks = 50)

A Answer the following questions in one word each. **(10 × 1 = 10)**

1. Name the process of keeping the food safe.
2. Which term describes a meal that contains all the nutrients in the right proportion?
3. What is the other name for aestivation?
4. What is the flat part of the leaf called?
5. Name the term used to describe the special features that allow a plant or animal to live in a particular place.
6. Name the time period during which animals protect their eggs until they hatch.
7. What is the visible part of the tooth called?
8. Name the set of teeth used to cut and bite the food.
9. What is the characteristic of animals that help them to merge with their surroundings?
10. In which stage of lifecycle in a butterfly does the larva form a protective covering around itself?

B In each question, two choices are correct. Identify the correct choices. **(9 × 2 = 18)**

1. Sameeksha has a fracture in her elbow. Which of the following food items does she need to have more in her diet to strengthen her bones?
   (a) Meat (b) Fish (c) Spinach (d) Milk
2. Identify the amphibians from the following.
   (a) Salamander (b) Bat (c) Frog (d) Camel
3. The midrib and veins help in
   (a) Transportation of substances (b) Photosynthesis
   (c) Giving support to the leaf (d) Storing food
4. Chlorophyll is necessary for
   (a) Photosynthesis (b) Preparing nectar
   (c) Imparting green colour (d) Attracting insects
5. Two categories of aquatic plants are:
   (a) Cacti (b) Floating plants (c) Insectivores plants (d) Fixed plants
6. Which of the following modifications are shown by desert plants?
   (a) Small roots (b) Spines (c) Large flowers (d) Thick stem
7. Identify the animals that do not reproduce by laying eggs.
   (a) Fish (b) Cow (c) Whale (d) Butterfly
8. Which of the following is not a stage in the lifecycle of a frog?
   (a) Young adult (b) Tadpoles (c) Pupa (d) Nymph
9. Which among the following are body-building food?
   (a) Butter (b) Meat (c) Fish (d) Oil

B Answer the following questions briefly **(2 × 3 = 6)**

1. Draw a neat labelled diagram of a tooth and label its parts.
2. Write a note on endangered and extinct species.

C Answer the following questions **(4 × 4 = 16)**

1. What are microorganisms? Explain their different types with examples.
2. List two insectivorous plants and explain their adaptations.
3. How are animals adapted to protect themselves?
4. Draw a food pyramid and explain the importance of a balanced diet.

SOCIAL STUDIES

1 Our Country India

I Know ...

- The capital of India is ....
- The southern part of India is a ....

FA Observe and Reflect

- Which continent does this map represent?
- How many water bodies surround India?
- Which water body is named after India?

India is the seventh largest country in the world and the third largest country in Asia. Located in the southern tip of Asia, it is surrounded by the Bay of Bengal on the east, the Arabian Sea on the west and the Indian Ocean on the south.

The countries that are located next to a particular country are known as its **neighbouring countries**. The neighbouring countries of India are Nepal, Bhutan, Pakistan, Bangladesh, Afghanistan, Sri Lanka, Maldives, China and Myanmar.

Afghanistan and Pakistan lie to the west of India. Sri Lanka and the Maldives lie to the south of India.

Find Out

Look at the world map. Find out the largest and the smallest country in Asia.

Fact Zone

Maldives is an **archipelago** in the Indian Ocean. It has 1190 coral islands.

Bangladesh, Nepal, Bhutan, Myanmar and China border its east.

Find Out

What is a subcontinent? Which countries make up the Indian subcontinent?

Political Divisions of India

Look at the political map of India. It represents the states and territories of India.

You already know that for the **convenience** of administration of the central government, India is divided into 29 states and seven union territories. The central government, called the Government of India, looks after the entire country, while the state governments look after their **respective** states. In India, the union territories are directly under the rule of the central government.

The city that is the base of all important government activities of a state is known as the **capital** of the state. The capital of a state is the seat of power of the state.

Look at the list of the 29 states and seven union territories with their respective capitals.

Political divisions of India

State	Capital
Andhra Pradesh	Hyderabad
Arunachal Pradesh	Itanagar
Assam	Dispur
Bihar	Patna

State	Capital
Manipur	Imphal
Meghalaya	Shillong
Mizoram	Aizawl
Nagaland	Kohima

State	Capital
Chhattisgarh	Raipur
Goa	Panaji
Gujarat	Gandhinagar
Haryana	Chandigarh
Himachal Pradesh	Shimla
Jammu and Kashmir	Srinagar and Jammu
Jharkhand	Ranchi
Karnataka	Bengaluru
Kerala	Thiruvananthapuram
Madhya Pradesh	Bhopal
Maharashtra	Mumbai

State	Capital
Odisha	Bhubaneshwar
Punjab	Chandigarh
Rajasthan	Jaipur
Sikkim	Gangtok
Tamil Nadu	Chennai
Telangana	Hyderabad
Tripura	Agartala
Uttar Pradesh	Lucknow
Uttarakhand	Dehradun
West Bengal	Kolkata

Union Territory	Capital
Andaman and Nicobar Islands	Port Blair
Chandigarh	Chandigarh
Dadra and Nagar Haveli	Silvassa

Union Territory	Capital
Daman and Diu	Daman
Lakshadweep	Kavaratti
Delhi – National Capital Territory	New Delhi
Puducherry	Puducherry

Do It Yourself

Look at the map and answer the questions.

1. When was this new state carved out?
2. The capital of this state is also the capital of the new state. Name the capital city.
3. Name the proposed new capital city of Andhra Pradesh.

Physical Features of India

When we look at the physical map of India, we see great diversity in the landforms in India.

Broadly, the six physical features of India are:

- The Northern Mountains
- The Northern Plains
- The Great Indian Desert
- The Southern Plateau
- The Coastal Plains
- The Islands

Eco Zone

New Delhi, India's capital city, is one of the most polluted cities in the world. What steps can we take to prevent pollution?

Physical features of India

Remember

- Pakistan, Afghanistan, Maldives, Myanmar, Bhutan, Nepal, Bangladesh and Sri Lanka are the neighbouring countries of India.
- India is divided into 29 states and seven union territories.
- India has six physical divisions.

Words Zone

archipelago: a group of islands and the sea surrounding it

convenience: something that can be done with ease

respective: each

Review Zone

A Fill in the blanks with the correct answers.

1. Pakistan lies to the .... of India.
   a. west   b. east   c. north
2. The south-east and south-west of India are bordered by the ....
   a. Coastal Plains   b. Northern Mountains   c. Southern Plateau
3. .... is the capital of Himachal Pradesh.
   a. Kolkata   b. Shimla   c. Gangtok
4. Chandigarh is the capital of ....
   a. Haryana   b. Bihar   c. Assam
5. The Great Indian Desert region consists of the state of ....
   a. Maharashtra   b. Rajasthan   c. Punjab

B Write T for True and F for False.

1. Sri Lanka is one of India's neighbours. ☐
2. West Bengal has two capitals. ☐
3. The Andaman and Nicobar Islands are administered by their own state government. ☐
4. Hyderabad is the capital of Telangana. ☐
5. The Great Indian Desert is located in the north-east of India. ☐

C Answer these questions in brief.

1. Name all the neighbouring countries of India.
2. India is divided into how many states and union territories.
3. Name the capitals of any three southern states of India.
4. State the capitals of three north-eastern states of India.
5. Who looks after the administration of the union territories?

D **Read the capital cities in different regions of India. Circle the odd one out.**

1. Srinagar Shimla Mohali Chandigarh
2. Agartala Imphal Itanagar Jorhat
3. Kochi Bengaluru Chennai Hyderabad
4. Mumbai Agra Bhopal Gandhinagar
5. Patna Ranchi Siliguri Kolkata

E **Answer these questions in detail.**

1. Describe India's location in Asia.
2. Name the neighbouring countries of India.
3. Name all the physical features of India and name one state which falls in each region.

FA

Map Zone

Take an outline map of India. Mark only the union territories of India.

Think Zone

A What do you think would happen if the political divisions of India were dissolved? Discuss in class.

B **Look at the picture and answer the questions.**

1. What do you see in the picture?
2. What are these called?
3. Where can these be found in India?

Life Skills Zone

How can the people of a region contribute to the wealth of that region?

Value Zone

A state is known by its people and their work. We must appreciate and respect people from all regions.

FA

Activity Zone

Take a quick quiz on India and answer these questions.

1. The third largest country of Asia: ....
2. The government that looks after all the states and union territories of India: ....
3. A city that serves as the capital of two states of India: ....
4. A landlocked neighbouring country of India: ....

FA

My Zone

Draw a smiley if you know and a star if you wish to know more.

1. I know the neighbouring countries of India. ....
2. I know the names and capitals of all the states and the union territories of India. ....
3. I know about the physical features of India. ....

Pin It Up

List the states of India with their capital cities and their current chief minister on a chart paper. Display it on your class notice board.

2 The Northern Mountains

I Know ...

- The Northern Mountains is one of the .... features of India.
- .... is a state that lies in the region of the Northern Mountains.

Observe and Reflect

- Which physical feature of India can you see in this picture?
- Where in India can we find such a landform?
- Name two states that have this type of landscape.

Look at the map of northern India. India is the land of the highest mountain **ranges** in the world, the Himalayas. They form the **crest** of the country. The **Northern Mountains** region stretches from the state of Arunachal Pradesh in the east to Jammu and Kashmir in the west. The total length of the Northern Mountains is around 2500 km. The width varies from 250 to 400 km. The Himalayan, Karakoram and Kailash ranges are all the part of the Northern Mountains.

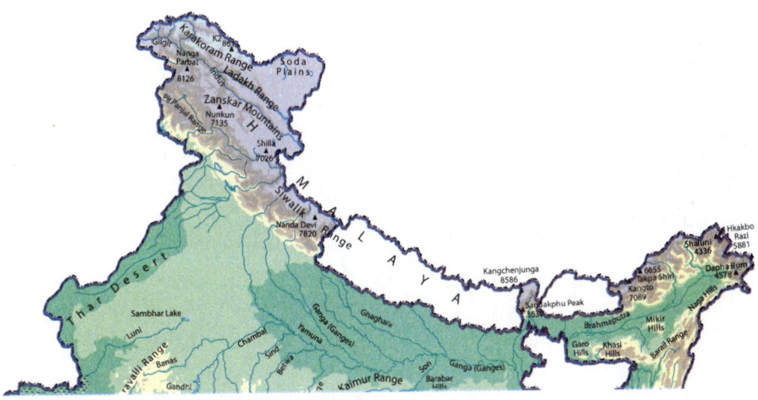

Northern Mountains

Importance of the Northern Mountains

The Northern Mountains play an important role in determining the climate of India.

They block the cold winds that blow from the north. The Himalayas are the natural barrier for rain-bearing clouds. As a result, the Northern Plains receive rains and have a moderate climate. The Himalayas are also the source of many important rivers. These rivers are the **lifeline** of the plains of India. The thick forests of the Northern Mountains are sources of timber and rich wildlife.

Parts of the Northern Mountains

The Northern Mountains consist of three ranges that run parallel to each other.

1. The Greater Himalayas or Himadri
2. The Middle Himalayas or Himachal
3. The Lesser Himalayas or Shiwalik

Find Out

Who were the first people to successfully climb Mt Everest and when?

Fact Zone

Khardung La, is the highest motorable road in the India.

^ Nanda Devi peak

Just as the name suggests, the **Greater Himalayan range** is the highest of all the three ranges. Also known as Himadri, the mountains of this region remain covered with snow and **glaciers** throughout the year and have an extremely cold climate. These glaciers are the source of many important rivers like Ganga, Yamuna, Indus and Brahmaputra. The vegetation is sparse as only a few plants like lichens, moss and wildflowers can survive the cold climate. Yak, snow leopard, goat and sheep are the only wildlife found in this region. Nanda Devi, at an **elevation** of 7,817 m, is the highest peak in India and Mt Everest, which stands at a height 8,848 m, is the highest peak in the world.

^ Hill station in Himachal

The **Middle Himalayas** or Himachal, lies to the south of Himadri. Since it is lower in altitude than the Greater Himalayas, it is not so cold here. With thick pine and deodar forests, the scenic beauty of the Himachal range has given rise to many hill stations. As a result, tourism is an important economic activity in this region.

Eco Zone

Deforestation in the hills for timber leads to landslides during heavy rains.

The **Lesser Himalayan ranges** are also known as the Shiwalik range. This range has the Shiwalik range in the north and the Purvanchal range in the north-east.

The Shiwalik range merges with the foothills of the Himalayas and is about 16 km wide in some places. It runs parallel to the main Himalayan range and is separated from it only by hills and valleys. This region is the most populated region of the Himalayas. Due to favourable climatic conditions, many food crops are grown here.

Mountain ranges and hills like the Patkai, Mishmi, Naga, Manipur, Tripura and Mizo run through the Lesser Himalayas in the north-east and are collectively called the Purvanchal range.

Life in the Northern Mountains

Some of the major states that lie in this region are Jammu and Kashmir, Uttarakhand, Himachal Pradesh and Sikkim. Most states of the north-east, such as Arunachal Pradesh, Nagaland, Manipur, Meghalaya and Mizoram, also fall in the Northern Mountain region.

Jammu and Kashmir has two capitals—Srinagar in summer and Jammu in winter. Ladakh is an important region of the state. Lying at the northernmost point of India, Jammu and Kashmir experience an extremely cold climate for several months at a stretch. Kashmir has a pleasant and cool summer and snowfall occurs during winters. Vegetation in the state varies from thick pine and cedar forests in the valleys to sparse vegetation in the Ladakh region.

Find Out

Kahwa and *kangri* are two important terms in Kashmir. What are they and what do they mean?

Farming is the main occupation during the summer season. Farmers grow kidney beans (*rajma*), maize, rice and vegetables. Saffron is an exclusive product of this region. The state is famous for apple, walnut and almond orchards.

Jammu and Kashmir is famous for handicrafts like woven woollen and silk clothes. The state is also famous for embroidered shawls and carpets, walnut wood handicrafts and papier-mâché products.

People speak in Urdu and Kashmiri in Srinagar and Kashmir, Dogri in Jammu and Ladakhi in the Ladakh region.

Wular lake

Kashmir is known for it's scenic Wular and Dal lakes. Tourists enjoy staying in houseboats, taking boat rides in the *shikaras*, trekking in Pahalgam and skiing in Gulmarg. The Vaishno Devi temple, the Amarnath caves, the city of Srinagar, the Sonmarg hill station and the town of Pahalgam are all places to visit in the state.

The Ladakh region with its monasteries is another important tourist destination of the state.

Do It Yourself

Look at the picture and answer the questions.

1. What is the boat known as?
2. Where in India can we find these boats?
3. What is the climate of this place?

Himachal Pradesh is another important state in the Northern Mountains. Farming is a major occupation and the people here grow maize, barley, rice and vegetables. The state is known for its fruit orchards.

Shimla

Himachal Pradesh is particularly famous for all its hill stations like Shimla, Kullu, Manali and Dalhousie. Many tourists visit them during the summer months. People here speak in Hindi, Punjabi, Kinnauri and Pahari. The state is famous for its warm *kullu* shawls with colourful woven borders.

Valley of Flowers

The beautiful state of **Uttarakhand** in the northern mountains is known for its Rhododendron forests. UNESCO World heritage site, the Valley of Flowers is located here. People here speak in Hindi or the Pahari language.

Sikkim

Farming and tourism are the two major occupations in the state. Tourists visit pilgrimage sites, such as Hemkund Sahib, Haridwar, Badrinath, Kedarnath, Gangotri and Yamunotri. Many hill stations like Ranikhet, Nainital and Mussoorie are located here too.

Bordered by Bhutan, Tibet and Nepal, **Sikkim** has cool summers and cold winters. It experiences heavy rainfall during the rainy season. People here speak Nepali, Sikkimese and Lepcha.

Tea plantations

Sikkim is a popular tourist destination. Farming and weaving are the two major occupations of the people of Sikkim. The red panda is found in this state.

Fact Zone

In 2013, flash floods damaged the Kedarnath shrine and left many pilgrims stranded.

Darjeeling, a hill station in the state of West Bengal, also comes under the Northern Mountains region. Vast plantations in Darjeeling produce tea, which is exported throughout the world.

In the north-east, five states, namely Arunachal Pradesh, Meghalaya, Manipur, Nagaland and Mizoram, are part of the Northern Mountains.

The largest state in the northeast is **Arunachal Pradesh**. It shares international borders with China, Myanmar and Bhutan. Farming and weaving are the two most important occupations. The state produces paddy, maize and wheat. Tourist places in Arunachal Pradesh are the Tawang Monastery and the Namdapha National Park which is famous for its snow leopard.

Tawang Monastery

Find Out

Why do people in some parts of Arunachal Pradesh live in **stilt** houses?

The northeastern state of **Meghalaya**, land of the Khasi, Garo and Jaintia hills, shares its international borders with Bangladesh. Mawsynram, a village in Meghalaya, is the wettest place in the world with high annual rainfall. Shillong, its capital, is a beautiful hill station. Farmers grow paddy, potato and maize. Meghalaya is known for its pineapple and banana plantations.

Meghalaya

Manipur shares its border with Myanmar. The beautiful Loktak Lake in Manipur is the largest freshwater lake in north-east India. The climate is generally pleasant throughout the year and cold only during the winter months. Farmers produce cash crops, such as rubber, cardamom, tea and coffee in the hills. The Manipuri classical dance originated here.

The state of **Nagaland** also shares an international border with Myanmar. The Naga hill range makes the terrain mountainous and the climate wet and cool. Farmers grow rice, millets, pulses, sugarcane, oilseeds and potatoes. Weaving and woodwork are the other major occupations.

Mizoram, a landlocked state in the northeast, shares its international border with Bangladesh and Myanmar. Agriculture is the main occupation of the Mizo people. They also make a variety of bamboo products. Mizoram has one of the highest literacy rates in India.

Mizoram

Remember

- The Northern Mountains consists of three parallel ranges—the Greater Himalayas, the Middle Himalayas and the Lesser Himalayas.
- The states that fall under the Northern Mountains are Jammu and Kashmir, Himachal Pradesh, Uttarakhand, Sikkim, parts of West Bengal, Arunachal Pradesh, Meghalaya, Manipur, Nagaland and Mizoram.

Words Zone

range: a line of mountains or hills

crest: the top of something

lifeline: a thing on which something or someone depends

glaciers: moving masses of ice formed due to the accumulation of layers of snow

elevation: the height of a place

stilt: a pair of straight poles that are generally used for support

Review Zone

A Fill in the blanks with the correct answers.

1. Jammu and Kashmir is located in the .... part of India.
   a. western   b. eastern   c. northern
2. The Lesser Himalayas are also known as the .... range.
   a. Shiwalik   b. Himachal   c. Terai

3. Pahalgam is located in ....
   a. Jammu and Kashmir   b. Himachal Pradesh   c. Uttarakhand

4. Patkai is a hill which is part of the .... range.
   a. Himachal   b. Himadri   c. Purvanchal

5. Rhododendron forests are found in the state of ....
   a. Sikkim   b. Uttarakhand   c. Himachal Pradesh

B Name the following.

1. The highest of the three parallel ranges of the Himalayas: ....
2. A place in Kashmir that tourists visit to ski: ....
3. Shawls with colourful borders made in Himachal Pradesh: ....
4. A state in north-east India shares its international borders with Myanmar: ....
5. The north-eastern state with a high literacy rate: ....

C Write T for True and F for False.

1. No vegetation is found in the Middle Himalayas. ☐
2. The river Ganga has its source in the Himadri. ☐
3. Mizoram has thick bamboo forests. ☐
4. People grow crops in Jammu and Kashmir during the summer months. ☐
5. The Loktak Lake is located in Manipur. ☐

D Answer these questions in brief.

1. Name the three parallel ranges of the Northern Mountains.
2. Which is the second highest peak in the Himalayas?
3. Name two famous lakes of Kashmir.
4. Which state has many pilgrimage sites?
5. In which states of north-east India do the Northern Mountains lie?

E Answer these questions in detail.

1. Describe briefly the Northern Mountain region of India.
2. What do you know about the Purvanchal range?

3. Briefly state the life and activities of the people of Jammu and Kashmir.
4. Discuss the lifestyle of the people living in any one north-eastern state.
5. Write about the vegetation found in the states in the Northern Mountains.

Map Zone

On an outline political map of India, mark the three states of Jammu and Kashmir, Himachal Pradesh and Uttarakhand.

Think Zone

A There are houseboats in Kashmir as well as in Kerala. Find out the similarities and differences between the houseboats of both the states.

B **Look at the picture and answer the questions.**

1. Which state has apple orchards?
2. Name two famous hill stations of this state.
3. What do the people of this state generally wear?

Life Skills Zone

How do you think the climate of a region affects the life of the local people?

Value Zone

The Northern Mountains have a rich wildlife and vegetation. We must respect the land and take steps to preserve its natural flora and fauna.

FA

Activity Zone

Divide the class into five groups. Let each group choose a state of north-east India. The group should collect information about the climate, vegetation, major crops, people and major places of interest. Make a PowerPoint presentation and present it in the class.

FA

My Zone

Draw a smiley if you know and a star if you wish to know more.

1. I know about the Northern Mountainous region of India. ....
2. I know about the life of the people that live in the states located in the Northern Mountains. ....
3. I know about the seven states in north-east India. ....

Pin It Up

Which state would you like to visit in the Northern Mountains? Collect pictures and prepare a single-page travel brochure about that state.

3 The Northern Plains of India

I Know ...

- Ancient civilizations flourished along the banks of the river ....
- Plains are low and .... lands.

Observe and Reflect

- What do you see in the picture?
- In which regions of India can you see such lands?
- What is the climate like in such places?

We know that plains are low-lying flat lands. A large part of India is occupied by the Northern Plains. These plains are fertile since they are watered by the **perennial rivers** which flow down from the Himalayas.

Importance of the Northern Plains

The Northern Plains are an important physical feature of India as it has a suitable climate for agriculture and other economic activities. The **alluvium** deposited by the rivers makes the plains fertile. Rivers help in the **irrigation** of fields. Since, the plains provide a means of livelihood to the people, many people settle here. Towns and cities easily develop along the banks of the rivers and river basins. A river basin is an area watered by a river and its **tributaries**.

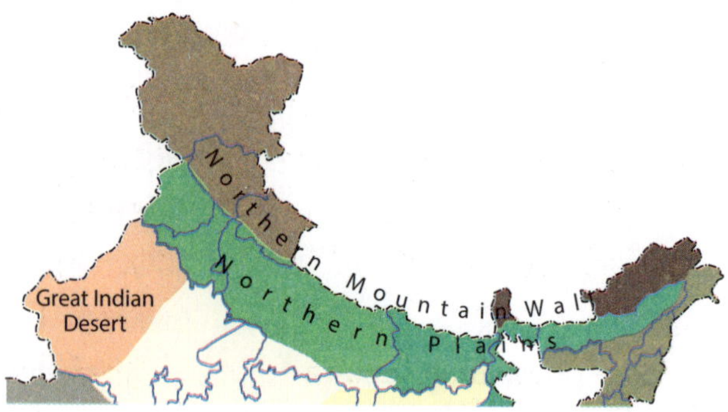

The Northern Plains

The river basins are ideal for agriculture and irrigation. The three major basins of the Northern Plains in India are the Indus basin, the Ganga basin and the Brahmaputra basin.

Eco Zone

Important river basins formed by the rivers Narmada, Tapti, Cauvery, Godavari, Krishna and Mahanadi are a source of irrigation and hydroelectric power.

The Indus Basin

The Indus river originates in the Tibetan Plateau. It flows through four countries, namely, India, Pakistan, China and Afghanistan. In the Northern Plains, the main tributaries of the Indus are the rivers Chenab, Jhelum, Satluj, Beas and Ravi. These rivers drain the states of Jammu and Kashmir, Punjab, Haryana and Himachal Pradesh.

The Indus river

The Ganga Basin

The Ganga, originating from the Gangotri glacier in the Himalayas, is the most important river of India. Flowing through the states of Uttar Pradesh, Uttarakhand and Bihar, it is in West Bengal that the Ganga branches out into small streams called distributaries.

A few tributaries of the Ganga are Gomti, Ghaghara, Kosi and Gandak. Some of the rivers that meet Ganga from the south are Son, Chambal and Betwa. The Ganga river basin is the most fertile region of the Northern Plains.

Ganga at Devprayag

Find Out

Where does the Ganga meet its largest tributary, the Yamuna?

The Brahmaputra Basin

Another important basin of India is the Brahmaputra basin. The river Brahmaputra originates in Tibet. It enters India through the state of Arunachal Pradesh where it is called river Dihang and flows into Assam as Brahmaputra. The Brahmaputra, like the Ganga, breaks off into distributaries before it finally drains into the Bay of Bengal.

River Brahmaputra

Fact Zone

The word 'delta' is derived from the Greek letter delta 'Δ', which is also triangular in shape.

The Ganga and Brahmaputra rivers form the world's largest delta known as the Sunderbans Delta.

Do It Yourself

List the rivers of the three major river basins of the Northern Plains.

Indus basin	Ganga basin	Brahmaputra basin

Life in the Northern Plains

Some of the most important states that lie in the Northern Plains are Punjab, Haryana, Uttar Pradesh, Bihar, West Bengal, Assam and Tripura. The union territory of Delhi is also located in the Northern Plains. Let us find out about the life of the people in the states that lie in this region.

Punjab is located in the Indus and Satluj river basins. It has very hot summers and cold winters with rainfall mainly during the monsoons. Punjab receives water from the rivers Satluj, Ravi and Beas which make the land fertile and ideal for agriculture. Being the largest producer of wheat, this state is known as the 'wheat bowl' of India. Other crops, such as rice, millet, sugarcane, mustard, oilseeds and gram are grown here.

The capital of Punjab is Chandigarh. A few other important cities of this state are Patiala, Amritsar, Jalandhar and Ludhiana. The Golden Temple in Amritsar is a famous pilgrimage site. People mainly speak Punjabi and Hindi. Though agriculture is the main occupation of the people in Punjab, many industries like food, paper and textile are found in the state.

Fact Zone

The popular Punjabi folk dances are *Gidda* and *Bhangra*.

Golden Temple

Rice fields in Haryana

Haryana lies in the Satluj basin. Chandigarh is the capital city. Haryana too has hot and dry summers, cold winters and receives rainfall during the monsoon months. The main crops of the state are wheat and rice. Farmers use pumps and tube wells for irrigation. The people in the state speak mainly in Hindi and Haryanvi. Many cities of Haryana are part of the National Capital Region of Delhi.

One of the important states of the Ganga basin is **Uttar Pradesh**. Yamuna and Ganga are the two main rivers that run through the state. The summer months are very hot and the winter months are very cold. Heavy or light rainfall might occur in the monsoons. The major crops of the state are rice, wheat, sugarcane, corn and pulses. People speak in Urdu, Bhojpuri and Hindi. The state is known for its sugar mills, leather and textile industries. Many service industries like tourism and hospitality flourish here. The cities of Agra, Mathura, Varanasi and Lucknow are major tourist destinations.

Varanasi

Nalanda university

Bihar lies on the Ganga basin. Its capital is Patna. Rice, wheat, jute and sugarcane are the major crops that are grown here. Bihar experiences hot summer months and cold winter months. Patna is an ancient city and the relics of the ancient university of Nalanda are found here. People here mainly speak Hindi, Urdu, Bhojpuri and Maithili.

West Bengal receives water from the Ganga and Brahmaputra rivers, making it very fertile. Jute and rice are the main crops of this region. The summer months are hot and humid, while the winter months are cool with heavy rainfall during the monsoons. Kolkata is the capital of West Bengal. People here mainly speak in Bangla and Hindi. The major occupation of the people is farming and manufacturing, which is an important industry in West Bengal.

The Northern Plains extend eastwards to the north-eastern states of **Assam** and **Tripura**. Both the states experience hot and humid summers, pleasant winters and heavy rainfall during the monsoon.

Howrah bridge

The Brahmaputra river flows through Assam, making the land fertile. Jute and rice are the major crops. Tea cultivation and silkworm rearing is also practised here. The capital of Assam is Dispur. Guwahati is one of the most important cities of Assam. People here speak Assamese and Hindi.

Assam

Tripura, surrounded by Bangladesh on three sides, is a small state in the northeast. People here grow jute, rice and bamboo. The main river of Tripura is Gumti.

Remember

- The Northern Plains of India consist of mainly three river basins—the Ganga basin, the Brahmaputra basin and the Indus basin.
- States that lie in the Northern Plains are Punjab, Haryana, Delhi, Uttar Pradesh, Bihar, West Bengal, Assam and Tripura.

Words Zone

perennial rivers: rivers that flow throughout the year

alluvium: the silt or clay that is left behind by rivers

irrigation: the practice of supplying water to fields for agriculture

tributary: a river flowing into a larger river

Review Zone

A Fill in the blanks with the correct answers.

1. The ancient university of Nalanda is located in the state of ....

   a. Haryana b. Uttar Pradesh c. Bihar

2. .... receives water from the Ganga and Brahmaputra rivers.

   a. West Bengal b. Bihar c. Uttar Pradesh

3. The capital of West Bengal is ....

   a. Lucknow b. Kolkata c. Chandigarh

4. Ganga rises from the .... glacier.

   a. Gangotri b. Yamunotri c. Tibetan Plateau

5. The Golden Temple is located in ....
   a. Tripura   b. Amritsar   c. Chandigarh

B **Write T for True and F for False.**

1. Assam is surrounded by Bangladesh on three sides. ☐
2. The Indus river passes through four countries. ☐
3. Yamuna is one of the major distributaries of the Ganga river. ☐
4. The Brahmaputra river drains into the Arabian Sea. ☐
5. Tea is grown in Assam. ☐

C **Answer these questions in brief.**

1. Define a river basin.
2. From where do the Ganga and Brahmaputra rivers originate?
3. Name the countries through which the Indus river flows.
4. Name the languages spoken by the people of Bihar.
5. In which basin does the state of Haryana lie?

D **Answer these questions in detail.**

1. Why are the Northern Plains so fertile?
2. Describe the life of the people living in Punjab.
3. Which state receives water from two major rivers? How is the life of the people in this state?
4. What kind of life do people have in the states of Assam and Tripura?

Map Zone

FA

On an outline map of India, mark the three major river basins.

Think Zone

A Imagine that you have to plan a trip to Assam. What should you keep in mind while planning the trip? What are the places that you plan to visit?

B **Look at the picture and answer the questions.**

1. Which monument is depicted in the picture?
2. In which state is it located?
3. In which river basin does this state lie?

Life Skills Zone

Both Haryana and Bihar lie in the same physical region of India, namely, the Northern Plains. However, the life of the people in both states is different. Why do you think there is a difference? Find out two reasons for it.

Value Zone

All states in India have a rich cultural heritage. One must respect and protect one's cultural heritage.

Activity Zone

Circle the names of rivers found in the Northern Plains in the word search.

- Beas
- Bhagirathi
- Brahmaputra
- Chenab
- Dihang
- Gandak
- Ganga
- Ghaggar
- Gomti
- Gumti
- Hooghly
- Kosi
- Ravi
- Satluj
- Son
- Yamuna

E	T	O	O	M	J	L	W	A	V	M	B	I	E	Y
B	E	A	S	U	R	S	G	K	G	R	B	T	L	L
G	A	O	L	D	X	A	G	V	A	N	W	M	G	H
V	G	T	D	B	S	C	G	H	R	Q	A	U	Z	G
Y	A	Q	E	X	U	J	M	G	U	A	Z	G	N	O
S	A	C	H	E	N	A	B	I	A	S	G	V	C	O
K	K	M	M	Q	P	U	G	E	Y	H	U	G	P	H
N	O	F	U	U	I	H	T	A	R	I	G	A	H	B
M	M	S	T	N	G	W	A	S	K	J	W	N	Q	V
H	S	R	I	F	A	D	W	C	Y	C	Y	D	A	W
E	A	D	L	V	I	S	K	Z	I	F	F	A	X	V
K	E	X	I	H	N	O	D	Z	Q	F	K	K	U	R
W	H	V	A	X	E	B	W	R	L	V	B	B	S	X
C	A	N	S	X	G	R	H	J	I	G	Q	R	O	V
R	G	I	T	M	O	G	R	U	A	N	R	O	N	R

FA

My Zone

Draw a smiley 😊 if you know and a star ⭐ if you wish to know more.

1. I know about the Northern Plains of India. ....
2. I know about the river basins of India. ....
3. I know about the states that are located in the Northern Plains. ....

Pin It Up

On a map of India, trace the course of the Ganga river starting from its point of origin.

4 The Western Desert

I Know ...

- One of the plants commonly found in the desert is the ....
- .... is a very important state that lies in the desert region of India.

Observe and Reflect

- Which landform is shown in the picture?
- Who is called the ship of the desert and why?
- Name two such famous landforms from around the world.

Take a look at the map. It shows the extent of the Great Indian Desert. You already know, a desert is covered with sand and gets very little rain.

The Western Desert

The **Great Indian Desert** is also known as the **Thar Desert**. It stretches from the Rann of Kutch in Gujarat to the borders of Haryana. A large part of Rajasthan lies in the Thar Desert. The Aravalli range is located to the east of the Thar Desert.

The Thar Desert is a dry and hot desert. It has many **sand dunes**. Sandstorms are a regular feature of the desert. Small streams and underground water are the only natural sources of water in this region. Sometimes, underground water comes to the surface and forms water bodies known as **oases**. The lands around these water bodies are fertile and hence, villages develop around them. Date palms are a characteristic feature of oases.

Camels are important to the people of the desert. They provide milk and are used for travelling and transporting goods from one place to another. Camels are also used to draw water from wells and to plough fields.

The climate in the Thar Desert remains very hot and dry throughout the year. While temperatures are high during the day, the nights are always cold. This region receives little or **scanty** rainfall.

Cactii in desert

Due to the **scarcity** of water, only plants that can draw underground water or store water can survive here. Cactus, keekar and babool are a few examples of such plants. People build houses with thick walls and small windows to keep away the heat.

Fact Zone

Deserts like the Gobi Desert get snow during the winter months and are known as cold deserts.

Find Out

Which river flows through the Thar Desert and why is it not of much use?

Eco Zone

The clearing of forests and overgrazing increases the spread of desert land.

Do It Yourself

Look at the picture and answer the questions.

1. Which physical feature is surrounding the water source?
2. Which tree can be seen growing around the water body?
3. What is this water body called?

Life in the Region

Rajasthan, known as the 'desert state', is located in the Western Desert region. Bikaner and Jodhpur are two cities in this region. Agriculture, sheep rearing, textile printing, tourism and making handicrafts are the main occupations of the people of Rajasthan. They grow bajra and oilseeds. Due to the scarcity of water, people sometimes move in groups from one place to another looking for water. These people are called *banjaras*.

The people of Rajasthan speak in Hindi and Rajasthani. Men wear white *dhoti* with colourful *kurta* and tie *pagri* on their head to keep the heat away. Women wear colourful *ghaghra*, *odhni* and *choli*. They wear large silver jewellery and several white bangles that completely cover their forearms. Jaisalmer, Jaipur and Chittorgarh have famous forts. Rajasthan is also known for its national parks and sanctuaries. Rann of Kutch is known for its uniquely embroidered clothes. The area is also known for animals like the wild ass and the desert fox.

Find Out

Why is making handicrafts an important occupation of people living in the deserts?

Remember

- The Great Indian Desert is also known as the Thar Desert.
- It stretches from the Rann of Kutch in Gujarat to the borders of Haryana.
- A large part of Rajasthan lies in the Thar Desert.
- Desert areas receive very little rainfall.

Words Zone

sand dunes: mounds of sand found in hot deserts

scanty: very little

scarcity: the lack of something

Review Zone

A Fill in the blanks with the correct answers.

1. The Aravalli hills lie to the .... of the desert region.
   a. southwest b. east c. south
2. Hot and .... winds blow in the deserts.
   a. cold b. moist c. dry

3. .... is one of the commonly found plants in the desert region.
   a. Croton   b. Cactus   c. Caucasia

4. .... is an important city of the desert region in Rajasthan.
   a. Udaipur   b. Bikaner   c. Ajmer

5. The desert region is .... populated.
   a. thickly   b. sparsely   c. highly

B Name the following.

1. A place in the desert that has a water source and date palms: ....
2. Rajasthani men wear this on their heads to stay cool in the heat: ....
3. Hills lying to the east of the Thar Desert: ....
4. A cold desert: ....

C Write T for True and F for False.

1. The winter months are very cold in the deserts. ☐
2. The Thar is a wet and white desert. ☐
3. The Rann of Kutch lies in the desert region. ☐
4. All types of vegetation are found in deserts. ☐

D Answer these questions in brief.

1. Where is the Thar Desert located?
2. What languages do the people of Rajasthan speak?
3. What are camels used for in deserts?
4. Why do villages develop around oases?
5. Name four important cities of Rajasthan.

E Answer these questions in detail.

1. How do desert plants adapt to the conditions of water scarcity?
2. Describe the clothes worn by the men and women of Rajasthan.
3. Why do deserts have cold nights?
4. What are the kind of houses that can be found in a desert and why?

Think Zone

A The Thar Desert is located in the western part of India. What are the factors that influence the climate of this regions?

B **Look at the picture and answer the questions.**

1. What bird is this—the stork or the Great Indian Bustard?
2. In which region is this bird found?
3. Name two animals found in the region where this bird is found.

Life Skills Zone

Rajasthan in a well-known tourist destination. Why do you think tourists like to visit Rajasthan?

Value Zone

People in the desert regions are generally hardworking. Life is much more difficult for them than it is in other areas.

FA

Activity Zone

Puppetry is a popular art performance in Rajasthan. Let us make sock puppets.

You will need an old pair of socks, buttons, some wool, paper, glue, scissors and different-coloured sketch pens.

1. Take an old pair of socks.
2. Mark the place for the eyes. Now, either glue buttons for the eyes or sew them on to the socks.
3. Take some wool for the hair of the puppet and stick it on the socks where the puppet's head should be. You can style the hair however you like.
4. Now that the puppet is ready, give it a name.
5. Wear the socks on your hand. You are now ready to stage a puppet show.

FA

My Zone

Draw a smiley ☺ if you know and a star ☆ if you wish to know more.

1. I know about the Western Desert region of India. ....
2. I know about the climate and vegetation of the desert region. ....
3. I know how the people in the desert region live. ....

Pin It Up

Collect pictures of flora and fauna found in the Thar Desert and make a colourful chart. Paste it on the class bulletin board.

5 The Southern Plateau

I Know ...

- The Southern Plateau lies to the .... of the Northern Plains.
- One of the important states in this region is ....
- The capital of Maharashtra is ....

Observe and Reflect

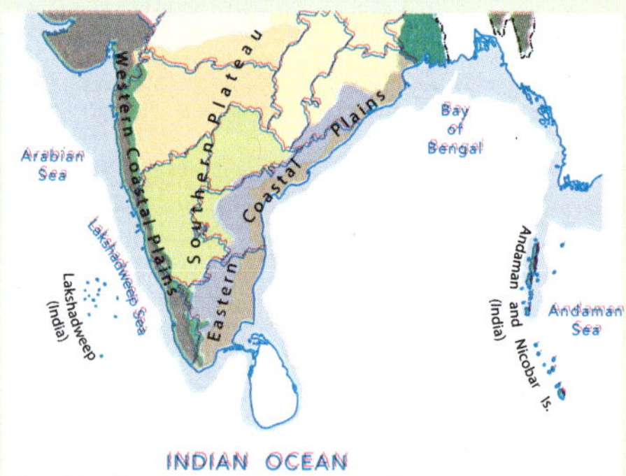

- Which part of India does this picture show?
- Name the seas on the western side and the eastern side of this part of India.
- What is the name of the neighbouring country visible in the picture?

Do you know what a plateau is? A plateau is a large stretch of high or elevated land that has a flat upper part.

The Southern Plateaus, also known as the 'peninsular plateaus', form a distinct physical feature of India. The rocky plateau is wide in the north and **tapers** as we travel towards the south. They are outlined by the Western Ghats in the west, the Aravalli hills and the Rajmahal hills in the north, the Eastern Ghats in the east and the Nilgiri hills in the south. The rivers in the Southern Plateaus are mainly rain-fed and flow with a great speed. Some flow into the Bay of Bengal and the others, like river Narmada and Tapi, flow into the Arabian Sea.

The Southern Plateau is divided into two parts by river Narmada. The northern part is called the **Central Highlands** and the southern part is called the **Deccan Plateau**.

The Central Highlands consist of the **Malwa Plateau** and the **Chhota Nagpur Plateau**. The Malwa Plateau is of volcanic origin. It is drained by the Chambal and Betwa rivers and bordered by the Aravalli hills and the Vindhya range.The southernmost part of Rajasthan and most of Madhya Pradesh fall in this plateau region.

Southern Plateau

Chhota Nagpur Plateau

The Chhota Nagpur Plateau also known as the 'mineral belt' of India is bordered by the Satpura range in the north-west and drained by river Damodar. It includes Jharkhand, northern Odisha and north-eastern Chhattisgarh.

The Central Highlands is rich in black soil, which is excellent for cultivating cotton and sugarcane. The region has vast resources of minerals like coal, iron, bauxite, manganese and mica.

The Deccan Plateau is surrounded by the Eastern Ghats and the Western Ghats, extending upto the southern tip of peninsular India. It is drained by the Godavari, Indravati, Krishna, Kaveri and Mahanadi rivers which flow eastwards into the Bay of Bengal. Some areas in the region have red soil, which is good for crops, such as groundnut, tobacco, millets, potato and sugarcane.

Western Ghats

Find Out

The area with black soil is also known as Deccan Trap. Find out why is it called so?

Life in the Plateau Region

Many states of India including Madhya Pradesh, parts of Maharashtra, Karnataka, Jharkhand, Odisha, Chhattisgarh, Andhra Pradesh, Telangana and Tamil Nadu lie in the plateau region. Let us look at the life of the people in these states.

Eco Zone

The Southern Plateau is rich in minerals yet, due to exploitation of these minerals, frequent landslides occur.

Madhya Pradesh lies in the centre of India in the Central Highlands region. It has a dry and wet climate.

Kanha National Park

Agriculture is the main occupation of the people here. Wheat, sugarcane, pulses, oilseeds and cotton are the main crops. Panna is a well-known diamond mine of the state. The state has rich forest reserves and has more than ten national parks. The Kanha National Park and Bandhavgarh National Park serve to protect tigers. The people of Madhya Pradesh speak Hindi and Marathi.

In the year 2000, the state of **Chhattisgarh** was formed out of Madhya Pradesh. The climate in the state is hot and humid. Chhattisgarh has both hills as well as plains. The main occupation of the people is farming and mining. The Bhilai steel plant, situated in Chhattisgarh, is a major producer of steel in the country. Chhattisgarh has scenic waterfalls, such as Chitrakote Falls, which attract tourists. The people here speak Hindi.

Fact Zone

Anai Mudi is the highest peak, Jog Falls, the highest waterfall, and Godavari is the longest river of the Deccan Plateau.

Some parts of **Odisha** towards southeast Chhattisgarh are located in the Central Highlands. Rice and jute are the main crops of this region.

Maharashtra lies in the north-western part of the Deccan Plateau. The state has an irregular monsoon climate. Farming is the main occupation of the people in the state. Mumbai is the capital. The black soil that is found abundantly in parts of Mumbai is suitable for growing cotton and sugarcane. Other crops include groundnut, wheat, *jowar*, pulses and *bajra*. Maharashtra has many textile industries. The people of Maharashtra speak Marathi, Hindi and Konkani.

Do It Yourself

Name this famous festival that is celebrated in Maharashtra during the monsoon season. Find out why this festival is celebrated.

Eco Zone

The tribal people living around the Southern Plateau worship nature and protect parts of the forests as sacred groves.

Jharkhand was carved out from the state of Bihar in the year 2000. The climate of the state is hot and humid. Jharkhand is rich in minerals and forest reserves. Farming, animal rearing and mining are the important occupations of Jharkhand. The major crops grown here are paddy, oilseeds, millets and sugarcane. A large section of the population in the state is tribal. The people of Jharkhand mainly speak Hindi, Bihari, Odia, Santhali and Munda.

A part of the state of **Andhra Pradesh** is located in the Deccan Plateau region. Farming, mining, animal rearing and handicrafts are the important occupations of the people. The region has rich deposits of mica and limestone. Farmers here grow rice, *jowar*, tobacco, sugarcane and groundnut. The state is the largest producer of tobacco in India. People speak in Telugu and Urdu.

Charminar

In 2014, a new state named **Telangana** was created from some parts of Andhra Pradesh. Farmers here grow rice, tobacco, maize and cotton. It shares its capital with Andhra Pradesh. People here speak Telugu. Nagarjuna Sagar Dam, one of the largest dams in the world, is located here.

Nilgiri Hills

Tamil Nadu lies to the south of Andhra Pradesh. Agriculture, weaving and fishing are the main occupations of the people in Tamil Nadu. Farmers grow rice, sugarcane, groundnut, bananas and oilseeds. Tea, coffee and rubber are also grown along the slopes of the Nilgiri hills. Tamil Nadu is also known for its textile and leather industry. Tamil is the main language of the people of Tamil Nadu.

The state of **Karnataka** lies to the south of Maharashtra. The farmers of Karnataka grow coffee, sugarcane, cotton, spices and jowar. The state has extensive teak and sandalwood forests and **hydroelectric** power. Karnataka has five national parks including Bandipur and Nagahole and Nilgiri Biosphere Reserve. Kannada is the state language. It is a major centre of the information technology (IT) industry.

Jog Falls

Remember

- The Southern Plateaus, also known as the 'peninsular plateaus', form a distinct physical feature of India.
- The Narmada river divides the plateau into two parts—the Central Highlands and the Deccan Plateau.
- Madhya Pradesh, Maharashtra, Odisha, Karnataka, Tamil Nadu, Chhattisgarh and Jharkhand are the major states of the Southern Plateau region.

Words Zone

tapers: to become narrower

hydroelectric: electricity generated by water

Review Zone

A. Fill in the blanks with the correct answers.

1. The Southern Plateaus, also known as the .... plateaus, form a distinct physical feature of India.

   a. table   b. peninsular   c. coastal

2. The river .... divides the entire plateau region into two parts.

   a. Tapi   b. Godavari   c. Narmada

3. .... is the highest peak in the Deccan plateau.

   a. Mt Abu   b. Anai Mudi   c. Mt Annapurna

4. .... Plateau is of volcanic origin.

   a. Malwa   b. Vindhya   c. Betwa

5. .... soil is found in the Central Highlands.

   a. Alluvial   b. Sandy   c. Black

B. Name the following.

1. A state of India that is known for its tobacco production: ....
2. A famous diamond mine located in Maharashtra: ....

3. Two rivers of the Deccan Plateau that drain into the Arabian Sea: ....
4. A type of soil suitable for growing cotton: ....
5. A state with rich tribal culture: ....

C **Write T for True and F for False.**

1. The Deccan Plateau is only surrounded by the Western Ghats. ☐
2. The Chhota Nagpur Plateau covers Jharkhand. ☐
3. The Godavari is the longest river in the Western Plateau. ☐
4. The people of Tamil Nadu speak Odia. ☐
5. Red soil is good for growing groundnut and tobacco. ☐

D **Answer these questions in brief.**

1. What is a plateau?
2. Name four rivers of the Southern Plateau that drain into the Bay of Bengal.
3. Which regions are included in the Chhota Nagpur Plateau?
4. Name three hills of the Western Ghats.
5. What are the main crops of the state of Maharashtra?
6. What is the state of Andhra Pradesh famous for?
7. Which rivers flow through the state of Karnataka?

E **Answer these questions in detail.**

1. Describe the Central Highlands.
2. Describe the rivers of the Deccan Plateau.
3. Write a short note on the states of Telangana and Jharkhand.
4. Describe the state of Karnataka.

Map Zone

On an outline map of India, mark the following:

1. Malwa Plateau
2. Narmada river
3. Chhota Nagpur Plateau
4. Nilgiri hills
5. Deccan Plateau

Think Zone

A Why does the state of Karnataka have extensive hydroelectric power?

B **Look at the picture and answer the questions.**

1. In which state are these trees found?
2. What is the wood of this tree used for?

Life Skills Zone

The plateau region has rain-fed rivers flowing through it. These rivers dry up during the summer months. Find out how the people of the region cope with this situation.

Value Zone

Every time a tree is being cut, we should see to it that a new one is planted in its place.

FA

Activity Zone

Make a chart on the rivers and dams of the Southern Plateau. Paste colourful pictures of the rivers and dams and write briefly about their location.

FA

My Zone

Draw a smiley if you know and a star if you wish to know more.

1. I know about the Southern Plateau region of India. ....
2. I know about the life of the people in the plateau region. ....
3. I know about all the states located in the plateaus of India. ....

Pin It Up

Find out all the interesting tourist spots of the Southern Plateau. Paste their pictures on a chart.

Assessment 1 (Chapters 1-5) — Maximum Marks: 25

A Fill in the blanks. (1 x 6 = 6)

1. The capital of a state is also called the seat of .... in that state.
2. Nagaland shares its international borders with ....
3. The Northern Plains enjoy .... summers and .... winters.
4. The Northern Plains are watered by .... rivers.
5. A large stretch of high land is called a ....
6. The Northern .... are fertile and are suitable for growing crops.

B Match the columns. (1 x 10 = 10)

Column A	Column B
1. Andhra Pradesh	a. Peninsular plateaus
2. Ganga	b. Raipur
3. Khardung La	c. Chota Nagpur Plateau
4. Southern Plateaus	d. High mountain pass
5. Thar desert	e. Bay of Bengal
6. Chhattisgarh	f. Hyderabad
7. Punjab	g. Srinagar
8. Central Highlands	h. Gangotri
9. Brahmaputra	i. Sand dunes
10. Jammu and Kashmir	j. Wheat bowl of India

C Tick (✓) the appropriate answer. (1 x 5 = 5)

1. Which of these is one of the physical features of India? (Northern Mountains/ Southern Mountains)
2. What are kidney beans called? (Maize/Rajma)
3. Which place is known as the mineral belt of India? (Chhota Nagpur Plateau/ Malwa Plateau)
4. Why is vegetation sparse in deserts? (Scarcity of water/Abundance of water)
5. Where does Ganga meet Yamuna? (Varanasi/Allahabad)

D Write True or False. (1 x 4 = 4)

1. Karnataka has six national parks. ....
2. Rajasthani men wear *pagris* on their heads to keep them cool. ....
3. The Northern Plains are very fertile. ....
4. Punjab is located in the Ganga basin. ....

6 The Coastal Plains and the Islands

I Know ...

- The Deccan plateau is surrounded by the .... and .... coastal plains.
- The capital of Kerala is ....

Observe and Reflect

- Name any two states that lie in the coastal plains.
- What is the name of the small group of islands located below the southern part of India?
- What does the green colour signify on the map?

When we visit the seaside, we see long sandy beaches where the land meets the sea. This is called a **coast**. The low-lying land along a coast is called a **coastal plain**.

Coastal plains

The Coastal Plains

We have already learned about the Deccan plateau. The coastal plains surround it from Gujarat in the west to West Bengal in the east. The coastal plains in the west are called the **Western Coastal**

Plains and the coastal plains in the east are called the **Eastern Coastal Plains**. The two plains meet at Kanyakumari.

The Eastern Coastal Plains is a wide stretch of land that stretches from West Bengal in the north to Tamil Nadu in the south. It lies between the Eastern Ghats and the Bay of Bengal. Tamil Nadu, Puducherry, Andhra Pradesh, Odisha and West Bengal lie along the Eastern Coastal Plains.

The Eastern Coastal Plains has two parts. The northern part is called the **Northern Circars** and the southern part is called the **Coromandel Coast**. Many rivers, such as the Godavari, Krishna, Kaveri and Mahanadi form large deltas along this coast. The Chilka Lake, the largest saltwater lake in India, is located along the eastern coast in the state of Odisha.

The Western Coastal Plains is a thin strip of land that stretches from the state of Gujarat in the north to Kerala in the south. It falls between the Western Ghats and the Arabian Sea. The Western Coastal Plains is divided into three parts. These are the **Gujarat Coast** in the north, the **Konkan Coast** in the middle and the **Malabar Coast** in the south. The Gulf of Khambat and the Gulf of Kutch lie in the Western Coastal Plain. The western coast is narrower than the eastern coast. The states of Gujarat, Maharashtra, Goa, Karnataka and Kerala are located in the Western Coastal Plain.

Find Out

Why are the coastal areas fertile?

Fact Zone

Indira Point is the southernmost point of India.

Life in the Coastal Plains

Let us look at the life of the people that live in the different states of the coastal plains.

We have already learned about **West Bengal** in the Northern Plains. If you look at the location of West Bengal on the map, you will find that some parts of it fall under the Northern Mountains, some under the Northern Plains and some in the Eastern Coastal Plain. Which parts of West Bengal fall in the Eastern Coastal Plain?

Located on the eastern coast, **Odisha** is a fertile state. Agriculture and fishing are the two most important occupations in the state. Rice is a major crop. Lentils, oilseeds and jute are also grown here. The coastal region is hit by major cyclones almost every year. The Chilka Lake is a major tourist attraction where **migratory** birds roost.

Chilka Lake

Andhra Pradesh is the eighth largest state of India. Some parts of this state are part of the Deccan Plateau while some parts make up the coastal plains. It is home to the Visakhapatnam port, which is an important seaport of India. The state has a shipbuilding yard, an oil refinery and an iron and steel plant.

Towards the southernmost part of India, **Tamil Nadu** has a long coastline called the Coromandel Coast. The river Kaveri, which flows through the state, provides it with water and makes the land fertile. Its capital, Chennai, is well known for cotton and silk *sarees*. The Marina Beach in Chennai is the longest beach in India.

Marina Beach

Matri Mandir

Once a French colony, **Puducherry** is now a union territory of India. It lies to the south of Chennai. The famous Aurobindo Ashram and the Matri Mandir are located here. Farming and fishing are the main occupations of the people here.

The state of **Gujarat** lies on the west coast of India. Gandhinagar is the capital of Gujarat. Ahmedabad is the largest city in this state. Farming is the main occupation of the people. The crops grown here are *jowar*, *bajra*, cotton, oilseeds, sugarcane and wheat. The famous Sabarmati Ashram is located here. Gujarat is home to the Asiatic lion, which is found in the Gir National Park.

Sabarmati Ashram

Located on the western side of the Indian peninsula, **Maharashtra** is the third largest state in the country. Mumbai, the capital of Maharashtra, is the largest seaport of India. It is also an important centre for business and industry. Bombay High is an offshore oilfield, which has large deposits of petroleum.

Eco Zone

Make no open fires. A small open fire can destroy an entire forest!

The smallest state of India, **Goa** is a land of beautiful sandy beaches, old churches, marvellous monuments, beautiful temples and well-maintained museums. Panaji is the capital of Goa. Agriculture is the main occupation of the people of Goa. The people here are also engaged in farming and fishing. Cashew nuts, rice, spices, coconuts and mangoes are the main crops grown here.

Goa

A part of the state of **Karnataka** lies in the Konkan Coast with the other parts lying in the Deccan Plateau. Bangalore is the capital of Karnataka and is known as the information technology or IT capital of India. Karnataka has thick teak forests along its coastal areas, making the state a major producer of sandalwood products. Mangalore is an important seaport of the state.

The state of **Kerala** lies on the Malabar Coast. Thiruvananthapuram is the capital city of Kerala. The state is known for its beautiful backwaters. Agriculture is the main occupation of the people. Coconut, rubber, cocoa, coffee and spices are the main crops grown here. Kerala has the highest literacy rate in India.

Kerala backwaters

The Islands

You already know that an island is a piece of land surrounded by water. A number of islands surround the coastal plains. Of these, the two biggest group of islands are the **Andaman and Nicobar Islands** and the **Lakshadweep Islands**. Look at the map of India and you will find exactly where the two island groups are situated.

Fact Zone

The Andaman Islands are a group of 300 islands out of which only 26 are inhabited.

Andaman and Nicobar Islands

These islands are situated in the Bay of Bengal. The Andaman and the Nicobar Islands are the two island groups forming one union territory. The Andaman lies to the north and Nicobar lies to the south. The capital of this union territory is Port Blair. The main occupations are agriculture, fishing, animal rearing and construction. Rice is the main food crop along with maize, coconut and rubber.

The smallest union territory of India, the Lakshadweep Islands, lies in the Arabian Sea. The Lakshwadeep Islands are a group of 36 islands out of which only 10 are **inhabited** by people. Kavaratti is the capital of the Lakshadweep Islands. This island is formed by the **deposition** of corals. Fishing is the main occupation of the people. The main crop grown here is coconut.

Do It Yourself

This is a famous dance form of Kerala. Find out its name. Find out how and where this style of dancing originated. You can browse the Internet to find out.

Remember

- A coastal plain is the lowland that runs along a coast.
- The Eastern Coastal Plains is divided into two parts—the Northern Circars and the Coromandel Coast.
- The Western Coastal Plains is divided into three parts—the Gujarat Coast, the Konkan Coast and the Malabar Coast.

Words Zone

migratory: going from one country to another country

inhabited: occupied by people and animals

deposition: process of leaving a layer on rocks or soil

Review Zone

A Fill in the blanks with the correct answers.

1. The southern part of the Eastern Coastal Plains is called the .... Coast.
   a. Malabar b. Coromandel c. Konkan
2. Kerala is famous for its ....
   a. museums b. backwaters c. islands
3. The Chilka Lake is in the state of ....
   a. Maharashtra b. Kerala c. Odisha
4. .... is a union territory.
   a. Puducherry b. Port Blair c. Kavaratti
5. Mangalore is an important seaport in ....
   a. Goa b. Karnataka c. West Bengal

B Name the following.

1. A river of the Eastern Coastal Plains that forms a delta in the eastern coast: ....
2. The capital of the Andaman and Nicobar Islands: ....
3. A group of islands formed by coral deposition: ....
4. The longest beach of India: ....

5. A famous ashram in Gujarat founded by Mahatma Gandhi: ....

C **Write T for True and F for False.**

1. An island is a piece of land surrounded by water on three sides. ☐
2. The Hirakud dam is built on the river Godavari. ☐
3. The coast of Tamil Nadu is called the Coromandel Coast. ☐
4. Bombay High is located in Maharashtra. ☐
5. The Marina Beach is located in Bangalore. ☐

D **Answer these questions in brief.**

1. Name the four rivers that form large deltas along the Eastern Coastal Plains.
2. What are the main occupations of the people in Goa?
3. What is an island? Name the group of islands in the Arabian Sea.
4. Which is the longest beach of India? Where is it located?
5. Which are the main crops of Gujarat?

E **Answer these questions in detail.**

1. Describe the extent and location of the Coastal Plains of India.
2. What do you know about the Western Coastal Plains of India?
3. Briefly describe the union territory of Puducherry.
4. Describe the state of Kerala.
5. Describe the Lakshadweep islands.

Map Zone

On an outline map of India, mark three of each of the following:

1. States of India located in the Western Coastal Plains
2. States of India located in the Eastern Coastal Plains

Think Zone

A Kerala is suitable for growing spices. Which spices are grown in Kerala? What do we use them for?

B Look at the picture and answer the questions.

1. Who is this person?
2. What is he carrying?
3. What does he do to earn a living?

Life Skills Zone

How does the location of a place affect the occupation of the people living there? Do people living in coastal areas have different livelihoods than people living in the mountains or deserts? Explain.

Value Zone

People of India follow different traditions and beliefs. We should respect these beliefs and traditions.

Activity Zone

Find out the names of the bird sanctuaries that are located along the coastal plains. Make a chart, paste pictures and write the names of the birds that are found there.

FA

My Zone

Draw a smiley if you know and a star if you wish to know more.

1. I know about the states and union territories that lie in the coastal plains of India. ....
2. I know about the islands of India. ....
3. I know how people live in the coastal plains and the islands. ....

Pin It Up

Make a list of the states covered in this chapter. Write the type of climate these places experience.

8 Natural Resources of India

I Know ...

- During the .... months, people burn coal to stay warm.
- Paper is obtained from ....
- Cars run on ....

Observe and Reflect

- What do you see in the picture?
- How does it help to grow crops?
- Can it be used for drinking?

Look around you. Where do you get all these things from? Our Earth provides us with everything that we need to live. Air, water and sunlight are some of the things that we get from the Earth. They are called **natural resources**. Natural resources are the **resources** that we get from nature and that help us in our day-to-day lives.

Natural resources are mainly of two types:

- **Renewable** or **inexhaustible** resources
- **Non-renewable** or **exhaustible** resources

Renewable Resources

Renewable or inexhaustible resources are the resources that never get used up as they are abundantly available in nature. Sunlight, air, water and soil are some natural resources that will never get used up. This makes them inexhaustible. Let us learn about the uses of some renewable resources.

Air is essential for all humans, animals and plants to survive. While plants use air to make their food, humans need air to breathe and live. The blanket of air on the Earth's surface also helps maintain the right temperature so that it is suitable for life. Without this blanket of air, life on the Earth would not have been possible.

Water makes up three-fourths of the Earth's surface. Just like air, water is essential for humans, animals and plants to survive.

Sunlight is one of the most important renewable resources. Sunlight warms us and provides light in the daytime. Plants use sunlight to make their food through a process called **photosynthesis**. Sunlight also serves as a source of **solar energy**. Many cars today run on solar energy. Cooking can also be done using solar energy.

Wind is another important natural resource. Windmills are used to create energy from the movement of the wind. Several states in India, like Tamil Nadu and West Bengal, produce wind energy.

Eco Zone

Although air, water and soil are inexhaustible, they can get polluted. These have an adverse effect on our health.

Fact Zone

Electricity produced by using water is called hydroelectricity. The Tehri dam in India is the highest dam of India.

Solar panels

Forests are a rich source of plants, trees, animals and soil. Plants and trees provide us with wood, medicines, gum, perfumes and raw materials to make many things. Most importantly, plants release oxygen in the air, which is essential for humans.

Animals provide us with food like milk, eggs and meat and other things like wool and leather. They are also sometimes used as a means of transport in hilly areas and deserts.

Soil, which forms the top layer of the Earth's surface, is essential for plants to grow and live.

Forests

Non-renewable Resources

Non-renewable resources are those resources that exist in limited quantities and it takes a long time for them to be created. Their supply is slowly getting over. They are also known as exhaustible resources. Some examples of non-renewable resources are coal, petroleum, metals, minerals, oil and gas. Coal, natural gas and petroleum are called **fossil fuels**. When plants and animals die, with time, their remains get buried under the earth. They are pressed further into the ground and after many years become fossil fuels.

Find Out

In which states of India are coal reserves found?

Coal is one of the most useful non-renewable natural resources. It is used for many purposes like cooking, producing electricity and for heating. It is used both in homes as well as industries. Machines and vehicles also run with the help of coal.

Petroleum is used to form diesel and petrol, which are used to run cars, ships and aeroplanes. It is a very rare natural resource as not many countries in the world have petroleum reserves. Petroleum is also known as liquid gold. Bombay High in India is a petroleum **reserve**.

Bombay High

Metals like iron, bauxite and copper are useful natural resources used to make many important objects of daily use.

Do It Yourself

Write the names of the natural resources that are used to make the following things.

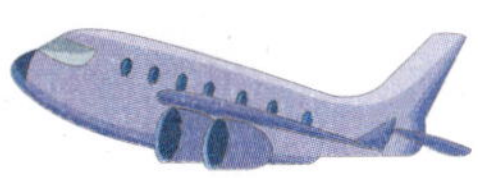 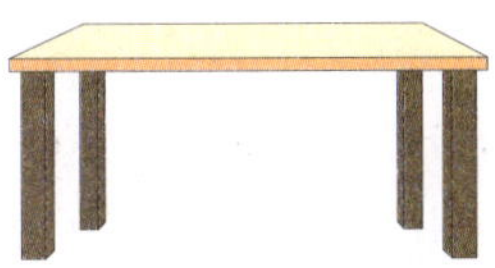   

....

Conservation of Natural Resources

It is very important for us to use both renewable as well as non-renewable natural resources carefully. Since non-renewable resources take a long time to form, it is very important for us to preserve them. Therefore, people have developed ways where sunlight, water and wind are used in place of renewable sources to produce energy. These are called **alternative** sources of energy.

Remember

- Minerals, metals, fossil fuels, air, water and other such resources, which are useful in our daily lives are known as natural resources.
- There are two types of natural resources—renewable and non-renewable.
- Air, water and sunlight are renewable resources.
- Petroleum, coal and metals are non-renewable resources.

Words Zone

resources: something that a country has, which it can use and which makes the country rich

exhaustible: something that can be completely used up

inexhaustible: something that cannot be completely used up

reserve: to keep for future use

alternative: something that can be used in place of something else

Review Zone

A. Fill in the blanks with the correct answers.

1. Non-renewable resources are also known as .... resources.
   a. exhaustible b. exhausting c. inexhaustible
2. Water is used to produce ....
   a. hydroelectricity b. solar energy c. wind energy
3. Bauxite is an .... resource.
   a. exhaustible b. inexhaustible c. renewable
4. Fossil fuels are made up of the remains of ....
   a. solar energy b. dead plants and animals c. water sources
5. We use .... to get solar energy.
   a. hydroelectricity b. wind c. sunlight

B **Each tile has a set of letters. Two or more tiles form a word in a phrase. Unscramble the tiles to reveal the phrase and read the message. The first tile has been unscrambled for you.**

O U R	D W	S E R	C E S	E	A N
I L D	L I F	V E	R E S		

CON										

C **Write T for True and F for False.**

1. Renewable natural resources do not need to be preserved. ☐
2. Windmills require wind and sunlight to work. ☐
3. Coal and petroleum are examples of fossil fuels. ☐
4. Plants make food through the process of photosynthesis. ☐
5. Sunlight is a non-renewable resource. ☐

D **Answer these questions in brief.**

1. Name some non-renewable natural resources.
2. Define natural resources.
3. What is solar energy?
4. How does soil help us?
5. Write one difference between renewable and non-renewable natural resources.

E **Answer these questions in detail.**

1. Describe two renewable natural resources.
2. Why is it important for us to conserve both renewable as well as non-renewable natural resources?
3. How are coal and petroleum useful as natural resources?

Think Zone

A How would your life be affected if there were no more coal and petroleum in the world? List the things that you would not be able to do.

B Look at the picture and answer the questions.

1. What do you see in the picture?
2. Which natural resource do they require in order to work?
3. What are they used to generate?

Life Skills Zone

Find out about one type of alternative energy and write a report on it.

Value Zone

Plants and forests may be inexhaustible but if we keep cutting down forests and don't plant new ones, they will run out.

Activity Zone

FA

Make a chart showing the renewable resources that are used to produce energy. Draw pictures along with each natural resource and explain their benefits in two or three sentences.

FA

My Zone

Draw a smiley if you know and a star if you wish to know more.

1. I know about the natural resources of India. ....
2. I know about renewable and non-renewable natural resources. ....
3. I know that we need to preserve natural resources. ....

Pin It Up

Write three ways in which a family can preserve non-renewable resources.

8 Soils of India

I Know ...

- Plants grow on ....
- Soil, unlike coal, is a .... resource.
- Plants get their food from soil and prepare their food through a process known as ....

Observe and Reflect

- What is the man in the picture doing?
- Why does this need to be done?
- What are the natural resources plants require to live?

The uppermost layer of the surface of Earth is known as **soil**. Also known as the **topsoil**, it forms on the surface of the land. Soil is a mixture of minerals, water, air and the decaying remains of plants and animals.

Formation of Soil

Soil takes a very long time to form. Large rocks, due to wind, water and sunlight, are broken down into smaller pieces. With time, these pieces are further broken down into smaller pieces, which form sand, **silt** and the different types of soil. But this is a process that takes millions of years!

Why is soil such an important natural resource? This is because plants, trees and crops require soil to grow. We have learned in the previous chapter that soil is a renewable resource.

Soil differs from place to place but all types of soil are composed of **particles** of clay, sand and silt in varying quantities. The nature of soil depends upon the rocks and other materials from which it is formed. Some types of soils are very fertile, while others are not depending upon the location of a region. The soils in areas that have plenty of water supply are very fertile. When soil is fertile, crops grow well. In places where the soil is not fertile, farmers use **manure** or fertilizers to make the soil more fertile.

Different Types of Soils

Different parts of India are rich in different types of soils. Look at the map and find out which part of India is rich in which type of soil.

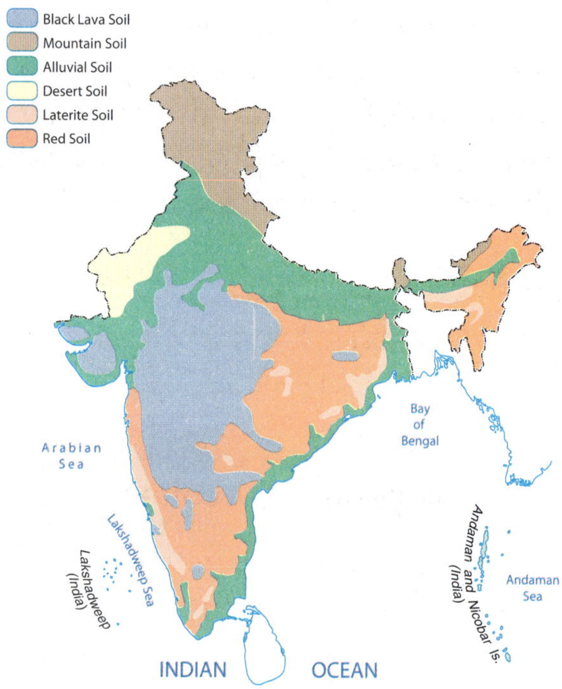

Soils in India

The soil that is formed due to the deposition of silt and sand brought down by rivers is known as **alluvial soil**. This type of soil is found in plenty in the Northern and Coastal Plains of India. These deposits are very fertile and soft in nature. Alluvial soil is rich in minerals.

Alluvial soil

Alluvial soil is good for growing crops, like rice, wheat, maize, tobacco, sugarcane, oilseeds, pulses and jute amongst many others. Fruits and vegetables also grow very well in this type of soil.

Black soil

The soil that is formed from **lava** after it **solidifies** is known as **black soil**. Black soil is mainly found in Gujarat, Maharashtra and Madhya Pradesh, which lie in the north-western part of the Deccan plateau.

Find Out

Which type of soil is found in the place where you live?

This soil is **clayey** and can retain a lot of moisture. It is most suitable for growing crops like cotton, millets, tobacco, oilseeds, wheat, sugarcane and even citrus fruits.

Take a look at the picture. The soil is red in colour and hence, it is known as **red soil**. The presence of iron makes this soil appear red in colour. This soil is not very fertile, still people grow crops such as pulses, rice, millets and certain vegetables. Red soil is found mainly in the states of Jharkhand, Madhya Pradesh, Maharashtra, Odisha, Andhra Pradesh, Tamil Nadu and Telangana.

Red soil

The soil that is produced by the process of **weathering** is known as **laterite soil**. This soil is found in regions that experience a lot of rainfall. As a result of the rain, the minerals in the soil get washed away. This process of washing away of minerals is known as leaching.

Fact Zone

Soil looses fertility when one variety of crop is grown for a long period. Farmers grow different crops in the same land to keep the soil fertile. This is known as crop rotation.

Laterite soil

It is found in some parts of Bihar, Odisha, Maharashtra, Karnataka, West Bengal, Meghalaya, Andhra Pradesh, Kerala and Telangana. Farmers of these regions apply fertilizers to the soil and mainly grow coffee, tea, coconut and rubber.

The soil that is found in the deserts is known as **desert soil**. Deserts receive little to no rainfall and hence, the soil is not at all fertile. It is only with the help of irrigation and fertilizers that a few crops like wheat, barley, millets, pulses and cotton can be grown here. This soil is mainly found in the desert regions of India, namely, Rajasthan and its surrounding areas.

Desert soil

Mountain soil

The soil that is found in the slopes of the hills is known as **mountain soil**. Rich in **humus**, this soil is very good for growing fruits and practising terrace farming. When the hilly slopes are divided into steps and various kinds of crops like maize, barley, coffee, fruits and spices are grown then it is known as terrace farming.

Eco Zone

For one week every year, trees are planted in different parts of the country. This is known as *van mahotsav*.

This type of soil is mostly found in the hilly areas of Uttarakhand, Jammu and Kashmir and Himachal Pradesh.

Do It Yourself

This is a picture of terrace farming. Find out more about how and where it is practised in India.

Soil Erosion and Conservation

Often due to natural as well as human activities, the top layer of the soil gets worn away. This is known as **soil erosion**.

Natural occurrences like heavy rainfall, excessive floods and strong winds **corrode** the top layer of the soil resulting in soil erosion. Some human activities like deforestation and land pollution cause soil erosion. The roots of the plants hold the soil together. When trees are cut down, the soil becomes loose. This results in the soil getting easily worn away. As a result, the land becomes less fertile and unsuitable for growing crops.

There are a few ways through which we can control soil erosion and increase fertility of the soil:

Planting a sapling

- Plant more trees instead of cutting them down as this leads to deforestation.
- Reduce land pollution by not throwing waste anywhere.
- Chemical fertilizers should be avoided because they decrease soil fertility.
- Natural and organic fertilizers like manure and **compost** should be used.

Remember

- Soil forms the top layer of the Earth's surface.
- There are various types of soils found in India, namely, alluvial, laterite, black, red, desert and mountain soil.
- Alluvial soil is very fertile and good for growing crops.

Words Zone

silt: sand and mud carried by flowing water

particles: tiny parts of a substance

manure: animal waste which acts as an organic fertilizer without harming the soil

fertilizer: substance added to the soil to make it fertile

- Black soil is formed from solidified lava.
- Red soil contains iron and hence, is red in colour.
- Laterite soil is not fertile because of leaching.
- Desert soil is not fertile and is found in the desert regions of India.
- Mountain soil is found on hill slopes and is ideal for practising terrace farming.
- The wearing away of the upper layer of soil is known as soil erosion.

lava: hot molten rock that comes from a volcano

solidify: to turn into the solid form

clayey: soil that contains large amounts of clay

weathering: to wear and wash away

corrode: to wear away

compost: a mixture of decayed plants and food that can be added to soil to help plants grow

Review Zone

A Fill in the blanks with the correct answers.

1. .... can prevent soil erosion.
   a. Rocks b. Trees c. Earthworms
2. The Northern Plains are rich in .... soil.
   a. laterite b. alluvial c. mountain
3. Spices grow well in .... soil.
   a. alluvial b. mountain c. desert
4. .... prevents the soil from becoming infertile.
   a. Crop rotation b. Crop farming c. Deforestation
5. Mountain soil is rich in ....
   a. clay b. lava c. humus

B Name the following.

1. The process of minerals being washed away from the soil due to rains: ....
2. The process of growing different crops in each season in the same area of land: ....

3. An organic fertilizer that makes the soil fertile without harming it: ....
4. The process by which the top layer of the soil is washed away by rains or winds: ....
5. A state in India where desert soil is found: ....

C Write T for True and F for False.

1. Land pollution results in soil erosion. ☐
2. Mountain soil is formed by the process of weathering. ☐
3. Black soil cannot retain moisture and hence, is ideal for growing cotton. ☐
4. Manure should be used instead of chemical fertilizers. ☐
5. Red soil is not very fertile. ☐

D Answer these questions in brief.

1. Define soil.
2. Name the various types of soil found in India.
3. Which crops are ideal for alluvial soil?
4. Where is black soil found in India?
5. What is leaching?

E Answer these questions in detail.

1. How is soil formed?
2. How and why is crop rotation practised?
3. How is laterite soil formed?
4. State a few ways in which soil erosion can be prevented.

Map Zone

On an outline map of India, mark the areas with fertile alluvial soil and black soil.

Think Zone

A Do you think that different types of soil in different parts of India affect the lives of the people in those parts? Select a type of soil and write about how it affects the life of the people living there.

B **Look at the picture and answer the questions.**

1. What type of soil is this?
2. Where is it found in India?
3. How can crops be grown here?

Life Skills Zone

Deforestation should not be practised but still it is done in many areas. Why do you think people still cut down trees? Make a list of things that are made from trees and suggest other resources that we can use to replace wood.

Value Zone

Planting trees reduces soil erosion. Make groups and spread awareness about the importance of trees in your neighbourhood.

Activity Zone

FA

You know soil is made up of clay, silt and sand. It also has humus and the remains of dead plants and animals. Take some topsoil, clay, sand and silt. Feel the texture of each separately. Compare the sizes of the particles of soil and fill in the table.

Particle	Clay	Silt	Sand	Humus
Size				
Texture				

My Zone

FA

Draw a smiley if you know and a star if you wish to know more.

1. I know about the different types of soils in different parts of India. ....
2. I know that soil is a renewable resource. ....
3. I know the ways in which we can control soil erosion. ....

Pin It Up

Collect pictures of the different types of soils that you have studied. Paste them on a sheet of paper and pin it up!

9 The Coastal Plains and the Islands

I Know ...

- Plants and trees are .... natural resources.
- .... is the national tree of India.

Observe and Reflect

- Identify the animal in the picture.
- Why are laws being made to prevent people from killing this animal?

Do you know what a forest is? A forest is a large area covered by trees, which is home to many wild animals. We have learned before that forests are an important source of renewable resources.

Importance of Forests

We know that plants take in carbon dioxide and give out oxygen which is essential for all animals and humans to survive. Trees prevent soil erosion. Soil erosion takes place when the topmost layer of soil wears away. This happens when there is too much water in a region, causing the soil to become loose. The roots of trees firmly hold the soil, thereby preventing soil erosion.

Eco Zone

Forests are considered as the 'lungs of the Earth' because they provide clean and fresh air, which is vital for our survival.

Forests provide food and shelter to wild animals. Trees give us products like gum, wood, medicines, fuel, furniture, paper, clothing and many more.

At least 33 per cent of a country should be covered by forests. However, only 20 per cent of India is covered by forests. Efforts have been made in various states to increase the forest cover and it has increased a little in recent times. Look at the map of India depicting India's forest cover.

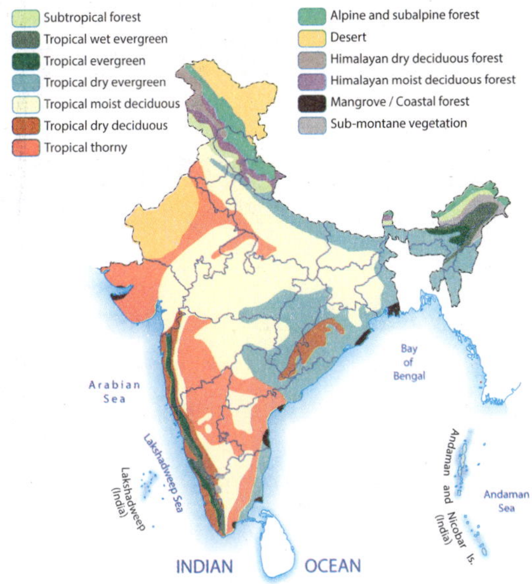

Forests of India

Different Types of Forests

We know that like soils, there are different types of forests too. Depending upon the nature of the trees found, the forests of India can be divided into five types—evergreen, deciduous, mountainous, thorn and mangrove or tidal forests. Let us learn more about these types of forests.

Evergreen forests have trees which never shed their leaves. These evergreen trees grow very tall and have a thick and woody bark. Since the trees grow very close to each other, the leaves at the top form a roof-like cover called canopy. These canopies do not allow much light to pass through them. Sometimes it rains heavily in these areas.

Find Out

Find out the names of the animals that are commonly found in evergreen forests.

Evergreen forests grow well in moist and wet places and are found mainly in the northeastern hills, the Andaman and Nicobar Islands and the hill slopes of the Western Ghats. The evergreen forests have mahogany, ebony and rosewood trees.

Evergreen forest

The trees that shed their leaves in the summer season form **deciduous forests**. These forests grow in areas that experience moderate rainfall.

They are mainly found in the foothills of the Himalayas, in the states of Uttarakhand and in Uttar Pradesh. Such forests are also found in the states of Maharashtra, Madhya Pradesh, Karnataka, Kerala, Tamil Nadu and Odisha.

Deciduous forest

Sal, teak, sandalwood, mahua, sheesham, bamboo and semul are the major trees found in deciduous forests. They are home to animals like deer, monkeys and birds like parrots. Deciduous forests form the largest forest cover in India.

Mostly coniferous trees such as pine, fir, spruce and deodar make up **mountainous forests**. These trees are conical in shape, very tall and bear fruits, which are also known as cones because of their shape. The leaves are pointed and hence, snow does not gather on the leaves. These forests are also known as coniferous forests.

Mountainous forest

Coniferous forests are mainly found in the higher parts of the Himalayan Mountains and also in the Nilgiris. Paper is made from the **pulp** of coniferous trees.

Thorn forests are mainly found in the desert regions of Rajasthan, parts of Haryana and the southern part of Punjab. The trees that have sharp thorns and small leaves to prevent loss of water, like *keekar* and *babool,* form thorn forests. The sharp thorns also keep animals away. These plants grow in desert areas and hence, they need long roots for survival. The roots of these plants spread out over a large area in order to absorb water and minerals. Various types of wild palms and cacti are also found in these forests.

Thorn forest

Mangrove forest

The forests that are found in deltas and in areas submerged in seawater are known as **mangrove** or **tidal forests**. These trees can grow well in both freshwater and seawater.

In India, tidal forests are found in the Ganga-Brahmaputra delta. The famous *Sundari* tree, a few **ferns**, shrubs and palms grow in these forests. Boats are made out of the wood of these trees. This forest is the home of the Royal Bengal tiger, spotted deer, crocodiles and many more animals.

Conservation of Forests

A number of movements have been launched in order to protect the forest cover of India. Of these, the Chipko movement which took place in the 1970s was the most famous. A group of villagers from the Reni village of Uttarakhand clung to the trees preventing woodcutters from cutting them down. The movement was successful and spread to many parts of the country.

Wildlife in India

Royal Bengal tiger

One-horned rhino

The wildlife of India includes a large number of birds, animals and insects. The Royal Bengal tiger, our national animal, is found in the Sundarbans. The one-horned rhinoceros found in the Kaziranga National Park is a protected animal. Rhinos, elephants, hippos and deer are also found in many forests in the north-eastern states. Deciduous forests give shelter to animals like the leopard, boar, bear and the wild buffalo. Camels and desert cats are found in thorn forests. Asiatic lions are found in the Gir forests of Gujarat. However, due to a large amount of deforestation and **poaching**, these animals are losing their natural homes. Hence, it is important for us to conserve both the forests as well as its wildlife.

In order to control poaching, the government has declared many areas as wildlife sanctuaries, bird sanctuaries and national parks. While a national park is meant to protect forest cover and wildlife, a wildlife sanctuary protects **endangered** species. Some of the important national parks and wildlife sanctuaries of India are given in the table below.

National Park	State
Jim Corbett National Park	Uttarakhand
Ranthambore	Rajasthan
Gir	Gujarat
Kaziranga	Assam
Sariska	Rajasthan

National Park	State
Sundarbans	West Bengal
Bandipur	Karnataka
Kanha	Madhya Pradesh
Panna	Madhya Pradesh
Periyar	Kerala
Bandhavgarh	Madhya Pradesh

Wildlife Sanctuary	States
Chilka Lake	Odisha
Sultanpur	Haryana
Periyar	Kerala
Hazaribagh	Jharkhand

Wildlife Sanctuary	States
Bharatpur	Rajasthan
Idukki	Kerala
Dachigam	Jammu & Kashmir

Do It Yourself

Based on the data given above, mark the locations of national parks and wildlife sanctuaries on an outline map of India. Put a ▭ for national parks and a ○ to show wildlife sanctuaries.

Remember

- Forests are an important renewable natural resource.
- The major types of forests in India are evergreen, deciduous, mountainous, thorn and mangrove or tidal.
- It is important to conserve both forests and wildlife.

Words Zone

pulp: wood that has been crushed into a soft substance

fern: a plant with large leaves and no flowers that grows in wet areas

poaching: illegal hunting and killing of animals

endangered: animals or plants at the risk of becoming extinct

Review Zone

A Fill in the blanks with the correct answers.

1. The pulp of .... trees is used to make paper.
   a. evergreen b. deciduous c. coniferous
2. .... trees can grow both in freshwater and seawater.
   a. Sal b. Sundari c. Teak
3. Coniferous trees are found in the ....
   a. Sundarbans b. Niligiri hills c. slopes of the Western Ghats
4. .... forests form the largest forest cover of India.
   a. Evergreen b. Deciduous c. Mangrove
5. Boats are made out of wood that can be obtained from .... forests.
   a. evergreen b. deciduous c. mangrove

B **Name the following.**

1. Trees that do not shed their leaves irrespective of the season: ....
2. Trees that shed their leaves in the dry season: ....
3. Trees whose pulp is used to make paper: ....
4. An animal found in the mangrove forests of Sundarbans: ....
5. An area enclosed for the protection of forest cover and wildlife: ....

C **Write T for True and F for False.**

1. Camels are found in the thorn forests of Rajasthan. ☐
2. The estimated forest cover of India is 33 per cent. ☐
3. Deciduous forests are found in the Andaman and Nicobar Islands. ☐
4. Mountainous forests are also known as coniferous forests. ☐
5. The Chipko Movement was launched to protest against deforestation. ☐

D **Answer these questions in brief.**

1. Name the types of forests found in India.
2. Which trees are mainly found in evergreen forests?
3. Write one difference between wildlife sanctuaries and national parks.
4. In which state was the Chipko Movement first launched?
5. Where are mountainous forests found in India?

E **Answer these questions in detail.**

1. Discuss the importance of forests.
2. Describe the mangrove forests of India.
3. What do you know about the Chipko Movement?
4. Describe the forests found in the desert regions of India.

Think Zone

A Do you think putting animals in zoos is a good way to prevent poaching? Give reasons for your answer.

B Look at the picture and answer the questions.

1. Name this animal.
2. Where is this animal mostly found?
3. In which national park can this animal be found?

Life Skills Zone

In what way, can you contribute to preserve trees and wildlife of your state?

Value Zone

Do you think animals like living in zoos?

FA Activity Zone

Make a group project on the topic 'Forests in India'. Divide the class into five groups. Each group can take up one type of forest found in India. Collect more information about the plants and animals in different types of forests. Make a PowerPoint presentation on it. You can also make colourful charts. Present the project report in the class.

FA My Zone

Draw a smiley if you know and a star if you wish to know more.

1. I know about the different types of forests. ....
2. I know about the different types of wildlife. ....
3. I know that forests and wildlife should be protected from becoming extinct. ....

Pin It Up

Make a list of the animals that are commonly found in each type of forest. Write how the animals have adapted to the conditions in which they live.

Assessment 2 (Chapters 6-9) **Maximum Marks: 25**

A Fill in the blanks. (1 x 6 = 6)

1. The low lying land along a coast is called .... plains.
2. Asiatic lions are found in the .... forests of Gujarat.
3. Renewable resources are also called .... resources.
4. Black soil is formed after the lava ....
5. Forests are called the .... of earth.
6. Migratory birds flock to .... lake in coastal India.

B Match the columns. (1 x 10 = 10)

Column A	Column B
1. Indira Point	a. Highest dam
2. Andhra Pradesh	b. Evergreen forests
3. Rajasthan	c. Vishakhapatnam port
4. Dras	d. Water
5. Hydroelectricity	e. Coldest place in India
6. Tehri dam	f. Driest state of India
7. Deposition	g. Southernmost point of the country
8. Black soil	h. Alluvial soil
9. Canopy	i. Paper
10. Pulp	j. Lava

C Tick (✓) the appropriate answer. (1 x 5 = 5)

1. Which of the following was once a French colony? (Delhi/Puducherry)
2. Which is one of the hottest cities of India? (Mawsynram/Nagpur)
3. What makes up three-fourths of Earth's surface? (Air/Water)
4. What is the soil produced by weathering called? (Laterite/Alluvial)
5. What is the other name for mangrove forests? (Tidal forests/Dry forests)

D Write True or False. (1 x 4 = 4)

1. Kaziranga National Park is located in Assam. ....
2. The leaves at the lowest level of a forest are called a canopy. ....
3. Manure is a natural fertilizer. ....
4. Coal is used to form diesel and petrol. ....

Different animals are found in different parts of India. On the map, mark where each of the animals given below are found.

Comprehensive Assessment (Chapters 1-9) **Maximum Marks: 50**

A Put a tick (✓) near the correct option. **(1 x 10 = 10)**

1. What is the capital of Himachal Pradesh?
   a. Jaisalmer b. Shimla
2. Which is the highest of the three parallel ranges of the Himalayas?
   a. Greater Himalayas b. Middle Himalayas
3. Which is of the following a desert plant?
   a. Cactus b. Tulsi
4. Which soil is suitable for sugarcane growth?
   a. Black b. Laterite
5. Which river divides the Southern Plateau into two?
   a. Ganges b. Narmada
6. Where is the Coromandel Coast situated?
   a. Tamil Nadu b. Assam
7. Which season is characterized by long and hot days?
   a. Summer b. Winter
8. What is the process through which plants make their food called?
   a. Photosynthesis b. Transpiration
9. What is the process of washing away of minerals called?
   a. Bleaching b. Leaching
10. What prevents soil erosion?
    a. Trees b. Land

B Match the columns. **(1 x 5 = 5)**

Column A	Column B
1. Mt Everest	a. Tibetan Plateau
2. Middle Himalayas	b. Chhota Nagpur Plateau
3. Indus river	c. Small water bodies
4. Oases	d. Himachal
5. River Damodar	e. Himalayan mountains

C Find an odd one in each line and write the reason why it is odd. **(2 x 10 = 20)**

1.	Northern Plains	Northern Mountains	Southern Plateaus	Canal
	Reason:			
2.	Khasi	Garo	Jaintia	Alps
	Reason:			
3.	Black	Laterite	Alluvium	Wells
	Reason:			
4.	Camel	Cow	Goat	Lion
	Reason:....................			
5.	Kanha	Gir	Sunderban	Madhya Pradesh
	Reason:			
6.	Chennai	Karnataka	Kerala	Bihar
	Reason:			
7.	Summer	Autumn	Winter	Wind
	Reason:			
8.	Water	Sunlight	Wind	Industries
	Reason:			
9.	Satpura	Himalaya	Aravalli	Thar
	Reason:			
10.	Evergreen	Deciduous	Mountainous	Plains
	Reason:			

D Answer the following questions. **(3 x 5 = 15)**

1. Describe in detail why are evergreen forests called so.
2. What are the components of soil?
3. Write a note on the wildlife of India.
4. Briefly describe the islands of India.
5. How are Himalayas important to us?

GENERAL KNOWLEDGE

1 Same Sound

Some words have the same sound but have different spellings. Read the words given in the box. Complete the sentences with the correct words.

1. a. The gardener dug a <u>hole</u> in the ground to make a compost pit.

   b. Dev was so hungry, he ate a <u>whole</u> pizza by himself.

2. a. She enjoyed the storybook so much that she __________ it over and over again.

   b. My mother bought me a new __________ scarf for my birthday.

3. a. Sam was sad because the new shirt that he got was too __________ for him.

   b. Mother told Farid that if he did not keep his new badge properly, he would __________ it.

4. a. Baby __________ enjoyed eating his bowl of honey.

   b. Tina got out of bed and walked to her door in her __________ feet.

5. a. The little mouse __________ up all the cheese.

   b. He had __________ marbles in his pocket.

hole	eight	bare	loose	ate	lose	whole	bear

Fact Zone

A homophone is a word that is pronounced like another word but has a different spelling or meaning, for example *some, sum.*

2 Sports Terms

Look at the sports icons given below. Choose two correct terms used in the sport from the box and fill in the blanks.

1.  Swimming ____________ ____________

2.  Golf ____________ ____________

3.  Hockey ____________ ____________

4.  Football ____________ ____________

5.  Tennis ____________ ____________

6.  Shooting ____________ ____________

7.  Basketball ____________ ____________

8.  Boxing ____________ ____________

Hook Free Hit Ace
Free Throw Bogey Keepie-Uppie
Knockout Heat Bulls Eye
Lap Bunker Scoop Deuce
Target Tackle Layup

Fact Zone

The terms 'penhold grip' and 'loop' are associated with table tennis and 'raider' and 'lobby' are used in the sport of *kabbadi*.

3 Find Fruits

Read the clues and name the fruits in the crossword.

Across

2. Grows in bunches of a climbing plant
5. Known as peru or amrood, this fruit has a white pulp
7. Soft, red and yellow, this fruit is juicy and pulpy inside with a hard seed in the middle
9. A small green fruit with sour juice
10. Called the king of fruits, eaten especially in summer

Down

1. A soft red fruit whose tiny seeds are on the outside
3. A round fruit whose inside is full of juicy pink-red seeds
4. A big fruit with a green and hard skin. The inside is pink or red and is full of water
6. Red or green fruits that grow in the states of Himachal Pradesh and Kashmir
8. Small soft round fruits usually used on top of the icing on a cake

Fact Zone

Jackfruit, originally from the Western Ghats region in India, is eaten both as a fruit and a vegetable.

4 Dances of India

India is known the world over for its classical dances. Identify the classical dances with the names of their state of origin. Choose the correct options from the two help boxes given below.

1. 
   ____
2. 
   ____
3. 
   ____
4. 
   ____
5. 
   ____
6. 
   ____
7. 
   ____
8. 
   ____

Kathak Mohiniyattam Kuchipudi
Odissi Sattriya Manipuri
Kathakali Bharatnatyam

Kerala Tamil Nadu Assam
Manipur Uttar Pradesh Odisha
Andhra Pradesh Kerala

Fact Zone

The origin of the Bharatnatyam dance can be traced to Sage Bharat Muni's ancient text *Natyashastra*.

5 Signs on a Hill Station

Have you ever noticed that traffic signs are different when you travel to a hill station? Look at the picture clues of traffic signs. Choose the correct words from the box and label the signs.

compulsory ahead or right	men at work	petrol pump ahead
narrow road ahead	hairpin bend	falling rocks

Fact Zone

Street signs have been there since the time of the Romans. They built pillars or milestones to let travellers know how far they've travelled and how far they are from a place.

6 Animal Groups

Read the description and name the animal groups. Choose the correct word from the help box.

1. Animals that live in water ________________
2. Animals that live on trees ________________
3. Animals that live both on land and in water ________________
4. Animals that live on land ________________
5. Animals that give birth to young ones ________________
6. Animals that lay eggs ________________
7. Animals that live in the sea ________________
8. Flesh eating animals ________________
9. Plant eating animals ________________
10. Animals that eat both animals and plants ________________

Herbivorous	Aquatic	Arboreal
Amphibia	Marine	Omnivorous
Terrestrial	Carnivorous	
Mammals	Oviparous	

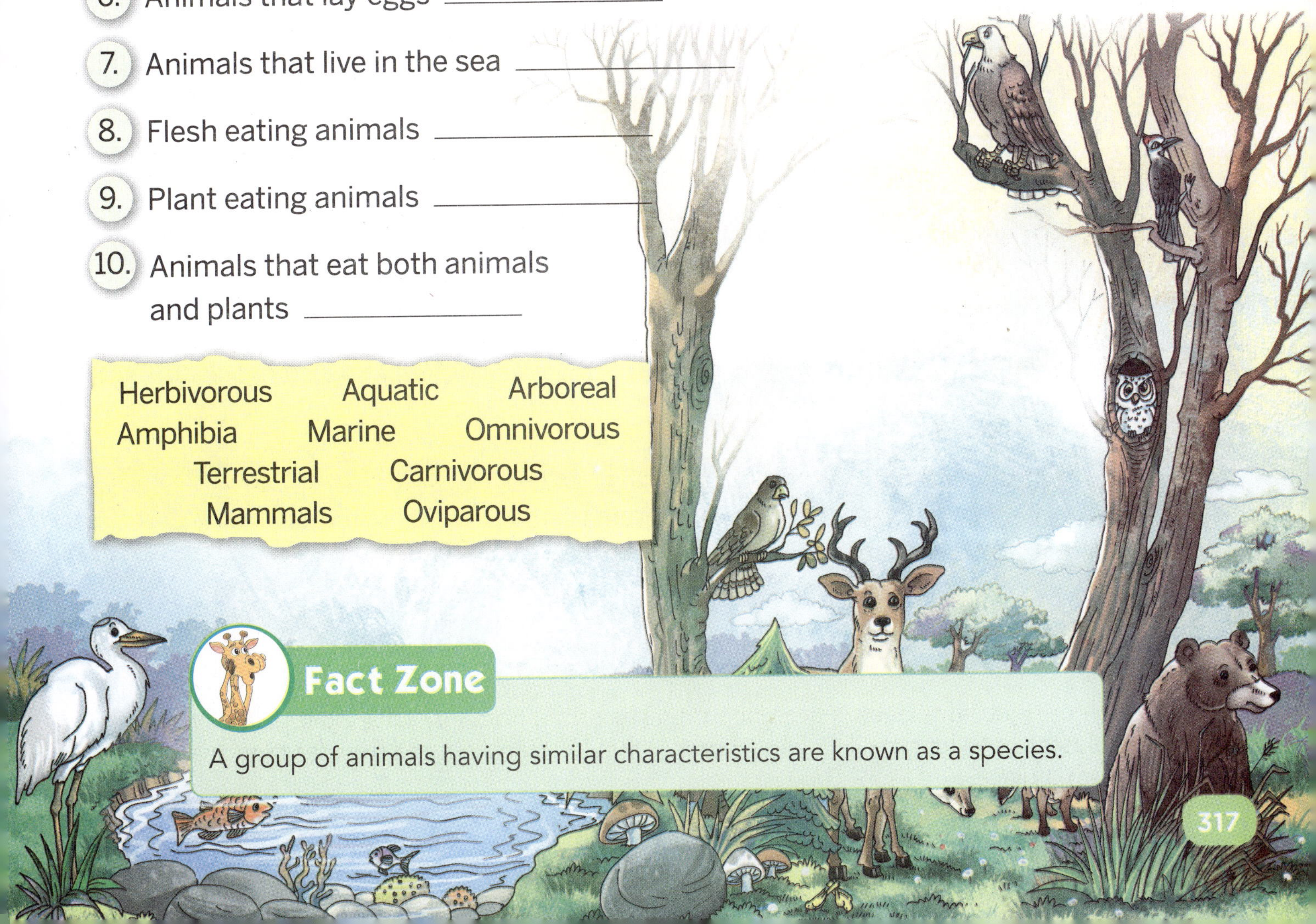

Fact Zone

A group of animals having similar characteristics are known as a species.

7 Communicating with People

Look at the icons used for means of communication. Label them and tick the ones you use to communicate.

SMS Email Telephone Letter Wifi
Megaphone Radio Blog Fax

8 Good Behaviour

Draw a smiley for good behavior and a sad face for careless behavior beside the given pictures.

1.

2.

3.

4.

5.

6.

7.

8.

9 Water on Earth

Read the clues and identify the water bodies found on earth. Choose the correct word from the help box.

1. The salt water that covers the earth is called an ocean.

2. Small white pieces of frozen water that falls from the sky in cold places is called ______________.

3. A natural flow of water that continues in a long line to the sea or ocean is called a ______________.

4. A small area of still water where fish and frogs live is called a ______________.

5. When water falls from the sky in separate drops, it is called a ______________.

6. Tiny water drops that fall on leaves or other cool surfaces at night are called ______________.

7. When a stream or river falls from a high place, it is called a ______________.

ocean	waterfall	pond	dew
river	snow	hailstorm	

Fact Zone

The Earth's surface has only 2.5% of freshwater as rest is saline water from oceans and seas.

10 Telling Time

Read the statements and draw hands on the clock to show the correct time these activities are completed. Write the time in the blanks too.

1. She left home at three-fifteen in the afternoon and it took forty-five minutes for her to reach the market.

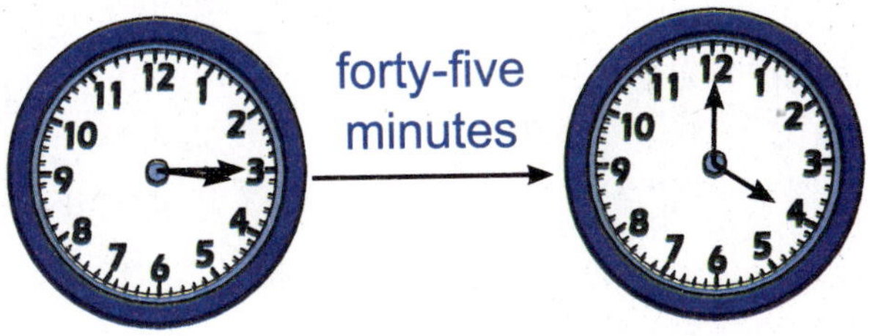

4:00 p.m.

2. Neha started cooking at ten past ten in the morning and finished in twenty minutes.

______

______

3. The show started at twelve-twenty-five and ended in two hours.

4. Sushil started studying for his test at three-forty in the afternoon and finished after two hours and thirty minutes.

______

______

5. The race started at 2 o' clock in the afternoon and lasted for eleven minutes.

6. Gurmeet wakes up at six-thirty and takes forty-five minutes to get ready for school.

______

Fact Zone

There are 24 Time Zones across the world.

11 States of India: North

Look at the pictures of the famous places and things from the different states of north India. Match two things for a state.

1.

Taj Mahal

2.

Corbett National Park

3.

Golden Temple

4.

phiran dress

5.

phulkari

6.

Kullu cap

7.

shikara

a. Uttar Pradesh

b. Jammu and Kashmir

c. Punjab

d. Himachal Pradesh

e. Uttarakhand

8.

Laxman Jhula

9.

chikan work

10.

Christ Church, Shimla

Fact Zone

The Northern Plains are called the 'food bowl of India.'

12 Flags of the World

Identify the flags of different countries in the world. Choose the correct answer from the help box.

1.  ____________

2.  ____________

3.  ____________

4.  ____________

5.  ____________

6.  ____________

7.  ____________

8.  ____________

9.  ____________

10.  ____________

11.  ____________

12.  ____________

France Thailand Japan India China Turkey Germany
Switzerland Saudi Arabia Portugal Russian Federation Iran

Fact Zone

The flag of the Netherlands was the oldest tricolour flag in the world.

13 Compost Pit

Look at these pictures. They show how a compost pit is made. Number each picture in the correct sequence.

1.

2.

3.

4.

5.

6.

7.

Fact Zone

Compost pit originated with the farmers in England.

14 Word Search

Find the words related to weather in the zigzag word search. One has been done for you.

C	S	N	O	W	C	L	O	U	M
A	K	A	L	F	D	E	W	D	I
L	E	G	B	H	A	I	L	W	S
M	L	N	L	R	S	Q	R	O	T
C	I	I	I	A	I	U	A	B	S
L	G	N	Z	Z	N	A	I	N	N
E	H	T	F	A	L	L	E	R	O
A	R	F	R	R	D	D	D	S	W
M	O	O	O	W	I	N	N	T	M
S	G	G	S	T	T	H	U	O	R

BLIZZARD	CALM	CLEAR	CLOUD	DEW
FOG	FROST	HAIL	LIGHTNING	MIST
RAIN	RAINBOW	SMOG	SNOW	SNOWFLAKE
SQUALL	THUNDERSTORM		WIND	

A **Match the following.**

1. 

2. 

3. 

a. Uttarakhand

b. Germany

c. Bharatnatyam

d. Ocean

e. Fax

f. Narrow road ahead

4. 

5. 

6. 

B **Choose the correct answer to fill in the blanks.**

1. A term associated with swimming is ________________ (lap/ace)
2. The tiny seeds of this small, red-pink fruit are on the outside are called ________________ (strawberry/cherry)
3. Animals that live both on land and in water are called ________________ (amphibian/arboreal)
4. Seema helped an old man in crossing the road. This was a ________________ action. (wrong/right)
5. Raj went out to play at five twenty- five and returned at twenty minutes past six. Raj played for ________________. (fifty minutes/fifty-five minutes)

NOTES

NOTES